T0192025

# Communications
# in Computer and Information Science     1501

Editorial Board Members

Joaquim Filipe ⓘ
   *Polytechnic Institute of Setúbal, Setúbal, Portugal*
Ashish Ghosh
   *Indian Statistical Institute, Kolkata, India*
Raquel Oliveira Prates ⓘ
   *Federal University of Minas Gerais (UFMG), Belo Horizonte, Brazil*
Lizhu Zhou
   *Tsinghua University, Beijing, China*

More information about this series at https://link.springer.com/bookseries/7899

Florian Niebling · Sander Münster ·
Heike Messemer (Eds.)

# Research and Education in Urban History in the Age of Digital Libraries

Second International Workshop, UHDL 2019
Dresden, Germany, October 10–11, 2019
Revised Selected Papers

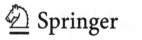

Springer

*Editors*
Florian Niebling (iD)
Universität Würzburg
Würzburg, Germany

Sander Münster (iD)
Friedrich-Schiller-Universität Jena
Jena, Germany

Heike Messemer
TU Dresden
Dresden, Germany

ISSN 1865-0929 ISSN 1865-0937 (electronic)
Communications in Computer and Information Science
ISBN 978-3-030-93185-8 ISBN 978-3-030-93186-5 (eBook)
https://doi.org/10.1007/978-3-030-93186-5

© Springer Nature Switzerland AG 2021
This work is subject to copyright. All rights are reserved by the Publisher, whether the whole or part of the material is concerned, specifically the rights of translation, reprinting, reuse of illustrations, recitation, broadcasting, reproduction on microfilms or in any other physical way, and transmission or information storage and retrieval, electronic adaptation, computer software, or by similar or dissimilar methodology now known or hereafter developed.
The use of general descriptive names, registered names, trademarks, service marks, etc. in this publication does not imply, even in the absence of a specific statement, that such names are exempt from the relevant protective laws and regulations and therefore free for general use.
The publisher, the authors and the editors are safe to assume that the advice and information in this book are believed to be true and accurate at the date of publication. Neither the publisher nor the authors or the editors give a warranty, expressed or implied, with respect to the material contained herein or for any errors or omissions that may have been made. The publisher remains neutral with regard to jurisdictional claims in published maps and institutional affiliations.

This Springer imprint is published by the registered company Springer Nature Switzerland AG
The registered company address is: Gewerbestrasse 11, 6330 Cham, Switzerland

# Preface

For art and architectural historians, historical photographs, paintings, and drawings of architecture are important sources for research. Over the last few decades, a large number of relevant documents have been digitized and made available to researchers by means of online repositories. These collections provide access to the captured data, but they also provide a greater infrastructure that allows the development of specific research efforts. Digital repositories meet a wide range of needs, from research in humanities and information technologies through museum contexts and library studies to tourist applications. The actual benefit of these applications for users highly depends on the usability, suitability, and efficiency of the technical solutions.

As investigated via a survey involving contributors to major international conference series on digital cultural heritage between 1990 and 2015, the majority of participants are humanists (Münster, 2019). Within the humanities cohort, a majority of around 90% are archaeologists, followed by art historians. With regards to methods used by participants of the survey, in particular statistical analysis, computer vision, or 3D modeling are of relevance. The data of relevance is primarily image and large scale point or polygon data as well as geo-located data and shapes (by GIS) and textual data.

Historically, digital heritage and digital humanities address different aspects of cultural heritage. While digital heritage refers to tangible and intangible cultural heritage objects and their preservation, education, and research (e.g. UNESCO, 2003), digital humanities focus on the application of digital technologies to support research in the humanities. Due to the predominance of textual content, spatial objects and images - as a common subject of both fields - are still a subordinate topic of the digital-humanities. Conversely, humanities-driven research is - compared to the recording, conservation, and exhibition of cultural heritage - a small field in digital cultural heritage. Besides the aspect of general relevance, there are many commonalities in this central area. Both fields share concepts such as the idea of spatialization, extensive information about an object as a basis for research, and a strong connection to the creation and perception of visualization and imagery. Technology and data are also important drivers, although whether the research is primarily data-driven or data-led remains an open question.

In this changing context, the question arises as to how research and education of urban history can be supported by digital libraries. The primary objective of the joint Time Machine Conference and CIPA Workshop on Research and Education in Urban History in the Age of Digital Libraries, held in October 2019 in Dresden, Germany, was to concentrate on the area of tension between the fields of culture, technologies, and education. This book presents major findings and aims to highlight crucial challenges for further research and to encourage debate between the sciences. We showcase contributions on theoretical and methodological issues, application scenarios, and projects, as well as novel approaches and tools. The 41 submissions to the joint event were reviewed by a joint Program Committee in a double-blind reviewing process.

After the conference, 11 papers were invited for this revised and selected papers volume. These cover the following four research areas:

1. **Theory, Methods, and Systematization**

   Digital humanities research as an inherently interdisciplinary field has created a high demand for critically reflected methods, techniques, valid strategies, classifications, and quality standards. But do computing methods also lead to new and ground-breaking research questions, approaches, or insights into architectural and urban cultural heritage research? In most cases, the use of computing simply extends nondigital possibilities, without much change to the pre-digital approaches and research questions. Nevertheless, digitalization has dramatically altered research qualities, quantities, and workflows. Against this background, this section includes three articles about methodologies, practices, and standards for utilizing digital technologies for cultural heritage research.

2. **Visualization and Presentation**

   Historians in cultural heritage research today are enabled to explore new research directions due to the availability of multitudes of digitized historical photographs in image repositories. Moreover, novel approaches such as the photogrammetric reconstruction of historical buildings from image databases allow for contextualization and intuitive access to data. Typical motivations for accessing these archives and repositories are scientific research, pedagogical applications, and the study of historical sites. These areas require advances in methods for visualization and presentation of data to support the different target groups. This section includes five articles focusing on technical workflows, methods, and tools to support research in the field of urban history.

3. **Machine Learning and Artificial Intelligence**

   During the past few years, various new technological opportunities have arisen from big data, Semantic Web technologies, and the exponential growth in data accessible via digital libraries such as EUROPEANA. Data-driven supervised and unsupervised classification approaches have been used to acquire high-level semantic concepts, especially from the interconnection of different types of data. Interdisciplinary collaborations between computer science and humanities disciplines are essential in developing methods and workflows to enable cultural heritage research to exploit machine learning approaches. Two articles are included in this section, exhibiting use cases and best practices of applied machine learning in digital humanities research.

4. **Policies, Legislation, and Standards**

   Academic culture, institutionalization of research, and the regulation and management of heritage are approached by international research and infrastructure projects involving key actors and stakeholders in this area. Research infrastructures aim at offering access to a wide range of high-level scientific instruments, methodologies, data, and tools for advancing knowledge and innovation in cultural heritage. Besides the further development of technical infrastructures like research environments and digital repositories, human resources, transnational knowledge exchange and cooperation, social and economic impacts, valorization and dissemination are increasingly important objects of funding. This last chapter is dedicated to gaining an insight into the implications of international policies for establishing and developing an academic culture, and also to highlighting the challenges and perspectives of cultural heritage on a global level.

We would like to acknowledge the important work done by the chapter reviewers. We also thank the sponsors, Program Committee members, supporting organizations, and volunteers for making the joint event held in Dresden in October 2019 a success. Without their efforts, the event would not have been possible.

July 2021

Florian Niebling
Sander Münster
Heike Messemer

# Organization

## Program Chairs

| | |
|---|---|
| Florian Niebling | Julius-Maximilians-Universität Würzburg, Germany |
| Sander Münster | Friedrich-Schiller-Universität Jena, Germany |
| Heike Messemer | TU Dresden, Germany |

## Reviewers

| | |
|---|---|
| Fabrizio I. Apollonio | University of Bologna, Italy |
| Maria Leonor Botelho | University of Porto, Portugal |
| Stefan Bürger | Julius-Maximilians-Universität Würzburg, Germany |
| Emanuel Demetrescu | Istituto per le Tecnologie Applicate ai Beni Culturali, Italy |
| Leyla Dewitz | Technische Universität Dresden, Germany |
| Isabella Friso | Università Iuav di Venezia, Italy |
| Andreas Georgopoulos | National Technical University of Athens, Greece |
| Andrea Giordano | Università degli Studi di Padova, Italy |
| Robert Hecht | IÖR Dresden, Germany |
| Isto Huvila | Uppsala University, Sweden |
| Christina Kamposiori | University College London, UK |
| Piotr Kuroczynski | Hochschule Mainz, Germany |
| Beate Loeffler | Technische Universität Dortmund, Germany |
| Ivan Lee | University of South Australia, Australia |
| Fotis Liarokapis | Cyprus University of Technology, Cyprus |
| Davide Mezzino | Carleton University, Canada |
| Nikolas Prechtel | Technische Universität Dresden, Germany |
| Claartje Rasterhoff | Maastricht University, The Netherlands |
| Fulvio Rinaudo | Politecnico di Torino, Italy |
| Chiara Ronchini | Historic Environment Scotland, UK |
| Antonio Rodríguez | Anahuac Mayab University, Mexico |
| Mauro Romanelli | Università degli Studi di Napoli, Italy |
| Mario Santana Quintero | Carleton University, Canada |
| Danilo Schneider | Technische Universität Dresden, Germany |
| Jin Shang | Tsinghua University, China |
| Alex Ya-Ning Yen | China University of Technology, Taiwan |

# Contents

**Theory, Methods and Systematization**

The Critical Digital Model for the Study of Unbuilt Architecture . . . . . . . .    3
    *Fabrizio I. Apollonio, Federico Fallavollita, and Riccardo Foschi*

Digital Reconstruction of the New Synagogue in Breslau: New Approaches
to Object-Oriented Research . . . . . . . . . . . . . . . . . . . . . . . . . . . . . . .    25
    *Piotr Kuroczyński, Igor Bajena, Peggy Große, Karolina Jara,*
    *and Kinga Wnęk*

User Involvement for Application Development: Methods, Opportunities
and Experiences from Three Different Academic Projects . . . . . . . . . . . . .    46
    *Cindy Kröber, Katharina Hammel, Cornelia Schade, Nicole Filz,*
    *and Leyla Dewitz*

**Visualization and Presentation**

Visual Representations in Digital 3D Modeling/Simulation
for Architectural Heritage . . . . . . . . . . . . . . . . . . . . . . . . . . . . . . . . . .    87
    *Krzysztof Koszewski*

Toward an Automated Pipeline for a Browser-Based, City-Scale Mobile 4D
VR Application Based on Historical Images . . . . . . . . . . . . . . . . . . . . . .    106
    *Sander Münster, Christoph Lehmann, Taras Lazariv,*
    *Ferdinand Maiwald, and Susanne Karsten*

Comparing Methods to Visualize Orientation of Photographs:
A User Study . . . . . . . . . . . . . . . . . . . . . . . . . . . . . . . . . . . . . . . . . .    129
    *Jonas Bruschke, Markus Wacker, and Florian Niebling*

In Which Images Does This Corner Appears? A Novel Approach
for Three-Dimensional Query of Historical Photographs Collections
in Urban Heritage Research . . . . . . . . . . . . . . . . . . . . . . . . . . . . . . . .    152
    *Antonio Suazo*

Visualizing Venice to Visualizing Cities - Advanced Technologies
for Historical Cities Visualization . . . . . . . . . . . . . . . . . . . . . . . . . . . .    171
    *Kristin L. Huffman and Andrea Giordano*

**Machine Learning and Artificial Intelligence**

Semantic Deep Mapping in the Amsterdam Time Machine: Viewing Late
19th- and Early 20th-Century Theatre and Cinema Culture Through
the Lens of Language Use and Socio-Economic Status . . . . . . . . . . . . . . .     191
    *Julia Noordegraaf, Marieke van Erp, Richard Zijdeman, Mark Raat,*
    *Thunnis van Oort, Ivo Zandhuis, Thomas Vermaut, Hans Mol,*
    *Nicoline van der Sijs, Kristel Doreleijers, Vincent Baptist,*
    *Charlotte Vrielink, Brenda Assendelft, Claartje Rasterhoff,*
    *and Ivan Kisjes*

Deep Learning from History: Unlocking Historical Visual Sources Through
Artificial Intelligence . . . . . . . . . . . . . . . . . . . . . . . . . . . . . . . . . . . . . .     213
    *Seyran Khademi, Tino Mager, and Ronald Siebes*

**Policies, Legislation and Standards**

A Framework to Support Digital Humanities and Cultural Heritage
Studies Research . . . . . . . . . . . . . . . . . . . . . . . . . . . . . . . . . . . . . . . . . .     237
    *Selda Ulutas Aydogan, Sander Münster, Dino Girardi,*
    *Monica Palmirani, and Fabio Vitali*

**Author Index** . . . . . . . . . . . . . . . . . . . . . . . . . . . . . . . . . . . . . . . . . .     269

# Theory, Methods and Systematization

# The Critical Digital Model for the Study of Unbuilt Architecture

Fabrizio I. Apollonio$^{(\boxtimes)}$, Federico Fallavollita⬛,
and Riccardo Foschi⬛

Department of Architecture, University of Bologna,
viale Risorgimento, 2, 40136 Bologna, Italy
{fabrizio.apollonio,federico.fallavollita,
riccardo.foschi2}@unibo.it

**Abstract.** The virtual (re-)construction of architectural artefacts that never existed or were destroyed is a research topic that currently presents several problems. This study, starting from a state of the art briefly described, tries to answer various questions: describe what a Critical Digital Model (CDM) is and what qualities it must fulfil to be scientifically constructed, visualized and evaluated. The qualities described are the followings: constructive aspects, the geometric accuracy and qualification of the 3D models; Traceability, use of sources and documentation, and the quality of historical (re-)construction; Accessibility and interoperability, compatibility with the publication on platforms/repositories and Data model Exchange formats; Visualization, graphic output to communicate scientific content throughout the 3D models. In particular, the latter quality is thorough, and some case studies are presented. Among these case studies, particular attention is given to the diplomatic representation and to the representation of the degree of uncertainty of the historical reconstruction of the model.

**Keywords:** Digital reconstruction · Hypothetical reconstruction · Architectural drawing

## 1 Introduction

Thanks to the advent of the digital revolution a new way of studying and representing the past has become increasingly important in the academic world and in the field of the digital entertainment (such as films and video games). This new way makes use of the so-called virtual 3D reconstructions, that is, figurative and textual sources-based 3D modelling of artefacts that no longer extant or have never been built.

Today architects, art historians, restorers and archaeologists [1–3] use this medium to study and represent the past. The large production of these studies and models has created an international debate [4–6] that concerns above all the scientific reliability [7] of these (re-)constructions. Two important guidelines have been drawn up in this regard; the London Charter [8] and the Seville Principles [9]. These documents have defined general guidelines on the scientific nature of Computer-based Visualisation of Architectural Cultural Heritage (CVCH) models, and for its use concerning intellectual

© Springer Nature Switzerland AG 2021
F. Niebling et al. (Eds.): UHDL 2019, CCIS 1501, pp. 3–24, 2021.
https://doi.org/10.1007/978-3-030-93186-5_1

integrity, reliability, documentation, sustainability and access of heritage artefacts. Despite some proposals [10–12] and several projects dedicated to the subject (e.g. CARARE [13]; 3D-ICONS [14]), the scientific community has not yet succeeded in establishing operational standards that would allow the visualization of the degree of the hypothesis of the data model adopted, or what the data model behind the 3D visualization looks like, or how the process adopted could be mapped or referenced in the 3D model.

The goal of this paper is to give, within the field of a CVCH 3D model, a scientific description, of the Critical Digital Model (CDM), and labels the main quality it should have. Among its qualities, we will study in depth the Visualization.

For the time being, the outputs/results of virtual 3D reconstructions are not yet fully considered scientific products due to the lack of any international strict guidelines to validate the models.

As we will see in more detail, the sources for virtual reconstruction can be both descriptive or figurative documents and archaeological remains. Here we will focus on the first case, even though the principles and qualities described are universal and are not related to a specific case.

If the reference documents are hand-made drawings (by the author or posthumous survey drawings), typical interpretation problems are known. For example, the original drawings of the plans and elevations may be inconsistent. In this case, the scholar will have to understand which path to take, whether to give greater importance to the plan or the prospect or look for an intermediate road that takes into account the information of the plan and that of the elevation together. More generally, the original documents are never exhaustive in their description and always leave gaps or parts to be interpreted. Besides, these gaps may affect the geometric architectural aspect, but it can also affect other characteristics such as construction and material. In conclusion, there is always an interpretative work in these (re-)constructions and the fundamental question is how to construct, represent and evaluate a 3D model of this type by limiting as much as possible subjectivity.

## 2   Research Topic and Case Studies

In the field of architectural representation, the advances of digital technologies walk side by side with the development of new tools and methods for 3D data acquisition, documentation and dissemination of information related to architectural-archaeological heritage. Virtual reconstruction in archaeology and architecture [15] opened the debate to a wide range of theoretical problems related to documentation [16], analysis and interpretation of hypothetical reconstruction [17], transparency in the reconstruction process [18], and to the definition of new protocols for processing spatial data (acquisition, manipulation and management) [19, 20]. Within this wide context, in order to validate the entire 3D modelling hypothetical reconstruction process and to facilitate the exchange and reuse of information, as well as collaboration between experts in various disciplines, a common and shared heritage of methods and practices is necessary in order to make the knowledge behind any 3D digital hypothetical reconstruction accessible and reusable [21]. The source-based reconstructive process is the result of a highly complex decision-making process [22], through which, the data used and the decision adopted, accumulates an unknown, thus unpredictable and unquantifiable, degree of uncertainty and/or reliability [23].

Without a properly degree of confidence, expressed by the uncertainty/reliability of the incorporated data, the 3D model final output cannot be adequately evaluated from a scholarly point of view. For that reason, a structured hypothetical reconstruction modelling process is based on different levels of interpretation, characterized by a progressively increasing level of uncertainty. It is a complex and interconnected analysis and interpretation of documentary sources affected and/or characterized by different degrees of (a) coherence/consistency, (b) accuracy/metric quality and (c) subjectivity/perceptiveness [24].

## 3 The Critical Digital Model (CDM)

### 3.1 What is a Critical Digital Model?

The name Critical Digital Model deliberately refers to two studies in the field of digital elaboration of original drawings. The idea of the CDM derives from the ecdotics of the written text. In philology, it is the theory and practice of the critical edition of the text. In textual criticism, the critical edition of a text is the reviewed and enriched republication of the same text aimed at restoring its original form, and responding to the author's will, on the basis of the comparative study (collation) of each passage of the different witnesses existing direct and indirect, whether they are manuscripts or printed texts. The edition, therefore, is presented with a critical apparatus that reports varying lessons. It may also present a *codicum* coat showing the familiarity between the various texts put together to trace its archetype.

*Ecdotica* of the written text has a well-established history and is a discipline that has shared rules and standards. The same cannot be said about the ecdotics of drawings that has seen the light only in recent years with the publication of the Critical National Edition of Piero della Francesca's De Prospectiva Pingendi [25]. In this work, a critical edition of Piero's drawings was proposed for the first time.

Another study in which the critical term is proposed is Hubertus Günther's Critical Computer Visualization in Art History Teaching [26]. In this study, some typical problems of the virtual (re-)construction of unbuilt architectures based on graphic sources, are presented. However, several complications remain open such as that of visualizing the procedures adopted and the differences made in the proposed solutions. Questions to which our study tries to give some possible answers.

However, these two apparently distant studies, i.e. the Ecdotics of Piero's Drawings and the Critical Computer Visualization, have one main idea in common: the reconstruction of the original document, by filling the gaps and inconsistencies of the sources. To do this work it is necessary to accurately describe the methodology used and to display the proposed results in a transparent and transmissible way.

In this sense, the CDM wants to be a step forward in the path traced by these studies in different areas. The CDM, therefore, is an attempt to accurately define a transmissible methodology for constructing, viewing and evaluating 3D models of architectures that never existed or were destroyed.

The first question is to give a shared and concise definition of CDM: it is a 3D Computer-based Visualization of Architectural Cultural Heritage model based on reference documents of architectures never extant or destroyed.

The reference documents can be textual, they can be more or less accurate descriptions of the original artefacts, or they can be figurative: original drawings, photos, study models, or architectural remains in situ or preserved in museums.

The CDM can be used for scientific dissemination or as a three-dimensional reference document for scholars of architectural heritage. For this latter objective, the digital CDM should limit as much as possible the personal contribution to the interpretation of the sources and should document the criteria followed for the construction and representation of the 3D model in the clearest and transmissible way.

However, this concise definition is not sufficient to define a virtual (re-)construction. Therefore, we will try to describe the qualities that a CDM model should have.

1. Constructive aspects: the geometric accuracy and qualification of the 3D models;
2. Traceability: use of sources and documentation, and the quality of historical (re-) construction;
3. Accessibility and interoperability: compatibility with the publication on platforms/repositories and Data model Exchange formats;
4. Visualization: graphic output to communicate scientific content throughout the 3D models;

For each of these qualities a scale of values expressed in the Latin alphabet is assigned: A, B, C, D, E, where A is the maximum score and E the minimum score. These four main qualities do not have a hierarchy between them and express autonomous qualities from each other. Therefore, each CDM can be associated with about five values; for example (DEABA) or (CCBDA). In this way, the qualitative value of a CDM will not be associated with a single judgment but will be the overall evaluation of various qualities. For example, the "Visualization" quality could have a high evaluation while having a mediocre "traceability" or vice versa. The next sections report a brief explanation of these four qualities and an in-depth analysis of the "visualization".

### 3.2   Constructive Aspects

The constructive aspects of the CDM are evaluated through five points of analysis:

- The digital representation method used;
- The level of detail (LoD);
- The geometric quality;
- The scale of representation;
- The semantic segmentation.

Regarding the first category, the author must declare the digital method adopted for the construction of CDM. There are two methods of digital representation: the mathematical (i.e. NURBS models) one and the numerical one (i.e. MESH models).

Then the CDM can be mathematical, numeric or hybrid (numeric and mathematical). Parametric representation methods are not considered true representation methods because they do not influence the intrinsic nature of the model. A parametric model can be mathematical or numerical.

About the second category. The level of detail refers to the scale of representation adopted for the construction of the CDM. The LoD could be evaluated with five grades: Poor, Low, Medium, Good and High and refer to it at reference scales according to building typologies: for example, a model of a villa that can be printed in 1:50 scale without losing detail is medium/good; while a model of a building that can be printed in 1:200 is low.

About the third category. The geometric quality regards two different aspects. The first is the use or not of mathematical geometric profiles for the construction of three-dimensional entities. For example, if the geometric generator curves used to model the mouldings or the sections used to model the vaults can be extracted and identified as mathematical curves. A CDM where it is not possible to extract precise geometric generator curves (e.g. mesh models with discretized surfaces) should be placed at the lowest-quality step on the scale of 5. The second geometric aspect concerns the topological nature of the model. The use of closed and non-self-intersecting volumes. This is a particularly important factor for the calculation of the average uncertainty level of the model, weighted on the volumes of the elements, explained in Sect. 4.7. Thus a model consisting of closed and not self-intersecting volumes is a high-quality CDM according to this category.

About the fourth category, the scale of representation is linked to the tolerance of the digital representation adopted and to the type of building in question. The author must report the unit of measurement adopted for the representation and construction of the model (e.g. centimetres, with a tolerance of 0.01).

The last category regards semantic segmentation by layers or groups. This quality does not consider the quality of the segmentation but only assesses whether the segmentation exists or not and if it is usable (semantic quality is part of the "quality of historical reconstruction"). For example, if a CDM presents a study of the architectural order, topologically divided from the geometric structure of the rest of the model, but not organized into layers and sublayers, in this case, the CDM would have an average semantic segmentation quality.

Accurate descriptions of all these qualities complement the CDM and are required for its scientific validation.

## 3.3 Traceability

The quality of the sources concerns the quantity and quality of the reference documents used for the construction of the CDM.

The sources can be textual or figurative. The formers are exclusively textual descriptions. The figurative documents are original drawings, photos, sculptures, or even still existing rests of the original object.

The evaluation of the quality of the sources can be assessed according to four criteria:

- Consistency of sources (e.g. if the plan is consistent with the section and the façade);
- Quality of the documents used (e.g. if the graphic source is a scan or a photo and what is its resolution. If it is colour-corrected or not, if it is grayscale. If the original drawing is damaged);
- Completeness of the sources with respect to the object described (are the sources sufficient to describe the object entirely?);
- Types of sources (e.g. Textual or figurative sources).

The quality of historical (re-)construction is based on five categories:

- Comparative quality with sources (e.g. if the section of the CDM is equal to the section of the source);
- Structural quality (e.g. structural reliability with the technologies of the time. Alternatively, similarity with the construction systems adopted by the author of the project).
- Surface quality (the fidelity and the reliability of the materials or textures adopted for the representation of the CDM according to material available in that age);
- Typological quality. Any conjecture must be aligned with the architectural configuration of analogous case studies, otherwise, the author of the CDM must justify with robust references any atypical choice (e.g. if the theme is a church, the altar is expected to be in front of the aisle and at a higher floor quote, differently, proves must be provided).
- Semantic quality. Whether the digital CDM presents a semantic study of architecture or not and if it is accurate with regards to the field of study.

### 3.4  Accessibility and Interoperability

The characteristics described above guarantee a certain level of quality of the CDM model. By consulting this documentation any scholar can immediately see if that particular CDM is reusable for specific scientific purposes. Nevertheless, a CDM well documented can serve both academics for scientific purposes and the public for educational or entertainment purposes (video game, films).

Thus, traceability is the key factor for re-usability. In this sense, the creation of a comprehensive reference platform for the storage and exchange of these three-dimensional models and data would be desirable. This platform should allow the users to classify, catalogue and filter these models effectively, and to present them to the public. In this sense, some studies and projects are already carrying out this idea (Patrimonium.net [27]).

Currently there are several internet platforms or projects (e.g. Inception-project Horizon 2020 [28]) on the digital collection of the European architectural heritage. Most of these platforms are note exclusively dedicated to architecture never extant or destroyed. Therefore, it would be useful to have a digital 3D repository able to store and transmit together with the finished product, that is the 3D model, also all the information essential for a critical evaluation of the work: the document sources; how these sources have been used (paradata); the technical nature of the three-dimensional model (numerical, mathematical or mixed); semantic study, if any, etc. This kind of platform would be able, therefore, to offer two different and complementary interpretations: the first dedicated to scholars, that is, architects, engineers, art historians, archaeologists and all experts in the sector; the second devoted to the general public, non-experts in the sector.

### 3.5 Visualization

Visualization is the quality of the CDM that describes the methodologies adopted for the representation of 3D models produced. In other words, the graphic methods adopted to describe the models.

The visualization can, therefore, vary from photorealistic to abstract, such as that to describe the degree of uncertainty adopted in the reconstruction of the 3D model. To date, there are several studies on this topic, but a shared standard has not yet been reached. The following paragraph is an attempt to describe a possible methodology for viewing the models without compromising the original information contained in the source drawings.

## 4 The Visualization of the CDM

### 4.1 Premise

The hypothetical reconstruction process of unbuilt architecture requires to find solutions to missing parts, inconsistencies, design deficiencies, substrate faults, geometry discrepancies, undefined materials. To add the third dimension and generate a complete model coherently, it is necessary to fulfil lacks and correct issues of different nature trying to limit as much as possible personal interpretations. Nevertheless, the deduction/induction process is necessary to make conjectures, this highlights that the subjective interpretation is an unavoidable aspect of the reconstruction process [19, 29]. These issues are not only present at the geometric level but also at the shading level.

To visualize the digital models resultant from the reconstruction of never built or no more existent architecture, today the operators in this field usually choose between photorealistic (PR) or non-photorealistic (NPR) solutions.

From a certain point of view, the PR solution is the one with a greater chance of adding subjective conjectures [30]. However also the NPR solution of using a single white or grey material has its risks. For example, applying a single precise material to the whole scene, even if it is as neutral as possible such as white or grey, may induce the observer to think that the entire building is covered with a continuous layer of plaster, or even more grayscale-like reconstructions under unfavourable circumstances can contribute to the erroneous idea that antiquity was a colourless age [31]. Either way, people may subconsciously still perceive a different atmosphere from the one drawn by the original author. Thus, depending on the material and colour that are chosen, if they are different from the ones of the original reference, the perception of the spaces might change significantly. Thus in the next sections, we will present alternatives, to PR or NPR mono-material shadings, that might contribute preserving the graphical quality of the sources while being at the same time a valid visualization solution that add as little subjective conjectures as possible.

## 4.2    Photorealistic (PR) Shading

With the traditional drawing techniques representing realistic materials was difficult or too time-consuming, in fact, in the ancient technical drawings of architectures, the definition of materials and surface texturing was often, schematized through simple hatches or monochromatic solid fillings, described with brief texts, or postponed to later not documented design phases. Furthermore, even when the surface chromatic aspects are represented accurately the natural colour of the paper or the ageing of the document may affect the shade of the drawing, adding chromatic aberration, that increases the uncertainty. Given that, even if clear documental sources about materials and colours are available, which is already rare, producing a photorealistic view of the model, free of subjective interpretations, is still challenging. However, for some applications (e.g. entertainment, games assets, movie sets) the photorealistic aspect is indispensable. In most of these cases, the scientific accuracy of the model has secondary importance [32] and the creation of a model transmissible and reusable is not crucial, however, it is still possible if the level of uncertainty and the sources used are precisely declared.

## 4.3    Non-photorealistic (NPR) Shading

If there are not enough documents on construction materials, surfaces appearance and colours, and if the PR representation is not necessary, to limit as much as possible ambiguities and misinterpretations, is preferable to apply an alternative NP representation method. The most widespread NP solutions in digital reconstructions are the following:

- Abstract multi-coloured textures (solid colours or patterns): usually used to indicate the level of uncertainty or other aspects of the models that are not directly visible from the shade-less model.
- Neutral mono-material: deliberate avoidance of the definition of the materials (usually single white or grey material applied to the whole scene).
- Wire (with hidden edges or not): only the edges of the model are visible, without shadows and textures.
- X-ray/translucent/alpha: usually adopted to show inside or behind the model, or to indicate uncertainty.
- Flat shading: a model coloured only without any shadow or highlight usually used to focus the attention on the texture colour or to represent models that are captured with photogrammetry techniques.
- Ambient Occlusion: proximity shadowed model, mostly used to enhance the perception of 3D details without needing to define any specific material or light emitter.

- Black and white: patterns textures and materials are recognizable from the renderings but there is no colour information which limits the conjectures.
- Texture derived from original drawings.
- Stylized hand-painted texture.

Most of these graphical styles, even if they do not add further subjective interpretations, if used as the only representation method, might be hard to read or might generate ambiguities. For example, the use of abstract coloured textures, especially if they present patterns, might disturb the perception of the object shape and proportions, or if the colours are similar to plausible construction materials they might be confused by laypersons for the actual colours of the object. Furthermore, when proper lights and shadows are not applied (wire, x-ray, flat shading) the third dimension might be hardly readable. A more readable solution which is borderline between photorealistic and abstract is the black and white graphical style, which are basically photorealistic renderings converted to greyscale, this might be a good solution for those cases where the surface textures and materials are known but not the colours.

### 4.4    The Surface Appearance of the CDM

Even if there are a lot of examples of architectural reconstructions that make use of the photorealistic style [33–36], a lot of times, the application of photorealistic shaders is deliberately avoided propending for a more abstract graphical style to limit the addition of further subjective conjectures at shading level [37, 38]. However, both the solutions, if not carefully documented and presented, might lead to ambiguities and misinterpretations. The CDM aims to address also the aspects related to the shading and texturing, that is why the photorealistic solution must be adopted only if reliable documental sources support it. For all the other cases abstract graphical styles are preferable. If reliable sources on the surface appearance are not available, the CDM might become an occasion not only to restore the third dimension of the authorial drawings but also to incorporate, at texture level, additional information which is most of the times lost in the process or hidden into the attached documental sources. In the next sections, possible graphical alternative to photorealism compatible with the vocation of the CDM will be proposed.

### 4.5    Tridimensional Transposition of Bidimensional Graphical Style (*Diplomatic* Representation)

The application of a neutral mono-material is often the preferred solution when there are no reliable sources on surface appearance. However, in this way, the graphical style of the original drawings used as sources would not be visible on the model anymore. One of the key characteristics of the critical version of texts is that no part of the original text is usually removed, only additional notes and parts of other texts are added to clarifying concepts, correcting errors, or interrelating sources. The CDM has the same ambition but transposed to 3D models.

Within the theoretical assumptions adopted to define and outline the Critical Digital Model (see Sect. 3.1), a method of representation, called *Diplomatic*, is established, which is focused on the conventions, protocols and formulae that have been used by original hand-made document creators, in order to increase understanding of the processes of document creation, of information transmission, and of the relationships between the artifacts which the documents purport to represent and reality, with the aim of reproducing the values, the knowledge and qualities of the original drawings. Thus instead of applying a neutral mono-material, that would not add any information to the reconstruction, a texture extracted from the original drawing might be preferable. In this way, the model would not be only a possible "what if" represented with an aseptic look, but it would be a medium to disseminate and transmit the graphical quality of the documental sources, the aesthetic of the strokes, the cultural value of the use of colours and hatches, the quality of the architectural spaces, the intrinsic cultural and historical value of all these and other aspects directly retrievable from the original drawings. This type of shading might also be considered as a secondary shading variant for the models where a photorealistic solution is possible, in this way both the information about the graphic quality of the sources and about materials and surface finishing can be stored into the model at once.

**Fig. 1.** Mauro Guidi, Sepolcro antico di figura quadrata con portico di due gradini, Cesena Nuova, Atlante 41, Carta 48 [39]: 3D CDM (top); Original drawing (bottom).

Images from 1 to 5 exemplifies this concept on five different case studies belonging to different authors, geographic areas, architectonic styles and periods. The techniques used to achieve these results were:

- texture projection and manual mesh painting (Fig. 1)
- texture projection and procedural mapping (Fig. 2)
- texture projection and texture cloning (Fig. 3)
- postproduction of render passes (Fig. 4)
- procedural mapping and postproduction (Fig. 5)

**Fig. 2.** Claude Nicolas Ledoux, Maison d'un employè, Cité idéale de Chaux, Tome 1, Pl. 17 [40]: 3D CMD (top); Original drawing (bottom).

**Fig. 3.** Claude Nicolas Ledoux, Atelier des gardes de la forêt, Cité idéale de Chaux, Tome 1, Pl. 102 [40]: 3D CMD (top); Original drawing (bottom).

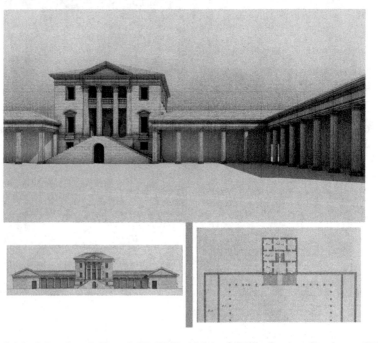

**Fig. 4.** Original drawing (left) and 3D CMD (right) of "Villa Ragona Cecchetto, Ghizzole, Montegaldella (PD)" by Andrea Palladio [41], tav. XLI

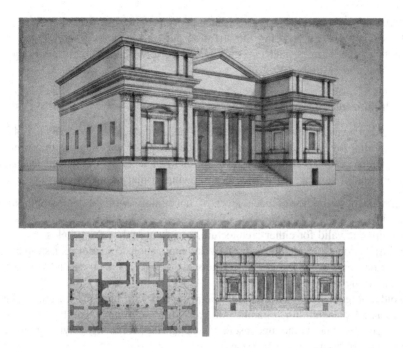

**Fig. 5.** Andrea Palladio, Villa Pisani, Bagnolo, RIBA collection, XVII/16 [42]: 3D CMD (top); Original drawing (bottom).

## 4.6   False Colours to Express the Uncertainty

When the sources are too many and too different and when they have not an adequate level of quality to be able to apply the technique proposed in Sect. 4.5, there are other ways to incorporate information about sources directly into the model. For example, shading the model with false colours. Adding information at texture level in the form of colours allows the viewers to retrieve information about the model without needing to access external sources. This method was widely used for example to add information about the type of sources used and/or information about the reliability of the reconstruction [43–45]. This idea was at the centre of international debate for many years because it is a process suitable to be standardised (Arbeitsgruppe Digitale 3D-Rekonstruktion [46]). The main reasons why in many years no method was adopted as a standard is probably because the proposed methodologies were specifically designed for single case studies or at most for specific application fields, but they were not flexible enough to be applied to other cases or fields, another reason might have been that the more all-inclusive methodologies were too complex and time-consuming to apply to simpler cases and/or some classifications of sources and models were ambiguous or overlapping if applied to other fields.

Given these premises, the scale of uncertainty proposed in Sect. 4.7 tries to be as flexible as possible by focusing the attention not on the type of sources but on the reliability of the sources, and every class is precisely defined to try avoiding overlapping and ambiguities.

## 4.7 Optimized Scale of Uncertainty

Starting from a vast series of proposals, developed over the past few years [21, 47–49], we tried to improve the several variations of the scales of uncertainties that were used in the various reconstruction projects in the field of architecture, design and archaeology to make it suitable to address the following primary issues:

- synthetic descriptions of each level of uncertainty with as less ambiguities as possible
- descriptions valid for either architecture, design or archaeology fields
- predisposition to granularity, to allow its application to harder and simpler cases while returning comparable results (the scale of 7 levels is compactable into 5 or 3 levels to the need)
- avoid ambiguous colours that might be perceived with opposite meanings (i.e. not used red for maximum reliability or green for minimum reliability, because the average observer would unconsciously apply the traffic light symbology to the colours, perceiving opposite meaning)
- HSV colour intervals as wide as possible (colours with too close HSV values might be hard to distinguish on the shaded model)
- Assign a colour also to neutral, irrelevant or not considered elements (they will not contribute to the average level of uncertainty of the model)

Concerning the number of colors for classification tasks (search and distinguishing), several publications showed that only a small number of different hues can be processed, by human vision, and use effectively with a low error rate. Healey [50] stated that only five to seven different hues can be found accurately and rapidly on a map. Furthermore, MacEachren [51] affirmed that, if the task is to precisely identify a certain color in a plot, the detection rate can plummet when the number of colors increases (detection rate for 10 colors: 98%; for 17 colors: 72%). Other issues that were considered were about people with colour perception problems and the cases where the model can only be visualized in greyscale. However in the former case, because the types of colour vision deficiencies are several and very different we were not able to find an acceptable solution that worked sufficiently well for every one of them, so we prioritized the perception of people with normal colour vision, or with minimal colour vision deficiencies. About the greyscale issue, we concluded that converting a scale of colours with a scale of shades of grey is not a good solution, because lights and shadows can always deceive the viewers (Fig. 8). So, for that, we think that it would be better to convert the colours to black and white graphical patterns instead of using different shadings of solid grey. However, also the patterns might be deceiving because they might be hard to distinguish in minute elements and they might mix up with the edges of the model making the shapes less distinguishable. Thus, these are issues that need further study.

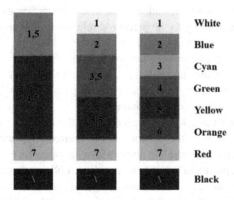

**Fig. 6.** Granularity of the scale of uncertainty.

To allow flexibility but at the same time to guarantee consistency we propose to use a scale of 7 + 1 steps (compactable to 5 + 1 and 3 + 1) assigned to colours that are easily nominable (black, red, orange, yellow, green, cyan, blue, white) (Fig. 6). We decided to not provide precise RGB values or RAL codes, but to assign wider intervals for each step of the scale, to improve flexibility. This choice was made to encourage the use of the same scale for projects were too bright or too dull colours would have not matched to the overall graphical style presentation and would have caused the adoption of a different colour scheme. The steps of the scale are no more than 7 + 1 to guarantee maximum recognizability. The red is assigned to the most uncertain level and blue to the less uncertain level. The colours are sorted following the order of the colours in the visible spectrum of light so once identified the lower and upper bounds the intermediate colours are easily derivable, the same colour schemes are used in many different scientific fields such as in the analysis of stress, deformation, temperature, pressure. We assigned the white colour (or light grey) to the level with maximum reliability. In some applications, this level of uncertainty might also be effectively substituted by the colour of the object in case of photographic textures extracted from real rests of the object. All those elements that will not be considered for the analysis but that are still useful to define spatial relationships with the object of study will be coloured with black (or dark grey).

A number from 1 to 7 is assigned to every level of the scale (the neutral level is identified with a backslash "\"), in this way it will be possible to extract an average numerical value for each model that would return the average uncertainty of the whole model. To achieve more reliable results not affected by the segmentation of the model, this number must be weighted with the volumes of each element that is why it is very important to model every single element with closed volume.

A theme of discussion regards the fact that some elements contribute more than others to the final aspects of the object especially in architectural cases, thus some elements are less important and should be considered less than others. For example, the walls against the soil of the cellars are a lot less relevant compared to the columns mouldings and architraves of the main façade, however, the volume of the walls might affect the global average value of uncertainty much more than the volume of the architectonic order. A solution for this might be providing two different average uncertainty values, one that is a simple average weighted with the volumes of each element which is more objective, and another one that applies multipliers to the volumes of the elements according to the perceived relative importance. This second value is a lot more subjective, but if the assigned weights are clearly provided it will be easily retro-traceable and might give more plausible results (Fig. 7).

Every level of uncertainty is carefully defined in Table 1 and clarified in Table 2. Every level is differentiated by the other according to the consistency, the state of conservation and the author of the sources used, in this way any overlapping is avoided. In the scale with five levels of uncertainty, the levels 3 and 4 are collapsed as well as 5 and 6, in this way the authors of the sources that are not direct/primary sources are not relevant anymore. In the scale with three levels of uncertainty, the levels 1 and 2 are collapsed and levels from 3 to 6 are collapsed as well, in this case, the elements derived from surveys of real remaining and elements derived from clear and consistent direct sources have the same level of uncertainty, and all the other sources except the elements modelled without sources will have the same uncertainty. To every level of the scale is assigned a number that will be used to calculate the average uncertainty level of the model, the collapsed levels in the scales with 3 and 5 steps will be numbered with the average of the collapsed levels. Even if the three scales are comparable, they have very different accuracy, especially the scale at three levels must not be used for cases where maximum accuracy is required.

**Table 1.** Level of uncertainty scale, with 7 + 1 steps, descriptive explanation of each level.

| | | Description |
|---|---|---|
| | 1 | Reliable assumption derived from reality-based data (i.e. the full real object or parts of it, well preserved archaeological founds, direct surveys, laser scans). |
| | 2 | Reliable conjecture based on clear and accurate direct/ primary sources* when the real object or parts of it are not available. |
| | 3 | Conjecture based on stylistic/ structural references by SAME AUTHORS when direct/ primary sources are available, but unclear/ damaged/ inconsistent/ inaccurate. Or logic deduction/selection of a variant derived by inconsistent direct sources. |
| | 4 | Conjecture based on stylistic/ structural references by DIFFERENT AUTHORS when direct/ primary sources are available, but unclear/ damaged/ inconsistent/ inaccurate. |
| | 5 | Conjecture based on stylistic/ structural references by SAME AUTHORS when direct/ primary sources are not available. |
| | 6 | Conjecture based on stylistic/ structural references by DIFFERENT AUTHORS when direct/ primary sources are not available. |
| | 7 | Conjecture based on personal knowledge due to missing or unreferenced sources. |
| | \ | Not relevant/ not considered/ left unsolved/ missing data and missing conjecture (it does not count for the calculation of the average uncertainty). |

* Direct/primary sources: all the sources where the object is directly represented, reported, recorded with any level of accuracy (i.e. drawings, sketches, surveys, pictures, paintings, texts, books, coins, medals, reliefs, physical models, sculptures)

**Table 2.** Level of uncertainty scale, with 7 + 1 levels, graphical explanation.

| Real object | Direct\primary sources | | Other sources | | Reliability |
|---|---|---|---|---|---|
| | Clear/ consistent | Damaged/ unclear | Same author/s | Other author/s | |
| 1 √ | \ | \ | \ | \ | Reality |
| 2 X | √ | \ | \ | \ | Reliable conjecture |
| 3 X | X | √ | √ | \ | Conjecture |
| 4 X | X | √ | X | √ | Conjecture |
| 5 X | X | X | √ | \ | Conjecture |
| 6 X | X | X | X | √ | Conjecture |
| 7 X | X | X | X | X | Conjecture |
| \ \ | \ | \ | \ | \ | Abstention |

1
2
3
4
5
6
7
\

Average Uncertainty
weighted on the Volume
of the elements
**AU-V** = 3.6

Average Uncertainty
weighted on the Volume and
the **Relevance** of the elements
**AU-VR**= 3.2
(capitals 5x, cornices 5x)

**Fig. 7.** Andrea Palladio, Villa Pisani, Bagnolo: Color map of level of uncertainty (7 + 1 levels) of 3D hypothetical reconstruction, after RIBA XVII/16 (left); Two average of uncertainties (right)

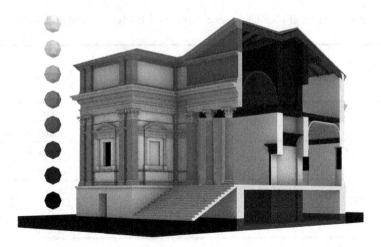

**Fig. 8.** Andrea Palladio, Villa Pisani, Bagnolo: Grey scale map of level of uncertainty (7 + 1 levels) of 3D hypothetical reconstruction after RIBA XVII/16.

## 5  Conclusion

In this study, we described the Digital Critical Model and what qualities it must possess to be scientifically assessed. The qualities described are the following. Constructive aspects: the geometric accuracy and qualification of the 3D models. Traceability: the use of sources and documentation, and the quality of historical (re-)construction. Accessibility and interoperability: compatibility with the publication on platforms/ repositories and Data model Exchange formats. Visualization: graphic output to communicate scientific content throughout the 3D models. In particular, the latter quality is thorough, and some case studies are presented. Among these case studies, particular attention is paid to the diplomatic representation and to the representation of the degree of uncertainty of the historical (re-)construction of the model. Some problems have not been explored here and will be addressed in future research and publications. The most important question remains the search for shared standards for the construction, visualization and evaluation of virtual (re-)constructions of drawn or no more extant architecture. Furthermore, the question of a shared and transmissible methodology that can visualize and communicate both the procedures adopted and the different qualities of the historical (re-)construction of the model is still central. In this sense, this study is a proposal to share reflections and possible solutions to well-known problems, with the scientific community and does not represent a definitive solution yet. The hope is that these studies (together with all the literature on the topic) can stimulate a debate and lead the research in the direction of shared standards between scholars and enthusiasts. In an increasingly globalized world, where virtual reality seems to be within everyone's reach, being able to share methodologies and standards on virtual reconstructions of architectural artefacts could be an important step forward for the valorisation, conservation and transmission of architectural heritage (existing and virtual).The definition of shared Standards, Methodology and Glossary can give a critical reference to the international scientific community working on historical virtual reconstructions and might set a scientifically recognized method to validate the models. These standards can be a reference also for the world of digital entertainment (films and video games) which have an increasingly important and powerful role in the collective perception of our past.

# References

1. Novitski, B.J.: Rendering Real and Imagined Buildings. The Art of Computer Modelling from the Palace of Kublai Khan to Le Corbusier's Villas. Rockport Pub, Gloucester (1998)
2. Barceló, J.A., Forte, M., Sanders, D.H.: Virtual Reality in Archaeology. ArcheoPress, Oxford (2000)
3. Bentkowska-Kafel, A., Denard, H., Baker, D.: Paradata and Transparency in Virtual Heritage. Routledge, Farnham (2012)
4. Hermon, S.: Reasoning in 3D. A critical appraisal of the role of 3D modelling and virtual reconstructions in archaeology. In: Frischer, B. (eds.) Beyond illustration: 2D and 3D Digital Technologies as Tools for Discovery in Archaeology, pp. 36–45. Tempus Reparatum, Oxford (2008)
5. Greengrass, M., Hughes, L.: The Virtual Representation of the Past. Ashgate, London (2008)
6. Münster, S., Köhler, T., Hoppe, S.: 3D modeling technologies as tools for the reconstruction and visualization of historic items in humanities. A literature-based survey. In: Traviglia, A. (eds.) Across Space and Time. Papers from the 41st Conference on Computer Applications and Quantitative Methods in Archaeology, Perth, 25–28 March 2013, pp. 430–441. Amsterdam University Press, Amsterdam (2015)
7. Pfarr-Harfst, M.: Virtual scientific models. In: Bowen, J.P., Keene, S., Ng, K. (eds.) Electronic Visualisation and the Arts, pp. 157–163. CDMaid, London (2013)
8. London Charter website. http://www.londoncharter.org/index.html. Accessed 30 Apr 2020
9. Seville Principles website. http://smartheritage.com/seville-principles/seville-principles. Accessed 30 Apr 2020
10. Demetrescu, E., Ferdani, D., Dell'Unto, N., Leander Touati, A.-M., Lindgren, S.: Reconstructing the original splendour of the House of Caecilius Iucundus. A complete methodology for virtual archaeology aimed at digital exhibition. SCIRES-IT 6(1), 51–66 (2016)
11. Gonzalez-Perez, C., Martín-Rodilla, P., Parcero-Oubiña, C., Fábrega-Álvarez, P., Güimil-Fariña, A.: Extending an abstract reference model for transdisciplinary work in cultural heritage. In: Dodero, J.M., Palomo-Duarte, M., Karampiperis, P. (eds.) MTSR 2012. CCIS, vol. 343, pp. 190–201. Springer, Heidelberg (2012). https://doi.org/10.1007/978-3-642-35233-1_20
12. Kuroczyński, P., Hauck, O., Dworak, D.: 3D models on triple paths – new pathways for docu-menting and visualizing virtual reconstructions. In: Münster, S., Pfarr-Harfst, M., Kuroczyński, P., Ioannides, M. (eds.) 3D Research Challenges in Cultural Heritage II. LNCS, vol. 10025, pp. 149–172. Springer, Heidelberg (2016). https://doi.org/10.1007/978-3-319-47647-6_8
13. CARARE homepage. https://www.carare.eu/. Accessed 30 Apr 2020
14. 3D-ICONS homepage. http://3dicons-project.eu/. Accessed 30 Apr 2020

15. Reily, P.: Towards a virtual archaeology. In: CAA 1990. Computer Applications and Quantitative Methods in Archaeology 1990 (BAR International Series 565), pp. 132–139. Tempus Reparatum, Oxford (1990)

16. Pfarr, M.: Dokumentationssystem für digitale Rekonstruktionen am Beispiel der Grabanlage Zhaoling, Provinz Shaanxi, China. TUprints, Darmstadt (2010). http://tuprints.ulb.tudarmstadt.de/2302/

17. Dell'Unto, N., Leander, A.-M., Ferdani, D., Dellepiane, M., Callieri, M., Lindgren, S.: Digital reconstruction and visualization in archaeology: Case-study drawn from the work of the Swedish Pompeii Project. In: 2013 Digital Heritage International Congress, pp. 621–628. IEEE, Marseille (2013)

18. Hermon, S., Sugimoto, G., Mara, H.: The London charter and its applicability. In: VAST 2007: Future Technologies to Empower Heritage Professionals, pp. 11–14. Graphics Art, Ioannina (2007)

19. Münster, S.: Workflows and the role of images for virtual 3D reconstruction of no longer extant historic objects. In: 24th International CIPA Symposium 2013, ISPRS II-5/W1, pp. 197–202 (2013)

20. Pfarr-Harfst, M., Grellert, M.: The reconstruction – argumentation method: proposal for a minimum standards of documentation in the context of virtual reconstructions. In: Ioannides, M., et al. (eds.) Digital Heritage Progress in Cultural Heritage: Documentation, Preservation, and Protection. LNCS, vol. 10058, pp. 39–50. Springer, Heidelberg (2016)

21. Apollonio, F.I.: Classification schemes for visualization of uncertainty in digital hypothetical reconstruction. In: Münster, S., Pfarr-Harfst, M., Kuroczyński, P., Ioannides, M. (eds.) 3D Research Challenges in Cultural Heritage II. LNCS, vol. 10025, pp. 173–197. Springer, Cham (2016). https://doi.org/10.1007/978-3-319-47647-6_9

22. Kőller, D., Frischer, B., Humphreys, G.: Research challenges for digital archives of 3D cultural heritage models. ACM J. Comput. Cult. Herit. 2(3) (2009). Article 7

23. Apollonio, F.I.: Classification schemes and model validation of 3D digital reconstruction process, In: 2015 20th International Conference on Cultural Heritage and New Technologies 2015 - CHNT 20. Museen der Stadt Wien – Stadtarchäologie, Wien (2016)

24. Grellert, M., Apollonio, F.I., Martens, B., Nußbaum, N.: Working experiences with the reconstruction argumentation method (RAM) – scientific documentation for virtual reconstruction. In: 2018 23rd International Conference on Cultural Heritage and New Technologies 2018 - CHNT 23, pp. 1–14. Museen der Stadt Wien – Stadtarchäologie, Wien (2019)

25. Migliari, R., et al.: Piero della Francesca: De prospectiva pingendi. TOMO II [Disegni]. Istituto Poligrafico e Zecca dello Stato, Roma (2016)

26. Günther, H.: Kritische Computer-Visualisierung in der kunsthistorischen Lehre. In: Frings, M. (ed.) Der Modelle Tugend. CAD und die neuen Räume der Kunstgeschichte, pp. 111–122. Weimar (2001)

27. Patrimonium.net homepage. http://www.patrimonium.net/. Accessed 30 Apr 2020

28. Inception EU-Project. https://www.inception-project.eu/en. Accessed 30 Apr 2020

29. Grellert, M., Pfarr-Harfst, M.: 25 Years of virtual reconstructions project report of department information and communication technology in architecture at Technische Universität Darmstadt. In: 18th International Conference on Cultural Heritage and New Technologies 2013 - CHNT 18, 2013. Museen der Stadt Wien – Stadtarchäologie, Wien (2014)

30. Grellert, M., Haas, F.: Sharpness versus uncertainty in 'complete models'. virtual reconstructions of the Dresden castle in 1678. In: Hoppe, S., Breitling, S. (eds.) Virtual Palaces, Part II. Lost Palaces and their Afterlife. Virtual Reconstruction between Science and Media, pp. 119–138. Palatium, München (2016)

31. Heeb, N., Christen, J.: Strategien zur Vermittlung von Fakt, Hypothese und Fiktion in der digitalen Architektur-Rekonstruktion. In: Kuroczyński, P., Pfarr-Harfst, M., Münster S. (eds.) Der Modelle Tugend 2.0. Digitale 3D-Rekonstruktion als virtueller Raum der architekturhistorischen Forschung, pp. 227–254. Arthistoricum.net, Heidelberg (2019)
32. Webster, A.: Building a Better Paris in Assassin's Creed Unity. Historical accuracy meets game design. The Verge (2019). https://www.theverge.com/2014/10/31/7132587/assassins-creed-unity-paris. Accessed 30 Apr 2020
33. Avella, F.: Il Gran Caffè di Giuseppe Damiani Almeyda. Caracol, Palermo (2015)
34. Apollonio, F.I., Gaiani, M., Fallavollita, F., Giovannini, E.C., Foschi, R.: Digital reconstruction of Piazza delle Erbe in Verona at XIVth century. In: Le ragioni del disegno. Pensiero, Forma e Modello nella gestione della complessità, pp. 57–62. Gangemi, Roma (2016)
35. Webster, A.: The Concept Art behind Assassin's Creed Syndicate's beautiful Victorian London. The Verge (2015). https://www.theverge.com/2015/11/10/9705396/assassins-creed-syndicate-london-concept-art. Accessed 30 Apr 2020
36. The TimeRide VR Experience Homepage. https://www.ronenbekerman.com/timeride-vr-experience/. Accessed 30 Apr 2020
37. Lengyel, D., Toulouse, C.: Visualisation of uncertainty in archaeological reconstructions. In: Hoppe, S., Breitling, S. (eds.) Virtual Palaces, Part II. Lost Palaces and their Afterlife. Virtual Reconstruction between Science and Media, pp. 103–117. Palatium, München (2016)
38. Sirbu, D.: Digital exploration of unbuilt architecture: a non-photorealistic approach. In: Klinger, K.R. (ed.) ACADIA22 - Connecting the Crossroads of Digital Discourse, pp. 235–245 (2003)
39. Guidi, M.: Pensieri d'architettura. Ms., Biblioteca Malatestiana, Cesena (1790)
40. Ledoux, C.-N.: L'architecture considérée sous le rapport de l'art, des moeurs et de la legislation, Tome 1. Paris (1804). Gallica. BNF. https://gallica.bnf.fr/ark:/12148/bpt6k1047050b.langFR. Accessed 30 Apr 2020
41. Muttoni, F.: Architettura di Andrea Palladio vicentino arricchita di tavole, Venezia, Angiolo Pasinelli (1740–1748). https://mediateca.palladiomuseum.org/palladio/immagine.php?id=7703. Accessed 30 Apr 2020
42. Palladio, A.: Design for Villa Pisani, Bagnolo: facade and plan (from RIBA archives). https://www.architecture.com/image-library/RIBApix/image-information/poster/design-for-villa-pisani-bagnolo-facade-and-plan/posterid/RIBA28582.html. Accessed 30 Apr 2020
43. Light, A., Bartlein, P.J.: The end of the rainbow? Color schemes for improved data graphics. EOS Trans. Am. Geophys. Union AQ5 **85**(40), 385–391 (2004)
44. Stone, M.: Choosing colors for data visualization. Business Intelligence Network (2006). http://www.perceptualedge.com/articles/b-eye/choosing_colors.pdf. Accessed 30 Apr 2020
45. Reichert, P., Borsuk, M.E.: Does high forecast uncertainty preclude effective decision support? Environ. Model Softw. **20**(8), 991–1001 (2005)
46. Arbeitsgruppe Digitale 3D-Rekonstruktion Homepage. https://digitale-rekonstruktion.info/. Accessed 30 Apr 2020
47. Apollonio, F.I., Gaiani, M., Sun, Z.: Characterization of uncertainty and approximation in digital reconstruction of CH artifacts. In: Heritage Architecture Landesign. Focus on Conservation Regeneration Innovation. Le vie dei Mercanti - XI Forum Internazionale di Studi, pp. 860–869. La scuola di Pitagora, Napoli (2013)
48. Apollonio, F.I., Giovannini, E.C.: A paradata documentation methodology for the Uncertainty Visualization in digital reconstruction of CH artifacts. SCIRES-IT **5**(2), 1–24 (2015)

49. Grellert, M., Apollonio, F.I., Martens, B., Nußbaum, N.: Working experiences with the reconstruction argumentation method (RAM) – scientific documentation for virtual reconstruction. In: 2018 23rd International Conference on Cultural Heritage and New Technologies 2018 - CHNT 23, vol. 23, pp. 1–14. Museen der Stadt Wien – Stadtarchäologie, Wien (2019)

50. Healey, C.: Choosing effective colours for data visualization. In: 7th Conference on Visualization 1996, pp.263–270. IEEE, San Francisco (1996)

51. MacEachren, A.: How maps are seen. In: How Maps Work. Representation, Visualization, and Design, pp. 51–147. Guilford Press, New York (1995)

# Digital Reconstruction of the New Synagogue in Breslau: New Approaches to Object-Oriented Research

Piotr Kuroczyński[1(✉)], Igor Bajena[1], Peggy Große[1,2],
Karolina Jara[1,3], and Kinga Wnęk[1]

[1] Institute of Architecture, Hochschule Mainz - University of Applied Sciences,
Mainz, Germany
piotr.kuroczynski@hs-mainz.de
[2] Heidelberg University Library, Heidelberg, Germany
[3] Institute of Art History, University of Wrocław, Wrocław, Poland

**Abstract.** Computer-aided 3D-modelling and visualisation are widely used in the examination and communication of historical architecture. In the case of a no-longer existing, demolished or seriously altered building, source-based, digital 3D-reconstruction represents an appropriate methodology of approach to this kind of research object. Digital models and their visualisation have, however, been criticised from the start for their lack of transparency as well as for the interoperability and sustainability of the research data.

The following article focuses on a new type of research methodology, presented by the digital 3D-reconstruction of the New Synagogue in Breslau (demolished 1938). In this case, the (Historic/Heritage) Building Information Modelling method adopted from contemporary building industry engages with concerns relating to a period building in a broad socio-cultural context as well as with the need of comprehensive documentation of the sources, their interpretation and a source-based hypothetical 3D-reconstruction in human- and machine-readable form.

**Keywords:** Historic/Heritage Building Information Modelling (HBIM) · Digital 3D reconstruction · Data modelling · CIDOC CRM · Web-based research environments · New Synagogue Breslau/Wrocław (Poland)

## 1 The Use of Digital Methods in the 3D-Reconstruction of Demolished Architecture

Both 3D-retrodigitisation of existing artefacts by 3D-laser scanning and photogrammetry and source-based, hypothetical 3D-reconstruction of physically non-existing objects or unexecuted designs represents an adequate, up-to-date and promising approach to research objects in the fields of archaeology, art and architectural history as well as in the preservation of historical monuments. The great potential of digital 3D-reconstruction models results from the exact reproduction of geometrical and material characteristics of a (no-longer) existing object as well as from a previous in-depth examination, evaluation and processing of the sources. The resulting creative,

© Springer Nature Switzerland AG 2021
F. Niebling et al. (Eds.): UHDL 2019, CCIS 1501, pp. 25–45, 2021.
https://doi.org/10.1007/978-3-030-93186-5_2

hypothetical replica of the buildings is matched by the in-depth understanding of the reconstruction's authors [1]. Therefore, any research object must be examined in its entirety in a (virtual) three-dimensional space by the authors of the reconstruction process. The spatial examination of an object in a 3D-software application does not allow for gaps and inconsistencies. Since traditional methods of architectural representation, e.g. the ground plan, sectional and elevation plans as well as fixed perspectives, are restricted to one side of an object at any given time, inconsistencies (gaps in knowledge) could only be recognised and corrected on the construction site. The digital 3D-reconstruction is based on the historical source material, the interpretation of the sources and a hypothetical reproduction of the object. During this process, knowledge is merged and generated, gaps in the sources (state of knowledge) are revealed and hypothetical suggestions (knowledge building) are presented.

For scientific research and its representatives, such as the Digital Humanities, the IT added value of a digital 3D-model originates in the sustainable link of academic issues with sources, their interpretation and with the resulting hypothetical findings in both human- and machine-readable form, as well as in the availability of interoperable research data [2]. The many possibilities of digital 3D-reconstruction of demolished or altered works of architecture or of unexecuted architectural designs have so far not been fully exploited due to the lack of digital methods and infrastructure. Above all, this situation affects the scientific documentation and publication of the results of 3D-reconstructions. Due to a lack of transparency of the information and decisions behind the reconstructions as well as of the availability of research data in the form of digital 3D-models, the scientific nature of most of these projects is still under debate.

As a result, urgent questions in the context of digital 3D-reconstructions must be asked, which concern aspects of content in data collecting and data modelling as well as technical criteria for data storage, infrastructure and data formats:

- How should source indexing, its interpretation and hypothetical suggestions be documented? To what extent should these types of work processing be represented?
- Which are the most appropriate working environments in which to use digital research data, for example administrative data (metadata) and creative data (paradata), and to develop them in accordance with the London Charter? [3] In which formats should the data be made available together with the visual material and the 3D-models?

As a progressive technology in the context of knowledge representation, the formalisation of knowledge in structured data models, the so-called "ontologies", is gaining acceptance. Computer-compatible formalisation and structuring of knowledge, as postulated by art historians back in the early 1980s, enables the operationalisation of data and promotes computer-assisted knowledge acquisition and web-based knowledge networking (Linked Data) [4]. A basic prerequisite for this modus operandi is provided by human- and machine-readable data models, which allow for a digitally networked representation of knowledge within an application ontology tailored to the needs of the respective discipline or to the issues at stake.

The integration of these technologies in the field of architectural research and monument preservation is pioneered by projects such as MonArch [5] and SACHER [6], which provide tools for the comprehensive and collaborative management of cultural heritage through the use of web-based 3D-viewers, for example 3DHOP. They allow for the thorough documentation of damage mapping and conservation work, as well as for the contextualisation of the object with the help of additional linked data resources.

In the case of source-based historical 3D-reconstruction, projects that engage with the process of source interpretation and creative, hypothetical 3D-modelling are particularly important. Projects such as www.patrimonium.net – Digital 3D-Reconstructions in Virtual Research Environments [7] or DokuVis [8] show the potential of a sustainable recording of these processes and the linking of 3D-data sets with events, sources and authors using WebGL-based visualisation and linked data technologies.

If we look at digitisation and associated methodologies in the building industry in which 3D-models are used for planning and construction work on historical buildings, a shared digital working method, termed Building Information Modeling (BIM), is emerging. Since the mid-1990s, object-oriented 3D-modelling has been introduced in civil engineering and a purpose-designed data exchange format, the Industry Foundation Classes (IFC), has been developed. The aim of this format is to facilitate communication between individual industries involved in construction work and to increase efficiency. In addition to minimising the loss of information during data transfer beyond the software applications of diverse specialist planners, the interoperability and sustainability of the models in the IFC format is thus guaranteed.

Although initial findings are already available from BIM-compliant modelling of historical objects [9] and additional guidelines in the field of civil engineering for the rebuilding of period architecture exist [10], a general digitally-oriented methodology that goes beyond object-oriented 3D-modelling to enable historical investigation and anchoring of the objects in the wider humanities context is still missing.

Against this background, the present paper aims to present a new type of methodology for the digital 3D-reconstruction of historical architecture, using the example of the New Synagogue in Breslau (nowadays Wrocław in Poland), which was destroyed in 1938, by combining our experience from previous projects with the application of the Building Information Modeling (BIM) method.

Therefore, this contribution focuses on the presentation of research issues concerning the historical object, the examination of sources, objects, events, people and places, as well as the visualisation of processes of 3D-reconstructions in a human- and machine-readable form. In this case, it will examine to what extent the BIM-method used in contemporary construction work can help with scientific (historical) 3D-reconstruction of demolished architecture and may contribute to the establishment of a new methodology within the Digital/Spatial Humanities.

## 2 The Historical Context of the New Synagogue in Breslau

### 2.1 The Source Material as a Basis for Reconstruction

The New Synagogue in Breslau (German: Neue Synagoge, also known as Synagoge am Anger) was erected from 1865 to 1872 in Schweidnitzer Vorstadt (now known as

Wrocław's Podwale Świdnickie) [11]. The building is, or used to be, a prominent piece of nineteenth-century synagogue architecture. When completed, it was also the second largest synagogue in the German-speaking region, preceded only by the New Synagogue in Berlin's Oranienburger Straße (by Eduard Knoblauch, Friedrich August Stüler, 1859–1866). The New Synagogue was designed by Edwin Oppler (1831–1880), one of the first Jewish architects and synagogue design theorists [12, 13]. On the night of 9th November 1938, this synagogue, like hundreds of other synagogues, including those designed by Oppler, was destroyed in a wave of pogroms that swept through Nazi Germany.

For art historians, the 3D-reconstruction of a perished synagogue brings the challenge of working in a Virtual Research Environment (VRE), a web-based collaborative platform for documenting and publishing research data (see Sect. 3.2). Additionally, it reveals how working in the VRE changes one's approach to source material and preliminary assumptions. The number and quality of source material, including original architectural designs from the mid-nineteenth century, was a key factor in ensuring that the reconstruction was as accurate as possible.

Relevant archive records are held in three museum collections: the Stadtarchiv Hannover [14], the Architectural Museum of the Technical University of Berlin [15], and the Museum of Architecture in Wrocław [16]. The extant photographs, prints, postcards, newspapers and publications from the era were a major source of information in our project.

A comparison of photographs and drawings from various design stages revealed that the initial design went through a number of alterations in the construction process. Therefore, any disputes on the final form of the synagogue were settled using photographs from the era. Unfortunately, both the photographs and designs represented only the two most visible elevations of the synagogue (the northern and the western); consequently, few insights into the synagogue's interior were provided. The dearth of colour photographs also proved to be a challenge. However, mural paintings were reconstructed based on a unique cross-section colourful representation of the New Synagogue.

Art historians were thus assigned with the task of providing and elaborating on examples of comparable buildings from the era, making necessary decisions on any disputed points. The Stadtarchiv Hannover sources (1864–1870) on the New Synagogue in Hanover proved to be particularly useful. Also created by Oppler, the Hanover Synagogue may be called a sister design to that of Breslaus; both of them were executed almost simultaneously [17].

Worthy of note were also extant material traces and buildings of Oppler's design; the latter were used as analogical examples (e.g. the sanatorium building in Görbersdorf, nowadays Sokołowsko in Lower Silesia/Poland). A section of painted wall fencing is now located where the synagogue once stood, and it is the only remaining ground-based vestige of the synagogue from its time. New findings were brought to light with an archaeological excavation survey that was completed in spring 2017. Carried out independently from the digital 3D-reconstruction, the survey revealed the almost fully intact foundations of the building underground [18].

In a nutshell, the number and quality of source materials on the New Synagogue in Breslau would instil enthusiasm in any art historian. However, this initial zeal soon gave way to the realities of digital 3D-modelling. With incoherent extant plans and insufficient findings on the topic, we began to seek architectural analogies and made decisions that would accurately reflect nineteenth-century construction practice. As a result, we have been able to produce a hypothetical model of the New Synagogue in Breslau. In the process, we also developed solutions that were recorded and described in the Virtual Research Environment.

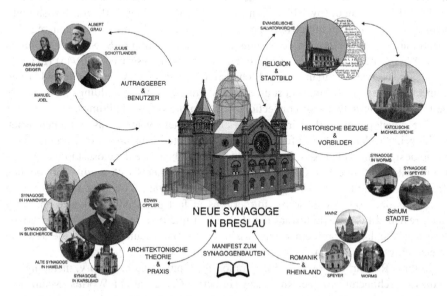

**Fig. 1.** The mind map representing the historical and socio-cultural context (AI MAINZ 2018/CC-BY-SA 4.0)

## 2.2 The Historical and Socio-cultural Context

The digital 3D-reconstruction of the New Synagogue in Breslau made it possible to showcase this building to a larger audience. As presented in the Mind Map (Fig. 1), we were also able to document and share findings on the context in which the synagogue was constructed. By connecting the synagogue's model to the sources, actors, buildings, and events, and by showing the interplay between them, we were able to outline the broader context and cover a number of areas, including religion, society, the economy, art, technology and engineering. We used our synagogue model as a time machine that took its users on a journey to experience and explore nineteenth-century Breslau.

The origins of the New Synagogue in Breslau are inextricably linked to the affairs of the local Jewish congregation, which, c. 13,000 people strong, was the third largest congregation of its kind in Germany, only preceded by those of Berlin and Hamburg [19]. It must be emphasised that the community was divided into Orthodox and Reform Judaism traditions, and it was the latter, mainly the wealthier members of the congregation, who commissioned the New Synagogue. The synagogue soon became an architectural manifesto; a marker of presence for Reform Judaism in Breslau's cityscape as well as a symbol of the community's identity.

Additionally, the context in which the synagogue was created reveals yet another intriguing phenomenon, namely, that of a competition involving the three largest denominations in the city: the Catholics, the Lutherans, and the Jews, each of whom strove to establish the largest and most impressive "house of God" in the city. While the Catholic community was committed to building the monumental Church of St Michael the Archangel (by Alexis Langer, 1862–1871, extant) [20], the Jewish community embarked on an initiative to erect a synagogue, and the Lutheran congregation commissioned just as impressive designs for the construction of St Salvator's Church (by C.J.Ch. Zimmermann, designed from 1867 to 1876, destroyed in 1945) [21].

This issue was our main research challenge in the VRE, where we recorded and connected the actors, events and sources that are linked to these buildings. In doing so, we presented the network of connections between these three buildings.

The development of Edwin Oppler's environement was just as important when working in the VRE. Oppler formulated an architectural manifesto concerning synagogue design, and in the New Synagogue in Breslau he came the closest to making his theoretical model a reality. One of the first Jewish architects with a university degree, Oppler was an avid supporter of the Neoromanesque style (as opposed to the Moorish style). His decision to choose the former was in fact politically motivated and very much revealed his attitude toward the state. On a micro scale, the Breslau synagogue illustrates the larger problem of the assimilation and acculturation of the Jews in nineteenth-century Prussia.

In the VRE various sources of inspiration for Oppler and his theory, including the medieval architecture of the Rhineland (Imperial Cathedrals in Worms, Mainz and Speyer) were documented. Quotations from other buildings are noticeable in Oppler's synagogue designs, a case in point being the dome, which could be considered his trademark, consciously modelled on Emperor Charlemagne's Palatine Chapel in Aachen Cathedral, his symbolic centre of power.

Further opportunities are revealed by the question of how resonant Oppler's ideas were, and on what scale they permeated synagogue designs at the turn of the nineteenth and twentieth centuries. Some of the buildings inspired by Oppler's architecture which were erected in Silesia include: the Glogau (nowadays Głogów) Synagogue (by Abesser & Kröger, 1892) and the Glatz (nowadays Kłodzko) Synagogue (1884–1885), designed by Albert Grau (1837–1900), who also supervised the construction of the New Synagogue in Breslau.

These examples illustrate only some of the opportunities that the VRE offers for drawing relations between different buildings, events and actors. However, in order to establish such links, researchers need a particular structure and tools that enable them to connect and analyse data and issues discussed in the humanities with a 3D-model.

# 3  The Model Behind the Model

Due to the interdisciplinary focus of this project, the 3D-model of the New Synagogue in Breslau was integrated into a more general enquiry. This had to be reflected both in the data model and the documentation scheme intended to contribute to the interdisciplinary nature of the project and present the collected data in a transparent way. Nonetheless, the main focus of the investigation remains on the presentation of the sources used during the reconstruction process and on the decisions made by the modeller (author) in relation to the interpretation of the sources, which are reflected in the 3D-model.

In addition, digital data and semantics should remain transparent and human- and machine-readable well into the future. This premise of the semantic web, i.e. to give data a semantic meaning, is guaranteed by the use of ontologies [22]. In the field of cultural heritage, the ISO-certified CIDOC CRM has established itself as the reference ontology [23]. Since one has to assume that no description system will ever be complete, it is possible to extend the reference ontology by an application [24]. In the application ontology "ontscidoc3D" [25], the specifics of a hypothetical 3D-reconstruction and visualisation are expressed. This ontology allows for a uniform description of all data collected in connection with the digital 3D-model of the New Synagogue, as well as of information about its socio-cultural context.

The data and documentation model described below is based on preliminary work carried out by the joint project "www.patrimonium.net" [26]. In this project, the ontology Cultural Markup Language (CHML) was adapted to the needs of hypothetical 3D-reconstruction based on sources and used after being implemented in the ISO standard CIDOC CRM [27, 28]. As a result, it served as the semantic back-end of the Virtual Research Environment "WissKI" [29], in which, same as in this current project, data was collected and presented.

## 3.1  Application Ontology and Data Model

The application ontology "ontscidoc3D" includes a total of 113 classes. Based on the research activities related to 3D-reconstruction (e.g. source examination and source creation, as well as creative 3D-modelling based on the interpretation of the sources), eight central concepts (classes) have emerged:

- osd 5a Historical Event
- osd 7a Research Activity
- osd 21a Person
- osd 22a Object
- osd 31b Source
- osd 55a Type
- osd 73a Reconstruction
- osd 74a Corporate Body.

The classes are linked to each other by relations; i.e. comparable to a simple sentence consisting of subject-predicate-object, source and target class are connected

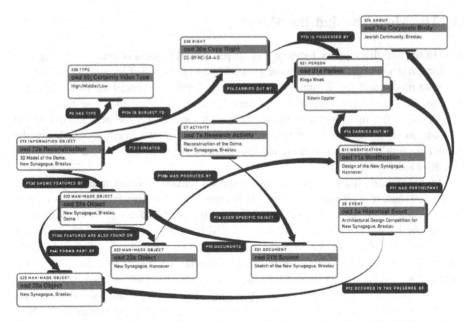

**Fig. 2.** Illustration of classes and relations of the application ontology "ontscidoc3D", together with additional classes of the reference ontology CIDOC CRM and illustrated by examples. (AI MAINZ 2020/CC-BY-SA 4.0)

by a relation. The possible relations are provided by the semantic framework of the CIDOC CRM.

The activity of 3D-modelling is in the centre of attention. It can be named or classified in accordance with the topology of the object to be reconstructed or in accordance with its structural semantics. All persons, sources and decisions involved in the 3D-reconstruction are connected by relations to the class "osd 7a Research Activity".

Based on the activity of 3D-reconstruction of the dome of the Synagogue, the above-mentioned concepts will be explained in more detail (Fig. 2): The reconstruction of the dome of the New Synagogue is to be understood as an example of the class "osd 7a Research Activity" (E7 Activity), from which the 3D-model of this component, an entity of the class "osd 73a Reconstruction" (E73 Information Object), is derived. The reconstruction is performed by persons, entities of the class "osd 21a Person" (E21 Person). Their 3D-reconstruction is based on the evaluation and interpretation of diverse source material, entities of the class "osd 31a Source" (E31 Document), to which reference is made. The 3D-model itself can be furnished with additional information, e.g. with a statement about its plausibility and copyrights. The documentation of the complex history of the building's origins is achieved by integrating historical events, entities of "osd 5a Historical Event" (E5 Event). Events related to the history of the Synagogue's origins, such as the selection of architects, can thus be documented. This mode offers the opportunity to gather information on the persons involved, for example the architect Edwin Oppler and the commissioning Jewish

Community of Breslau. Important comparable buildings can be documented to elucidate architectural and historical issues, entities of the class "osd 22a Object" (E22 Human Made Object), to which Edwin Oppler referred, when designing the New Synagogue.

Initially, CIDOC CRM and the application ontology "ontscidoc3D" were so-called "paper standards" impossible to process by machines. The application ontology was therefore implemented in Erlangen CRM [30]. It can be implemented in the guise of an owl-file into the VFU "WissKI".

## 3.2   The Documentation Scheme

In the input fields of the WissKI (front-end), the documentation scheme reflects the main classes of the application ontology mentioned above (Fig. 3). During the reconstruction process, data about research activities, sources, the objects and persons involved are collected. The research activity documents either the creation of a 3D-model or the creation of a source that can be used as basis for the modelling process. The latter activities include photo or measuring campaigns and drawings together with interviews and discussions among experts. The resulting content is then treated as source material and documented to be used during future reconstruction activities.

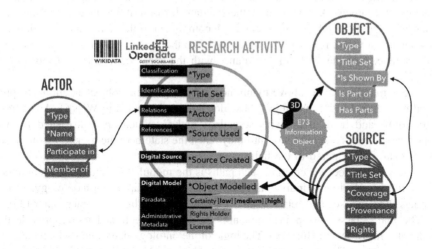

**Fig. 3.** Documentation scheme illustrating the most important entry fields as minimum requirements for documentation used in https://www.new-synagogue-breslau-3d.hs-mainz.de (AI MAINZ 2020/CC-BY-SA 4.0)

This scheme makes it possible to document the research, measurements, discussions, etc. carried out during the reconstruction process in a transparent way. The same applies to the documentation of (partial) 3D-reconstructions in which a distinction is made between variants and versions. Variants represent diverse levels of knowledge. A variant may include a range of versions, which represent individual work phases. Central to this scheme is the documentation of the sources used during the modelling process. The hypotheses based on the evaluation or interpretation of the sources, implemented in the 3D-model, are documented by the respective research activity. It usually happens in descriptive format. In addition, information on the degree of plausibility or the level of detail can also be provided.

Information on the socio-cultural context is recorded under the historical events category. The matching sources may also be linked to this context, as well as information on the building for which the historical event played a role.

The transparency required by the London Charter [31], i.e. who constructed which hypotheses within the reconstruction process and on which basis, is considered in this scheme. In addition, the 3D-model of the demolished New Synagogue is linked with information on the socio-cultural context surrounding the complex history of the Synagogue's origins, as well as with comparable buildings relevant to architectural history. By networking this information, it is possible to present diverse levels of knowledge and to close any existing gaps in our understanding.

The documentation scheme is mapped in WissKI, a module of the CMS Drupal, in the guise of entry forms, in which both data entries and descriptions are possible. The, preferably, standardised recording of personal names, titles, designations, information about place and time is time-consuming, but the effort is justified when considering the achievement of high data quality and the subsequent use of this data as Linked Data.

Semantically enriched data is stored as triples in the RDF schema. RDF (Resource Description Framework) has become the standard for describing metadata in the form of a subject-predicate-object statement. Each component of the statement, right down to the actual data value, is assigned a unique URI so that it can be individually addressed and referenced on the Web, in accordance with the specifications for Linked (Open) Data [32].

The semantics of the above-mentioned subject-predicate-object relation are provided by the application ontology "ontscidoc3D" implemented in WissKI. Apart from entry forms and fields it contains so-called "paths", which are constructed from a sequence of classes and relations until they reach the statement the user wishes to make by the data value entered in the field.

A very useful tool for creating such paths is the module "Pathbuilder". Pathbuilder allows for the selection of individual components from the application ontology. It only displays those classes and relations that may be logically linked to each other [33].

The main classes of application ontology already mentioned above provide the main entry forms (Main-Bundles). The logic of the ontology determines which data can be entered where. Therefore, information on a "historical event" cannot be documented via the "research activity" entry form. The entry forms may include several sub-bundles. Here, the descriptive logic of the application ontology is also decisive. The fields in a sub-bundle are always grouped together if their paths consist of the same components.

The previous remarks are to be illustrated by the example of the entry mask for the recording of information on the research activity (Table 1). The input form (Main-Bundle) includes all data for an entity of the class "osd 7a Research Activity", such as its name, the executors and the reference to the sources used for the modelling. These are referenced by their title. Data on the 3D-model resulting from the activity are summarised in the subgroup "3D-model", since this group includes the same path components. This grouping explains that the following information refers to the 3D-model. Sources only refer to the 3D-model through the interpretation executed by the person (author) performing the reconstruction, i.e. through research activity. This process must be considered in the data model. Therefore, the entities of "osd 31b Source" and "osd 73a Reconstruction" are linked via the shared research activity. The source does not explicitly annotate an entity of "osd 73a Reconstruction" (since it is not directly connected to it), but only implicitly via the research activity. The data structure is used to build a network (graph), which also allows the evaluation of implicit knowledge.

**Table 1.** Extract from the Pathbuilder (schematic) of "research activity" (https://www.new-synagogue-breslau-3d.hs-mainz.de)

| | |
|---|---|
| Research activity | Group [https://www.ontscidoc3d.hs-mainz.de/osd_7a_Research_Activity] |
| Title | https://www.ontscidoc3d.hs-mainz.de/osd_7a_Research_Activity → ecrm: P1_is_identified_by → https://www.ontscidoc3d.hs-mainz.de/osd_41a_ Research_Activity_Appellation |
| Source created | https://www.ontscidoc3d.hs-mainz.de/osd_7a_Research_Activity → ecrm: P9_consists_of → https://www.ontscidoc3d.hs-mainz.de/osd_65a_ Production → ecrm:P92_brought_into_existence → https://www. ontscidoc3d.hs-mainz.de/osd_31b_Source → ecrm:P102_has_ti- tle → https://www.ontscidoc3d.hs-mainz.de/osd_35b_Source_Title |
| Source used | https://www.ontscidoc3d.hs-mainz.de/ontology/osd_7a_Research_Activity → ecrm:P16_used_specific_object → https://www.ontscidoc3d.hs-mainz. de/ontology/osd_31b_Source → ecrm:P102_has_title → https://www. ontscidoc3d.hs-mainz.de/ontology/osd_35b_Source_Title |
| 3D-Model | [https://www.ontscidoc3d.hs-mainz.de/osd_7a_Research_Activity → https://www.ontscidoc3d.hs-mainz.de/P12.1_created → https://www. ontscidoc3d.hs-mainz.de/73a_3D_Reconstruction] |
| Object modelled | https://www.ontscidoc3d.hs-mainz.de/osd_7a_Research_Activity → https:// www.ontscidoc3d.hs-mainz.de/P12.1_created → https://www.ontscidoc3d. hs-mainz.de/73a_3D_Reconstruction → ecrm:P130_shows_features_of → https://www.ontscidoc3d.hs-mainz.de/osd_22a_Object |
| Certainty | https://www.ontscidoc3d.hs-mainz.de/osd_7a_Research_Activity → https:// www.ontscidoc3d.hs-mainz.de/P12.1_created → https://www.ontscidoc3d. hs-mainz.de/73a_3D_Reconstruction → ecrm:P2_has_type → https:// www.ontscidoc3d.hs-mainz.de/osd_55j_Certianty_Value_Type → ecrm: P149_is_identified_by → https://www.ontscidoc3d.hs-mainz.de/osd_75e_ Certainty_Value_Type_Appellation |

By applying application ontology, the semantics of the collected data is structurally mapped as both human- and machine-readable. Since it is based on the ISO standard CIDOC CRM, the long-term interpretability and interoperability of the data is guaranteed. The meta- and paradata of entities of the class "osd 73a Reconstruction" are thus traceable and sustainably documented. For the documentation of the geometry and material data of a 3D-model, the HBIM approach is presented below.

# 4   Reconstruction Methodology in the HBIM Environment: 3D Modelling in ARCHICAD

The digital 3D-models provide a visual summary of the entire modelling process and serve as a crucial element in the digital reconstruction of lost architectural heritage. However, it is only the geometry and material of a building that can be rendered in the traditional modelling system. That is why the reconstruction of the New Synagogue was completed in HBIM (Historic/Heritage Building Information Modelling), a digital environment developed specifically for design purposes when working on architectural heritage [34]. The system enables the recording of additional datasets in the model, and it also requires a particular working methodology. The reconstruction project was completed in ARCHICAD 22 by Graphisoft, a software designed to support the HBIM environment.

## 4.1   Preparation for the Reconstruction Process in BIM-Supporting Software

The modelling stage was preceded by an examination of the collected sources and their comparative analysis. These two components served as a starting point for the digital reconstruction of the synagogue. Given the multitude and diversity of the sources, we had to choose a set of specific and possibly coherent drawings which was later used as the core research material; this became the basis for the reconstruction process. The remaining sources were used as auxiliary materials.

The historic plans, cross-sections and elevation plans of the synagogue were available as hand drawings of relatively low accuracy. As such, they had to be "translated" so as to meet the requirements of our digital working environment. For the purpose, we decided to establish a module based on the dimension values of the bricks used for the construction of the synagogue (the dimensions were established using the archaeological research findings). We then used the module to establish the dimensions and levels of the building. These in turn were used for the development of a reference model that provided a representation of the synagogue's geometry and its volume. The model was later used as reference by all the modelers in the reconstruction process. This in turn facilitated the coordination of the individual tasks and secured the integration of the entire model.

One of the challenges in the modelling process was to use software primarily developed for designing contemporary architecture. We, however, had a different goal in mind: we wanted to provide a sourced-based reconstruction of a historic (destroyed) building. The ARCHICAD design process is based on object-oriented modelling and storey-driven construction techniques. The model is rendered using objects that represent the building's physical components and are assigned to particular storeys. This type of modelling facilitates the process of adding project modifications without necessarily adjusting the whole model (modifications are added automatically).

When creating a historic building model, the segmentation of a building into classical storeys may hamper the whole process and be ineffective. For this reason, we used a system of storeys to designate a dozen or so characteristic levels of the building, starting from the level of terrain and ending at the top of the lantern that crowned the synagogue. The object-oriented development technique was also a challenge. In historic architecture, objects are more complex, and as such they call for the creative use of various tools. In the workflow, these tools are often combined, which in turn produces objects that do not always allow the entire model to be adjusted smoothly and automatically.

The division of the synagogue's building marked the final stage in the preparations for the reconstruction process. We had two types of division available: topological division (into structural components), which is traditionally used when modelling in ARCHICAD, or geometric division (identifying particular sections of the building). The mixed division proved to be the optimal choice for the reconstruction of the synagogue. When distributing the tasks, it was necessary that we divided the building into several geometric segments. Accordingly, the building was split into five parts: central (CP), northern (NP), southern (SP), eastern (EP), and western (WP), each of which was assigned to a different modeler (author). Subsequently, each of these parts was split into two or three smaller geometric segments that would be easy to identify in the building's body, e.g. in the central part (CP), two segments were identified: the main part (CPMP) and the dome part (CPDP). The final and third step in the process involved the topological division, which was performed by particular modelers assigned to particular parts of the synagogue (the object identification process).

The modelling of the synagogue was distributed among several modelers, each of whom was assigned with a task to elaborate one main part (except for the central part (CP). Once the task distribution was completed, we could proceed with the object identification. This topological division allowed the reconstruction of the selected parts of the synagogue with the object-oriented modelling technique (Fig. 4). It was essential that we also identify the objects as we had to attribute these to the sources that were used as a basis for the reconstruction. The identified objects were modelled in separate files and then inserted in a particular part of the synagogue. The objects were then copied if they appeared several times in a particular part.

The sources, or the lack thereof, were another challenge; some sources were also contradictory (when used as a reference for particular objects). In many cases, the representation of a particular object in one source was cancelled out by another. In those cases, the comparative analysis of the extant sources was followed by a creative process. The modelling staff were seeking solutions by offering their own interpretations recorded in sketches. These newly created sources were then part of a further consultation with art historians. Subsequently, the disputed objects were then reconstructed in their agreed form.

The windows in the dome are a case in point (central part (CP). The analysis of the sources revealed differences between the outside view of the dome (featuring a row of five windows) and the inside view (featuring four biforas in analogical places: two underneath the rosette and another two underneath them). This challenge was navigated by the following means: we assumed that the lower row of the windows on the inside was in fact composed of blind arches. The same solution was applied to the middle

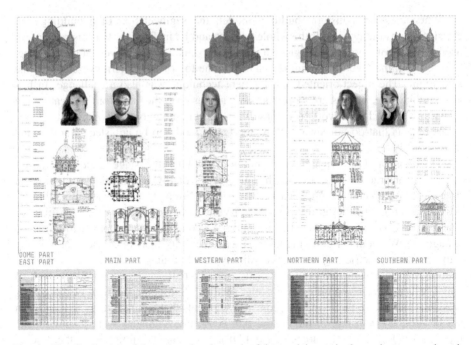

**Fig. 4.** The distribution of the tasks whereby each of the participants in the project was assigned a particular part in the geometric segmentation of the synagogue. The drawings of the middle part represent the object identification process. (AI MAINZ 2020/CC-BY-SA 4.0)

aperture on the outside: it was nowhere to be seen on the inside and, therefore, we recreated it as a fascia.

The ARCHICAD-created objects were also provided with object classification and attributes; the latter were to be entered manually. Object classification was intended to provide information on a particular object and the building component it represented (e.g. the rosette was coded as a window). Other basic attributes of a given object included two categories: its structural function (load bearing/non-bearing walls) and positioning (outside/inside). The modelling staff could also create attributes on their own. In the previous BIM reconstruction projects of historic buildings, only standard attributes were allowed. The reconstruction of a synagogue in Bielsko-Biała, Poland, is a case in point. One of the reconstruction projects carried out at the Technical University of Vienna, the Bielsko-Biała project was far from harnessing the full potential of BIM methodology [35]. Instead, it only used standard and simplified documentation methods.

In the New Synagogue reconstruction project, the "VFU-Oppler" attribute was created. For each object, it was provided with a link to its reconstruction in the VFU. These data could also be recorded directly in ARCHICAD, together with new object attributes and other data such as the age determination of an object, materials used, and the list of sources used in the reconstruction process (Fig. 5).

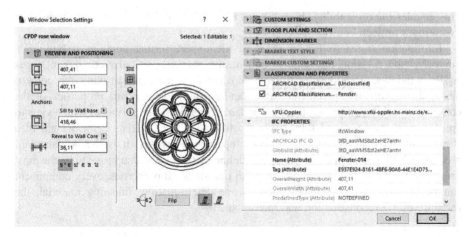

**Fig. 5.** Object attributes and classification with a parameter providing a reference (URL-link) to the VRE (AI MAINZ 2020/CC-BY-SA 4.0)

In the final step of the modelling process, we combined all the separate parts of the synagogue into one coherent model. We did so by creating a new coordination file in which we placed all the reconstructed parts as Hotlink modules. As a result, the imported parts contained all the objects with their textures and parameters. By using Hotlink modules we were also able to test connections between particular parts of the synagogue: if the model of a particular part required an improvement, it could be adjusted in the home file and a new updated Hotlink was provided. In the final and complete version of the reconstruction model, all the Hotlink modules were deleted to obtain the final model in one file.

The final coordination file that we submitted at the end of the project turned out to be too large (ca. 1 GB); as such, it was rather slow and increasingly difficult to use. The ARCHICAD file (.pln) was not satisfactory as a final format for yet another reason: the proprietary files are not commonly used 3D format files, which means that they can be accessed by only a relatively limited number of users (by ARCHICAD users only). However, when exported to a more common file, e.g. .3ds or.skp, object attributes would be lost. Therefore, we decided to use a format that would be the most common and, at the same time, guaranteed that all data would be suitably recorded.

### 4.2    Data Stored in the HBIM Model for Reconstruction Purposes

Available only to ARCHICAD users, the .pln-format turned out to be a serious limitation to our model. However, a dedicated open IFC-format (Industry Foundation Classes) was used to enable the transfer of data between different software users in the BIM environment. The format enables the recording of critical structural and project management data in a globally standardised format. Users choose the data to be exported in an IFC file. With IFC, users can export not only geometric data but also alphanumeric information on the classification and properties of particular objects [36].

This enables interoperability, higher work efficiency and better communication when executing a project.

Information transferred in a standard file export format contains a building's hierarchy (the division into storeys and design stages), particular component types (walls, windows, stairs, beams, pillars, etc.), the dynamic between particular components, their geometric parameters and standard and non-standard properties of the components attributed to the objects. Standard properties were attributed with a view to the designing process, and they cover the following characteristics: the weight of a component, its material and fire safety properties. However, it is the non-standard properties, which each and every user can define on their own, that prove to be the most important for reconstruction purposes. With non-standard properties, every component can be provided with attributes such as age determination, finishing material, the certainty of 3D-reconstruction and many more.

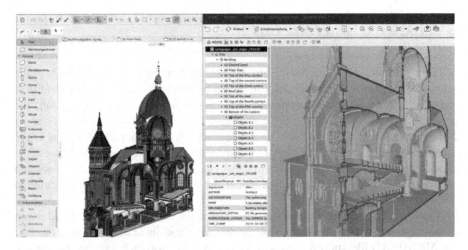

**Fig. 6.** The comparison of a 3D cross-section in the final ARCHICAD 22 file submitted for the entire synagogue (on the left) and in the IFC export file viewed in the Solibri Model Checker (on the right) (AI MAINZ 2020/CC-BY-SA 4.0)

IFC's additional strength is that it can be read in a dedicated viewer (e.g. the Solibri Model Checker). The software is fairly easy to manage by any type of users and it enables not only a geometric visualisation but also the reading of information encoded in the model [37]. The growing popularity of the BIM environment for design purposes promotes the development of more accessible solutions such as free viewers that are available for web browsers. One such viewer is a webpage developed by Bimspot IFC [38]. Naturally, the functionality is limited, but it is nonetheless sufficient for viewing of a model and the data encoded in it.

However, the amount of data to be transferred in the IFC format was insufficient to provide a full display of the entire reconstruction. We found it impossible to export the textures, which were an essential part of the design that captured the atmosphere of the building and expressed its genius loci (Fig. 6). That is why the final design was exported in several 3D formats, both supporting the BIM environment (.pln, .ifc) and more traditional modelling software (.skp, .fbx).

Nevertheless, due to the fact that we could create independent links between the model and the external database used in the project, we decided to test IFC for the purpose of the scientific documentation of the reconstruction. For the New Synagogue, it was the "VFU-Oppler" parameter that proved the most important as it provided a link to the "research activity" within the VRE containing all the essential information on a particular object and its reconstruction process (Fig. 7). This parameter was not defined as a standard object property and was added manually. In so doing, we were able to develop a connection between the 3D-models and the comprehensive documentation and further socio-cultural information within the VRE.

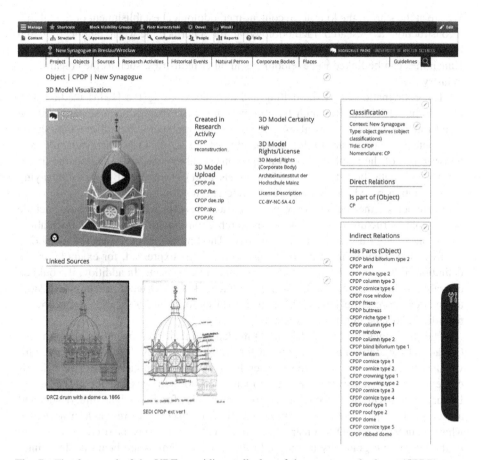

**Fig. 7.** The front-end of the VRE providing a display of the synagogue's dome (CPDP), see: https://www.new-synagogue-breslau-3d.hs-mainz.de/wisski/navigate/326/view    (AI    MAINZ 2020/CC-BY-SA 4.0)

By creating such a link, we were able to anchor BIM-compliant reconstruction in the digital humanities and define the broader historical context of the 3D-models through their comprehensive presentation within the VRE in a broad context. The IFC format and modelling in the HBIM environment allowed the development of a larger database that showcases, not only the geometric form of the building, but also provides a detailed overview of the project documentation. More importantly, however, this methodology enables an encounter between engineering and the humanities. The tools we tested have opened up a cooperation between architects and art historians and provided interpretive input data for further scientific research on the reconstruction of lost architectural heritage.

## 5   Conclusion

We are at the start of the long-term content-methodological establishment of digital 3D-reconstruction as research methodology at the interface between engineering and humanities. In the area of handling and utilisation of 3D-data sets, Digital/Spatial Humanities can be linked to developments in other industries, such as the construction industry.

The combination of 3D-modelling and attribution, using the HBIM method with the web-based Virtual Research Environment for a transparent documentation of the reconstruction process, as well as the sources and the socio-cultural context, shows great potential with regard to the sustainability of the 3D-data sets, the availability and transparency of the results. The advantage consists above all in the interoperability of the research data, both the case of 3D-models in IFC format and the accompanying documentation based on a CIDOC CRM referenced data model.

Nonetheless, the methodology presented also reveals weaknesses. These include the complex structure of a web-based research environment used for documentation, which places high demands on data curation. The limitations of the HBIM method to the free modelling of historical buildings are however expressed, for example, in the definition of the stories or in the merging of individual objects. In addition, it would be desirable to link the individual working framework for 3D-reconstruction and -documentation more closely by developing interfaces to ensure a seamless workflow in recording and labelling research results.

The challenges of accessibility of 3D-models and their accompanying research data (meta- and paradata) have been known for a long time. In an academic context, university libraries are the ideal repositories for scientific 3D-models. Interesting developments can be discovered in arthistoricum.net, located at Heidelberg University Library and providing a specialised information service for art, architecture, design and artistic photography. Here, the requirements of interdisciplinary research projects, for which source-based 3D-reconstruction of historical buildings is used as scientific methodology, are gradually coming into focus. First attempts are being made to integrate research data into the infrastructure of digital collections to ensure their accessibility and long-term availability for object-oriented research subjects [39].

The establishment of 3D-reconstruction as research methodology requires the implementation of shared standards for data preparation and data management in addition to necessary infrastructure. It must be the goal of any scientific work to place traceable research data into a larger context. In the digital age, it is necessary to make this type of data available in interoperable formats, using Linked (Open) Data standards and Semantic Web technologies, to be able to contribute to knowledge creation and debate within innovative projects such as Time Machine Europe [40].

# References

1. Favro, D.: Se Non e Vero, e Ben Trovato (If Not True, It Is Well Conceived): Digital immersive reconstructions of historical environments. J. Soc. Architect. Historians **71**(3), 273–277 (2012)
2. Kuroczyński, P.: Virtual Research Environment for digital 3D reconstructions – standards, thresholds and prospects. In: Frischer, B., Guidi, G., Börner, W. (eds.) Cultural Heritage and New Technologies 2016 Proceedings, Studies in Digital Heritage, Open Access Journal, vol. 1, no. 2, pp. 456–476 (2017). https://doi.org/10.14434/sdh.v1i2.23330. Accessed 05 Nov 2020
3. Baker, D.: Defining paradata in heritage visualization. In: Bentkowska-Kafel, A., Denard, H., Baker, D. (eds.) Paradata and Transparency in Virtual Heritage, pp. 163–175. Ashgate, Franham (2012)
4. Heusinger, L.: Kunstgeschichte und EDV: 8 Thesen. In: Kritische Berichte - Zeitschrift Für Kunst- und Kulturwissenschaften, vol. 11/4, pp. 67–70 (1983). http://journals.ub.uni-heidelberg.de/index.php/kb/article/view/9808. Accessed 05 Nov 2020
5. Freitag, B., Stenzer, A.: MonArch – a digital archive for cultural heritage. In: Franz, B., Vinken, G. (eds.) Das Digitale und die Denkmalpflege: Bestandserfassung - Denkmalver-mittlung - Datenarchivierung - Rekonstruktion verlorener Objekte, Veröffentlichungen des Arbeitskreises Theorie und Lehre der Denkmalpflege e.V., pp. 122–129. arthistoricum.net, Heidelberg (2017)
6. Apollonio, F.I., Rizzo, F., Bertacchi, S., Dall'Osso, G., Corbelli, A., Grana, C.: SACHER: smart architecture for cultural heritage in Emilia Romagna. In: Grana, C., Baraldi, L. (eds.) IRCDL 2017. CCIS, vol. 733, pp. 142–156. Springer, Cham (2017). https://doi.org/10.1007/978-3-319-68130-6_12. Accessed 05 Nov 2020
7. Kuroczyński, P., Hauck, O., Dworak, D.: 3D models on triple paths - new pathways for documenting and visualizing virtual reconstructions. In: Münster, S., Pfarr-Harfst, M., Kuroczyński, P., Ioannides, M. (eds.) 3D Research Challenges in Cultural Heritage II. LNCS, vol. 10025, pp. 149–172. Springer, Cham (2016). https://doi.org/10.1007/978-3-319-47647-6_8. Accessed 05 Nov 2020
8. Bruschke, J., Wacker, M.: Simplifying documentation of digital reconstruction processes. In: Münster, S., Pfarr-Harfst, M., Kuroczyński, P., Ioannides, M. (eds.) 3D Research Challenges in Cultural Heritage II. LNCS, vol. 10025, pp. 256–271. Springer, Cham (2016). https://doi.org/10.1007/978-3-319-47647-6_12. Accessed 05 Nov 2020
9. Murphy, M.: Historic Building Information Modelling (HBIM) for Recording and Documenting Classical Architecture in Dublin 1700 to 1830, Dublin, Trinity College (2012)
10. Antonopoulou, S., Bryan, P.: BIM for Heritage – Developing a Historic Building Information Model, Historic England, Liverpool (2017)
11. Jara, K.: Synagoga na Wygonie we Wrocławiu (1865–1872) i jej twórca Edwin Oppler (1831–1880). Wrocław, University of Wrocław (2013)

12. Oppler, E.: Synagogen und jüdische Begräbnisplätze. In: Baukunde des Architekten, vol. 2, pp. 270–285. Toeche, Berlin (1884)
13. Hammer-Schenk, H.: Edwin Opplers Theorie des Synagogenbaus. Emanzipationsversuche durch Architektur. In: Hannoversche Geschichtsblätter, vol. N.F. 33, pp. 99–117 (1979)
14. Stadtarchiv Hannover, Nachlass Oppler, Mappe 60 (Synagoge Breslau)
15. Architekturmuseum der Technischen Universität Berlin in der Universitätsbibliothek, Inv. Nr. 14047, 14048, 14049, 14050, 14051, 14052, 14053
16. Architekturmuseum in Breslau, Bauarchiv der Stadt Breslau, Mappe 246, 1472 und Baupolizei Akten, Mappe 4045, 4046
17. Stadtarchiv Hannover, Nachlass Oppler, Mappe 13 (Synagoge Hannover)
18. Gliński, R.: Sprawozdanie z sondażowych badań archeologiczno- architektonicznych w miejscu dawnej Synagogi na Wygonie przy ul. Łąkowej we Wrocławiu. Wrocław (2017)
19. Hammer-Schenk, H.: Synagogen in Deutschland. Geschichte einer Baugattung im 19.und 20. Jahrhundert, p. 213. Hamburg, Christians (1981)
20. Zabłocka-Kos, A.: Sztuka, wiara, uczucie. Alexis Langer – śląski architekt neogotyku, Wrocław (1996)
21. Pikulska, D.: Carl Johann Christian Zimmermann (1831–1911). Architekt w służbie miasta, Wrocław (2005)
22. Hitzler, P., Krötzsch, M., Rudolph, S., Sure, Y.: Semantic Web: Grundlagen. Springer, Heidelberg (2008). https://doi.org/10.1007/978-3-540-33994-6
23. CIDOC CRM. http://www.cidoc-crm.org/. Accessed 12 Nov 2020
24. Hohmann, G., Fichtner, M.: Chancen und Herausforderungen in der praktischen Anwendung von Ontologien für das Kulturerbe. In: Robertson – von Trotta, C., Schneider, R. (eds.) Digitales Kulturerbe. Bewahrung und Zugänglichkeit in der wissenschaftlichen Praxis (= Kulturelle Überlieferung – digital 2), pp. 115–128. KIT Scientific Publishing, Karlsruhe (2015)
25. Ontscidoc3D owl-file. https://www.ontscidoc3d.hs-mainz.de/. Accessed 20 Nov 2020
26. Patrimonium.net. http://www.patrimonium.net/. Accessed 20 Nov 2020
27. Hauck, O., Kuroczyński, P.: Cultural Heritage Markup Language – designing a domain ontology for digital reconstructions. In: Виртуальная археология – эффективность методов: материалы Второй Международной конференции. Изд-во Государственного Эрмитажа, pp. 250–255. The State Hermitage, St. Petersburg (2015)
28. Bruseker, G., Guillem, A., Zarnic, R.: Building an argumentation platform for 3D reconstruction using CIDOC-CRM and Drupal. In: Proceedings of the 2015 Digital Heritage International Congress, vol. 2, pp. 383–386. IEEE, Piscataway (2015)
29. WissKI (= Wissenschaftliche Kommunikationsinfrastruktur). http://wiss-ki.eu/. Accessed 20 Nov 2020
30. Erlangen CRM. http://erlangen-crm.org/. Accessed 20 Nov 2020
31. The London Charter (2.1, February 2009) principle 3. http://www.londoncharter.org/principles/research-sources.html. Accessed 20 Nov 2020 and principle 4 http://www.londoncharter.org/principles/documentation.html. Accessed 20 Nov 2020
32. Tim Berners-Lee on Linked Data. https://www.w3.org/DesignIssues/LinkedData.html. Accessed 20 Nov 2020
33. Fichtner, M., Ribaud, V.: Paths and shortcuts in an event-oriented ontology. In: Dodero, J. M., Palomo-Duarte, M., Karampiperis, P. (eds.) MTSR 2012. CCIS, vol. 343, pp. 214–226. Springer, Heidelberg (2012). https://doi.org/10.1007/978-3-642-35233-1_22
34. Arayici, Y., Counsell, J., Mahdjoubi, L., Nagy, G., Soheir, H., Khaled, D.: Heritage Building Information Modeling. Routledge, New York (2017)
35. Seitner, M.: Virtuelle Rekonstruktion der Synagoge in Bielsko-Biala. Technische Universität Wien, Wien (2015)

36. McPartland R.: What is IFC. https://www.thenbs.com/knowledge/what-is-ifc. Accessed 01 Nov 2020
37. Solibri. https://www.solibri.com/. Accessed 01 Nov 2020
38. Bimspot IFC viewer. https://ifc-view.com/. Accessed 01 Nov 2020
39. Projekt zur virtuellen Rekonstruktion von Kulturliegenschaften der Staatlichen Schlösser und Gärten Baden Württemberg. https://architekturinstitut.hs-mainz.de/projekte/virtuelle-rekonstruktion-kulturliegenschaften-4-0/. Accessed 20 Nov 2020
40. Timemachine-Project. https://www.timemachine.eu/. Accessed 20 Nov 2020

# User Involvement for Application Development: Methods, Opportunities and Experiences from Three Different Academic Projects

Cindy Kröber[1], Katharina Hammel[1], Cornelia Schade[1],
Nicole Filz[1(✉)], and Leyla Dewitz[2]

[1] Center for Open Digital Innovation and Participation,
TU Dresden, 01062 Dresden, Germany
{cindy.kroeber, nicole.filz}@tu-dresden.de
[2] University of Applied Sciences, Kiepenheuerallee 5, 14469 Potsdam, Germany

**Abstract.** This paper introduces several tools and methods of user inquiry and usability testing by means of three academic software development projects. The projects have different objectives and user groups and address different issues. This makes it possible to show the diverse ways of involving users in the development of solutions and allows to evaluate which human-centered approach might be suitable for similar projects and problems.

**Keywords:** UX · Usability · Human-centered design · Personas · Prototype testing

## 1 Introduction

It has become quite popular for academic projects to conceptualize and develop applications and software solutions for very specific issues. Users may benefit from the creation and availability of new applications, but they are usually hesitant to adopt them into their routine or workflow. With more and more software being developed, the competition is heavy, the market is saturated and it is impossible to test everything or even to keep track of advancements. Of course, the goal for every project is to develop a solution that reaches a large audience and stands the test of time (at least for a few years). One way of increasing the acceptance and use is to heavily cater to the user's needs. A thorough user involvement right from the beginning of the project accompanied by extensive usability testing ensures a high success rate. Even funding institutions of academic projects are increasingly interested in this kind of sustainability for software development projects.

User involvement and usability testing are common ways to gain subjective opinions about a specific application. Assessment and feedback by user groups is used to design and adapt applications and interfaces [1]. How much users actually benefit from applications and interfaces depends on the usability, suitability, and efficiency of technological solutions.

© Springer Nature Switzerland AG 2021
F. Niebling et al. (Eds.): UHDL 2019, CCIS 1501, pp. 46–83, 2021.
https://doi.org/10.1007/978-3-030-93186-5_3

Relying on the user's feedback shows how important it is to define the user group early on in the project and keep them in mind during the whole development process considering their technical abilities and skills as well as their resources, e.g., time. The user's satisfaction should not be neglected and entertainment and emotional involvement when using software are becoming more important to stand out from the crowd.

While some aspects connected to the users are clear from the beginning, like their low tolerance for slow and difficult solutions as well as expectations based on known norms and standards, others may not be anticipated and are only identified through interviews and testing.

Professional software development projects nowadays are more user-oriented and less technology-oriented to ensure they will actually be used. However, this trend is not as apparent for academic projects because of the costs and time necessary for user involvement. An employee is needed to plan and execute the required activities and prepare the data for integration into the development process. This competency is sometimes not available for academic projects where funding is very tight. This contribution tries to introduce tools and methods to incorporate usability efforts into different academic projects at different stages of the project cycle. The focus is on the inquiry of the users through questionnaires and interviews and the use of different levels of prototypes for testing. Three cases provide the examples and assessment of several tools and methods.

Case 1 explains how different usability and user experience methods can be deployed during various stages of the development process of a serious game. E.F.A. is a serious game on the topic of occupational health and safety addressing the target group of leaders in social service companies. On the basis of the project, it is explained how the methods questionnaire, interview, empathy map, user journey map, and paper prototyping can contribute to a more human-centered game development approach.

Case 2 describes a method for creating a template for digitally supported learning scenarios for professional further training in small and micro enterprises as well as medium-sized companies. The template provides the basic framework for the creation of micro-learnings and is based on a human-centered design. Through interacting with a high-fidelity prototype in the form of a click-dummy users can experience the possibilities and the functionalities of the authoring tool Adobe Captivate. In a pre-test the template will be evaluated and further developed.

Case 3 explores a framework for the evaluation and testing of a web application for research and exploration of historical images in a 3D interface. This part of the article gives a broad insight into implementing a user-centered study with heterogeneous user groups from digital humanities by adapting usability methods like personas and thinking aloud. The data was gathered during a workshop which was given on usability testing for 3D image repositories.

## 2 Research Questions

The three studies described below deal with usability and user experience of different applications. All three heavily rely on user involvement, but regarding their human-centered approaches, they are located at different points of the spectrum. Nevertheless, the actual goals are very similar and focus on either designing or adapting and improving an application based on user's needs and feedback. At the beginning, all projects had to deal with the assessment and definition of the user group as well as the selection of methods to develop and test a user interface. Further, the research questions for the three studies are largely connected to usability components of applications (cf. [2–4]):

- Are the selected methods appropriate for the development and testing/evaluation of a user interface? (Suitability of methods)
- In what physical and social environment does the user use the application? (User proximity)
- How does the user solve tasks during interaction with the user interface? Does he/she find and understand the functionalities as intended? (Learnability)
- How much time does the user need to solve tasks after getting familiar with the user interface? (Efficiency)
- What difficulties and errors were reported by users or committed by a user when performing tasks through the web application? (Errors and difficulties)
- How satisfied were the users after interacting with the user interface? (Satisfaction)

## 3 Case 1 – User Group Analysis and User Experience Testing at an Early Stage of the Development Process of a Serious Game

### 3.1 Introduction to the Project E.F.A.

The project "E.F.A.[1] – Digitales adaptives Lernspiel für die berufliche Aus- und Weiterbildung" (E.F.A. – Digital adaptive learning game for vocational education and training) aims at enhancing the acquisition of knowledge in the field of occupational health and safety. For this purpose, an adaptive serious game is to be developed, which enables employees, especially leaders of social service companies, to carry out a comprehensive risk assessment. In the game the player takes on the role of a workplace safety expert and has to fight the way through the "jungle of obligations" of risk assessment. Methodical and content-related knowledge is carried out during the course of the game. The "jungle of obligations" consists of four "temples" which reflect content aspects of occupational safety and contain various tasks that the player must complete in order to return to the "real world". Each "temple" contains a set of mission goals mirroring the learning objective the player must achieve. Each mission goal resp. learning objective is linked to a knowledge repository where all important knowledge and information conveyed by the game is organized.

The development of the serious game E.F.A. includes three different and strongly interwoven processes: conception, design and technical development. During the

---

[1] The project is funded by the European Social Fund (ESF) and the Free State of Saxony. The project term is 36 months (01.05.2019–30.04.2022).

conception phase learning objectives and learning contents need to be developed and meaningfully linked to the player's actions within the game as well as to gamification elements such as story, rewards or characters. According to the (didactic) serious game concept an appealing and customized graphic design must be developed. Usability and user experience aspects must be taken into account. Simultaneously the game concept and graphic design must be implemented into an appropriate technical environment. In order to foster the game's learning success and attractiveness the project team follows a human-centered approach meaning that the future user is regularly involved in different stages of the development process. Formulating project goals and defining target audiences are essential components for planning human-centered design activities. This consecutively allows describing, human-centered quality goals' out of the users' perspective [5, pp. 4].

Prior to the conception and development of the serious game the project team discussed and defined the following aspects:

1. Who are the user groups/target audiences?
2. What are the goals, tasks and requirements of the project?

Regarding 1: As pointed out above, target audiences of E.F.A are microenterprises and small businesses of the social service sector in Saxony, especially management personnel and staff members being responsible for work and health security. It is one task of the project to develop this image and characteristics of the user further in order to make him/her more tangible for the whole project team.

Regarding 2: A list of the following goals was defined prior to the project start:

- Development of a digital adaptive serious game that enables staff members to execute a comprehensive risk assessment ensuring complete legal compliance
- Positive impact to behavior and attitude regarding the topic occupational health and safety
- Support of knowledge acquisition of microenterprises and small businesses in Saxony regarding occupational health and safety in order to enable them to react to changing job requirements as well as new risks and health threats.

Based on this first knowledge about target audiences and the project goals, the E.F. A. team was able to describe human-centered goals and hence define user specific requirements, e.g.:

- Users are provided with practical, close to reality knowledge in small packages
- Users can deepen their knowledge regarding specific topics
- Users can freely determine place and time to play the game
- Users experience a risk assessment
- Users gain more recognition for acquiring competencies.

Furthermore, within a creative workshop at the beginning of the project the team developed a set of specific learning objective as well as a concrete aim of the game.

The result of the joint definition for the aim of the game was: "Find the way through the jungle of obligations and become expert in occupational health and safety".

Defining these (learning) goals of the game is a gold mine for setting further directions of game development regarding "human-centered quality goals".

## 3.2 Challenges in Developing Human-Centered Serious Game Concepts

**Learning Experience Design Approach.** A serious game always deals with the challenge of fulfilling a specific set of learning objectives and simultaneously also providing a playful and entertaining game experience [6]. During the development process of such a serious game the project team always has to master this balance between learning and playing. On the one hand a serious game aims at meeting the pre-defined learning objectives and on the other hand at creating game mechanics and elements which evoke motivation and positive emotions for the player. The challenge of creating those catchy and engaging learning experiences is captured by the concept of learning experience design (LXD) [7]. LXD feeds its fundamentals from the field of user experience design (UXD) as well as form learning science [7, 8]. It states that vivid and emotional learning experiences that are developed in a user-centered and goal-oriented way are expected to promote the learner's motivation and thus also the learning outcome [9].

**Human-Centered Design Approach.** As the name states the concept of human-centered design (HCD) puts the human in the center of development, not the interactive system [10, p. 31]. The process consists of a cycle of fields of activity. It is entered by planning the HCD process and contains understanding and specification of context of use, specification of requirements of use, generation of design solutions to satisfy requirements of use and evaluation of design against requirements (see Fig. 1). These were conducted in our project on a basic level (see Sect. 3.1 Introduction to the Project E.F.A., p. 3).

As depicted in the process flow 'Understanding and specification of context of use' is followed by consecutive steps. In case that the evaluation of the product shows that user requirements are not met, the context of use should be in the focus again. It is a crucial step to capture needs and desires of the user. The more information can be gathered about the context of use in the analysis phase, the more detailed and better founded requirements can be created for the product [5, p. 13]. The importance of a broad knowledge about the target user group as well as developing the product in cooperation with the user was already key to previous projects, turning out in improved quality of use. The basic idea is integrating user desires and needs right from the beginning into the development process. This paper will present the following methods used to uncover those user desires and needs:

- Questionnaire
- User context map
- Interview
- Empathy map
- User journey map
- Paper prototyping

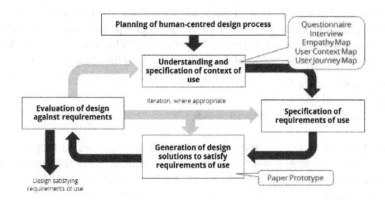

**Fig. 1.** Human-centered design process [10, p. 38] with methods to better uncover user desires and needs.

The basics of LXD and UXD or the concept of human-centered design form challenges for small research projects. The number of team members and the projects duration are limited, not allowing deep analyses. However, the project team's ambitions are high to conduct the project based on HCD fields of activity [5, p. 7]. In order to sufficiently explore the user's game and learning experience within the project E.F. A. the team was keen to evaluate the user and the serious game concept at an early stage. In the following sections there will be explained how a different methods have been applied in the course of the project and how they contributed to a more user-centered and efficient development process.

### 3.3  Methodology for User Group Analysis and Early Stage User Experience Testing

**Method: Questionnaire – Analysis of Desires and Requirements.** In conjunction with a master thesis as part of the E.F.A. project the questionnaire to analyze user desires and requirements could be adapted highly user specific. It is divided into four parts:

1. Previous knowledge and importance regarding workplace health and safety, desired outcome of an educational game
2. Requirements regarding work organization for development of on-the-job training measures
3. Attitude towards computers, e-learning and other technical pre-requisites
4. Demographic information (age, sex, work experience, etc.)

This questionnaire was distributed to the target group of 43 member institutions of *Trägerwerke Soziale Dienste* (TWSD) *Sachsen GmbH* (an agency of social services in Saxony) by e-mail. The time to complete the questionnaire was approximately 20 to 25 min. A total of 25 questionnaires were completed.

The results of the analysis of desires and requirements provided important information on attitudes and points of view of the target group. This was visualized for all team members by a user context map. The main user characteristics were deducted based on the general description of user group profiles [10, pp. 69], e.g.:

- Demographic characteristics
- Function based characteristics
- Work organization based characteristics

**Method: Context of Use – User Context Map.** The User Context Map is a visualization tool for the development team to identify different impacts in user behavior, understand the user and consider various requirements in the conceptual design of the interactive system.

Context of use contains conditions "under which an interactive system is being used" [10, p. 52], in human-centered design conditions are split into four areas (see Fig. 2).

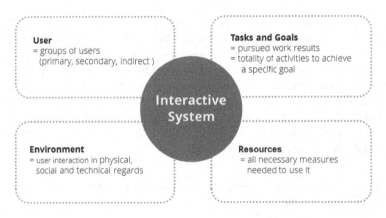

**Fig. 2.** The four areas of the user context map indicate the conditions in which a user interacts with the interactive system.

Data gathered in the project entry phase (e.g. from questionnaire survey) gets assigned to the various areas, in most cases this is unambiguous. At project start normally not all data is available yet so hypotheses need to be employed which will get validated or adjusted at a later stage by means of methods like interviews, focus group discussions or observations.

The visualization of the context of use represents an overview of the "reality of use" and should be accessible and resorted to by the team at any time.

**Method: Interview.** The interview is a method to gather data on users and user groups. Thoroughly selected persons are being interviewed individually to discover further commonalities and differences between potential user groups of the interactive system [10, p. 60]. Due to knowledge from the analysis of desires and requirements the general part can be left out. On the contrary, the focus needs to lie on the interviewee's knowledge on specific tasks so he or she explains and provides insight. An interviewer guideline or checklist is advisable so all team members acting as interviewers work through the same topics and generate information that can easily be compared and summarized. The interview itself follows the Master-Student-Model [10, p. 61] in order to cover tasks and goals of users to a sufficient detail. Closed and suggestive questions should be avoided; open and neutral questions are always preferable. If possible, the contextual place where the user executes his or her tasks is a preferable interview location to facilitate asking situation based question.

The interviews in the E.F.A. project could be conducted in a nearly contextual location. Some heads of institutions belonged to the local staff of the venue where the interviews took place and the E.F.A project team was able to get a firsthand impression of their day to day work. Six interviews with heads of institutions could be organized in separate group meeting rooms. The interviewers used an extensive guideline and recording tools to ask specific questions for 20 to 40 min. Based on the knowledge from the previous analysis of desires and requirements questions regarding safety at work were asked, e.g.: "Which requirements and templates regarding safety at work do you know?" This question helped to find out which sources these persons were already using for this topic.

Some creative questions were also included like: "Which picture comes to your mind when thinking of a jungle of obligations?" The interviewee could also use pen and paper to better visualize his or her imagination. This led to an improved understanding of the user's perception of tasks in daily routines.

**Method: Empathy Map.** Another method used with the project partner *TWSD Sachsen GmbH* was the empathy map. In this method future users were asked to describe their wishes and needs in respect to their physical senses while dealing with aspects and tasks in relation to safety and health at work. This enabled a deep insight into users' sensorial and emotional perception and hence the orientation of the game development to positive sensations.

It was important to adjust the empathy map questionnaire to the project's target audience. Members of this audience were not expected to have seen such a questionnaire before or have been asked similar questions. A question like "What are your emotional and sensorial associations regarding safety and health at work?" directly addresses the user. The interviewee should respond in four free text fields (see Fig. 3) to hearing (What do superiors, coworkers and people in the environment say?), seeing (environment, visual requests), thinking & feeling (What is important to you? What are your personal concerns and requirements?) and saying & doing (public point of view, activities, behavior towards others). In the lower section of the questionnaire the interviewee commented on pressure (Which negative experiences did you encounter? Please explain with example and situation.) and recognition (Which positive experiences did you encounter? Please explain with example and situation.).

The questionnaire was tested internally in the project team before handing it to the interviewees to validate and adjust the empathy map for this specific project and target audience.

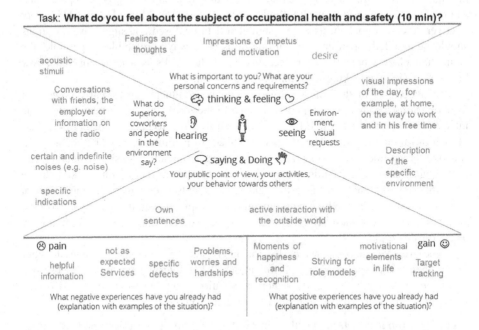

**Fig. 3.** Empathy map questionnaire specifically adjusted for the project's target audience.

It is important to note that the questionnaire was only employed after explaining to the user group in person what the cooperation was expected to look like (human-centered design approach) and that a close collaboration with the end user was fundamental for this. At the project kickoff with TWSD the empathy map questionnaire was used as first tool of the user experience method. Within ten minutes users were asked to note down their insights. As observers of the test the project team could realize that it was not easy for the users to fill in the questionnaire. As the evaluation showed as well, the users are concerned with the general topic but this is barely recognized or appreciated.

**Method: User Journey Map.** The user journey map provides an overview of touchpoints of the users with the product while dealing with their tasks. This also includes user experience touchpoints outside of the interactive system [10, p. 79]. The user journey map contains three areas:

- Before the interactive application,
- While using the interactive application and
- After the interactive application.

Primary communication of the user to or with the interactive system can be arranged in these three areas. It also helps to identify early where to focus on in the human-centered design process.

In the course of a creative workshop (about 30 min) different groups of the project team went through three stages "'before the game", "through the game" and "after the game". In each phase various aspects of the specific stage were visualized on a flip chart. For the "before the game" phase question were for example:

- By which touchpoints does the user arrive at the game?
- What are the user's interest regarding the game?
- Which type of user could the user be? (see list)
- What are the user's expectations regarding the game?
- By which requirements is the user characterized?
- Which emotion drive the user to the game?

Participants of the workshop answered these questions from a user's point of view using stickers on the poster. Every 10 min the groups moved on to another stage to complete contents. By this a first user journey map of the educational game E.F.A. was generated in 30 min.

**Method: Paper Prototyping.** For sufficiently testing the game mechanics and the didactic concept of the serious game E.F.A. at an early stage of the development the project team made use of a low-fidelity paper-based prototype. A paper prototype is defined as: "a variation of usability testing where representative users perform realistic tasks by interacting with a paper version of the interface that is manipulated by a person "playing computer", who doesn't explain how the interface is intended to work" [11, p. 4]. Thus, the paper prototype functions as a kind of board game version of the intended digital serious game. Since board games and digital games often follow the same logics and mechanics the game concepts and its playability can be evaluated with the help of a paper-based version [12]. For the first two sections of the serious game E. F.A. (section "organization of workplace health and safety" and "risk assessment") a paper prototype made of movable paper and cardboard pieces representing the contents and navigation elements was developed. The purpose of paper prototyping was to assess how a potential user group perceives the functionality of the game characteristics such as storylines, game mechanics, rules and navigation. The project team conducted several test runs with different user groups. Each test run was embedded into a semi-structured interview and during the game play the thinking aloud method was used [13]. Data on the following evaluation criteria was collected:

- Previous experiences with digital/non-digital (serious) games
- Expectations of the game/expected increase of knowledge
- General impression
- Perceived complexity/navigation
- Perceived playing time
- Dialogs
- Mini games
- Increase of knowledge

- Positive/negative aspects of the game
- Transfer between jungle scenario and workplace
- Willingness to play again

The answers of the interviews where descriptively analyzed and compared during the course of the test run phase. After each test run the prototype was modified according to the feedback given by the player. Thus, by using a slightly different version of the prototype in each test run a continuous and iterative improvement process was established. Each section of the serious game is planned to be tested separately by different user groups. As a starting point for testing and improvement the project team choose to ask experts in the field of media didactics to take on the role as players who primarily focus on aspects like game mechanics as well as didactical and medial preparation of the contents. Later on also experts in the respective field are involved and only at a later stage when game mechanics and contents already were subject of improvement the actual target group gets involved. In the course of the project also the digital prototype of the game will be evaluated by those user groups. The concept for the ongoing evaluation process of the low- and high-fidelity prototype is shown in Fig. 4.

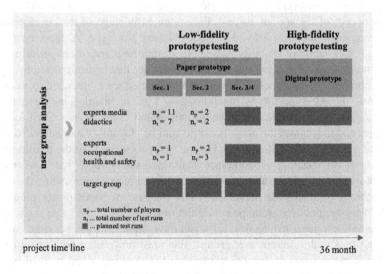

**Fig. 4.** User experience and usability testing concept for the serious game E.F.A.

### 3.4 Results and Recommendation for Early Stage User Experience Methods

**Questionnaire Results.** The results of the survey provide a first impression of the serious game's future user. One major finding indicated that 66% of the participants have already experiences with e-learning. 44% state that they use digital games and 55% of them play between 10 and 29 min per week [14, p. 84]. Thus, regarding the serious game conception the project team can build on prior gameplay experience of the target group. The respondents (n = 25) hope for a an increase in health and well-being within their company (M = 1,48), for a personal knowledge growth (M = 1,60)[2] as well as for an individual development (M = 1,60) as long-term effects of the serious game [14, p.67]. Regarding the integration of the serious game into the working life 88% of the participants indicate that they are able to use the game during work. 32% of them have a time frame of 10 to 19 min for continuously using the serious game [14, p. 69].

**User Context Map Results.** The User Context Map resulted in a large wall paper depicting numerous little details in all four areas: Users, Tasks and Goals, Environment and Resources. For fast digital access in day to day use this large map had to be boiled down to a compressed summary (Fig. 5).

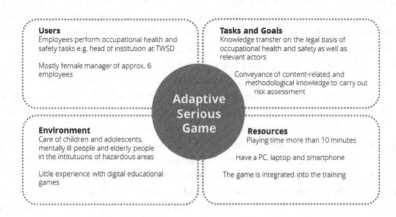

**Fig. 5.** Mini User Context Map.

The users are mostly female (88%) head of institutions, leading approximately 6 employees. Tasks and goals of the E.F.A. serious game are mainly knowledge transfer regarding basics of occupational health safety as well as a methodological knowledge focus for the execution of risk assessment.

Regarding the field of operation the user group is made up of child and youth care (60%), care of mentally ill persons (28%) and care of elderly persons, handicapped persons and others. One example out of our user group is a supervised youth accommodation where about eight persons aged 13 and older are taken care of as a kind of substitute family.

Danger areas are broken down into office rooms, group rooms, kitchen, living rooms and meeting rooms partly with play areas. Users are not used to digital learning games regarding further training.

---

[2] on a 4-step scale from 1 = "fully agree" to 4 = "completely disagree".

Resources are especially limited regarding time for learning games. PC, laptop and smartphone are available, however, playback of sound is an issue as speakers and headphones are missing.

For the next step of the human-centered design process of the serious game user requirements can easily be extracted and formulated out of these aspects of the situation of users.

**Interview Results.** Summarizing all results from six interviews a clear goal of the game needs to be visible from the first moment on. A common thread, e.g. given by a concrete story line, must be identifiable. This does not mean a given path needs to be followed. Rather users should be challenged while making decisions. They may see a serious game as a kind of puzzle, thereby raising their motivation. It is important though not to lose reference to work and health safety. A creative, open question like "What images come into your mind when thinking of jungle of obligations?" led to a picture of chaos for most interviewees. This chaos results from the vast amount of information and its interrelations. Orientation in this jungle is regarded as complicated. However, according to one person interviewed you should not get lost in the game. The jungle more often gets depicted by paragraphs and paper rather than vegetation, as can be seen in Fig. 6 where paragraphs are hanging from the trees instead of leafs.

Many of the interviewees listed time issues, hence it is important to focus on fundamental aspects of work and health safety. Deepening knowledge can be conveyed by the means of additional or bonus missions and areas. The implementation as a mobile game enables the user to play it on the way. Content may be packaged in form of levels or subject areas. This also allows the user to deal goal-oriented with a specific subarea. Hence, the game is adapting to individual needs and requirements. This in turn fosters learning motivation and success as well as fun in the process.

The interviews do not allow a specific kind of presentation, individual preferences vary widely. Some could imagine a more abstract kind of game, e.g. with talking animals, others considered this as too creative. A happy medium seems advisable.

The serious game also should work against the user's sensation of stress and being overburdened by information material regarding occupational health and safety. A high pressure and a lack of time demand for an effective use of the learning medium.

**Fig. 6.** Image of a user regarding the question: "What images come into your mind when thinking of jungle of obligations?"

Free decision making, clear actions, demanding and supporting, humorous and close to reality, but always constructive – all these are expectations regarding the serious game by the interviewed management staff.

**Empathy Map Results – the User's Emotions towards Occupational Health and Safety.** The respondent's empathy maps revealed that they often wish for transparency, comprehensibility, a clear structure as well as division of tasks regarding their obligations of occupational health and safety. Despite, they often experience a lack of time and a missing guidance in fulfilling these task. The participants feel the need for a more structured and simpler way of imparting the necessary knowledge. Healthcare and safety topics are recognized during the daily working life, however, work-related emotional stress still belongs to the rather unrecognized aspects. Moreover, the respondents value the cooperation with the employees and count on teamwork. The greatest burden they see in instructing and motivating the employees in occupational health and safety.

The results of the empathy map provided the project team with an insight into the future user's emotions regarding the topic. For the conception and development of the serious game could be concluded that contents should be well-structured and on the point in order to enable an easy and time-efficient access to the topic. Furthermore, the concept of cooperation and teamwork is recommended to be implemented into the game – e.g. with creating employees as decisive game characters.

**User Journey Map Results.** After switching stations every ten minutes results were shortly discussed in the group. Participants of the creative workshop realized how big the challenge of following the user on his/her path and how (see Fig. 7) this process is.

Development of the game becomes lively through positive emotions of the user. Therefore, potential motivations to play the game need to be inquired "before the game":

- Curiosity
- Refusal
- Lack of interest and
- Fear of consequences not observing all rules

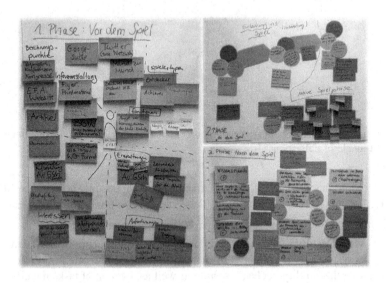

**Fig. 7.** First result of the User Journey Map.

An interesting aspect was that the E.F.A. project team apparently encountered a target audience that is not confident using new media but just curious.

In the second phase the anticipated game emotions for example to event "registration" are for example:

- Anticipation
- Cheerfulness
- Curiosity

The "before the game" process seems to be crucial in order to lead to the registration and a change of emotions.

The User Journey Map collects experiences, interests, expectations and satisfaction of users throughout the detailed game process. The User Journey Map helps revealing additional potential obstacles for the user. Further supportive interactions can be integrated into the game as help or offered before or after the game. In the example mentioned above a tutorial unit may guide the user before the game and trigger her/his curiosity. An example regarding the sense of being overburdened would be a helping character that is always right by the user's side. The results of the creative workshop are a good guideline for further digital refinement and improvement of the user journey map. It can be run through again with additional target audiences for further adjustment.

**Paper Prototyping Results.** The outcomes of the different test runs with the paper prototype enabled the project team to continuously improve the serious game concept. With the help of the semi-structured interviews and the thinking aloud method useful feedback for all pre-defined evaluation criteria could be collected at an early stage and prior to the digital implementation. In contrast to a high-fidelity digital prototype the paper prototype made quick improvements, e.g. small adjustments of dialogs or screen instruction, between different test runs possible. However, feedback that requires fundamental changes of game mechanics was better carried out when several test runs in a row showed the necessity of improvement.

The result of the descriptive analysis of the interviews and the expressed thoughts while playing game Sect.1 show that both weaknesses with game mechanics as well as problems in knowledge acquisition could be observed. First, the operation and handling of the paper prototype caused problems for some of the players since buttons were distributed over a large gaming board and were not always recognized. Also orientation difficulties occurred. A rather smaller gaming board compared to a computer desktop size might solve those problems. Second, the post-playing interview revealed a rather positive impression of the game and its contents. The participants praised the funny and varied dialogs and all of them understood the overall aim of the game. Inconsistencies in the story or in game characters could be identified and adjusted between the test runs. Regarding knowledge acquisition the results indicate that testers within the group of media didactics experts were able to recall specific learning contents after playing. Nevertheless, learning outcomes were not as high as anticipated by the players. The transfer of learning contents through mini-games was improved and thus, a superior paper prototype was tested with the expert of occupational health and safety. The comparison of the results between both expert groups shows that experts in the field of media didactics rather focus on game elements such as rules, rewards or story and rather question those than content-related aspects. Experts in the field of occupational health and safety, however, rather take a look at learning contents than on the underlying game mechanics.

During the course of the ongoing development process all game sections will be evaluated with the help of the paper prototype and with the three different user groups. Then, the digital prototype will be evaluated with the same evaluation pattern and criteria. The results will provide data of how different game elements were perceived first in the paper prototype and later, after their improvement according to the feedback, within the digital prototype. This comparison will provide more profound research findings of paper prototyping being an efficient and user-centered method for the development of vivid and experienceable learning environments according to LXD.

## 4  Case 2 – Development of a Click-Dummy Prototype for the User-Centered Creation of a Template with Adobe Captivate

### 4.1  Introduction of the Project weiter.digital

The project weiter.digital[3] is a transfer project that develops, introduces and tests digitally supported learning scenarios for professional further training in small and micro enterprises as well as medium-sized companies. It is a cooperation of the Center for Open Digital Innovation and Participation (CODIP), formerly Media Center of the TU Dresden under supervision of the *Verband Sächsischer Bildungsinstitute e.V.* (Association of Saxon Educational Institutes, short: VSBI). The partners preparing and testing the educational services are the *Akademie für Wirtschaft und Verwaltung GmbH* (Academy for Economy and Administration), the *future Training & Consulting GmbH* and the *AMS Ausbildungsgesellschaft für Metalltechnik und Schweißer mbH* (training company for metal technology and welders).

The project goal is to use barrier-free mobile learning scenarios in order to facilitate access to further education offers and increase the participation of small and micro enterprises as well as medium-sized companies in further education in the Saxon region. Through the development of innovative learning and media formats, the groups should be able to acquire technical and media related skills right at their own workplace. Different media formats will be tested, for example with Adobe Captivate, an authoring tool for learning applications. All applications developed in the project will be published as Open Educational Resources (OER).

### 4.2  The Target Group and Connected Challenges

Due to the ubiquitous digitalization, companies, their employees, and customers have to deal with profound changes. Therefore, new skills and competencies are required of the employees while the companies also have to cope with staff retention and shortage of skilled professionals. Knowledge and expertise additional to the actual production are essential components that make up the value of a company. Further training and professional development will help to ensure that companies can keep up with the technological and process-related advances. Small and micro enterprises (SME) are much more reluctant to engage in professional training than medium-sized or large companies [15, p. 348] and their staff structure often does not allow their employees to be absent from work for several days to complete further training. In order to overcome the distinct challenges service providers need to redesign their trainings.

Digital formats for professional training may be a promising solution to this problem. Hence, an idea is to minimize actual physical attendance at training sessions and make use of smaller not dedicated time slots. In addition, the workplace may be

---

[3] The project is funded by the European Union, the European Social Fund (ESF) as well as by funding approved by the members of the Saxon state parliament. It runs from June 2019 to June 2022.

integrated into the digitally supported training tools in order to further promote the professional training behavior.

Another important success for further training is to involve the providers of professional training and properly introduce them to micro-learnings and its possibilities and challenges. On the one hand providers need to offer topics which are individually tailored for the SME and on the other hand they have to keep an eye on cost-efficiency since there will be fewer participants. Therefore, the providers of the training programs should be supported in terms of transfer and development of digital (self-) learning competencies, e.g., through assistance and tutorials for the implementation of content that enables training anywhere and anytime using digital media. The prototype, which will be described in more detail in the next section, will help the employees to get familiar with the process of creating micro-learnings. Their involvement early on will also ensure to pay attention to usability aspects. Ambiguity and aversion to the template will be reduced due to the involvement of the service providers during the creation process.

### 4.3 Creation and Testing of a High-Fidelity Prototype for Micro-learnings

**Micro-learning.** Micro-learnings aim to impart knowledge to the learners as small learning snippets keeping the amount of time and content to a minimum [16, 17].

Within the project weiter.digital a micro-learning on media competence is set up which is based on the four major aspects (media theory, media analysis, media use, and media design) defined by German media pedagogue Dieter Baacke [16]. A high-fidelity prototype is used for the development and testing of the media skills micro-learning application.

The micro-learning is divided into: introduction, learning objective, media skills, summary, quiz and outlook. In the beginning the terminology is introduced and the learning objective is described. Focusing on media skills, the knowledge transfer is connected to an entry-level test which allows the user to assess their prior knowledge on the topic and if sufficient, move on quickly. Answering correctly will directly lead to the next question, but in case of an incorrect answer the user has to study the relevant information before continuing. The test results are not included in any evaluation and the test can only be taken once. A subsequent session will always show all relevant information. At the end the user can access a summary on the topic and finally start the examination of his newly acquired knowledge. This final examination is done in form of a quiz. The micro-learning is concluded by an outlook on how to deal with the new knowledge on a practical level. The course does not follow a fixed structure, the user can freely choose the order in which to proceed.

**High-Fidelity Prototype.** A high-fidelity prototype is a detailed prototype and allows the simulation of the real application. It is similar to mockups, but interactive and introduces the full functionality of the application [18]. The creation of a high-fidelity prototype is very time consuming and requires several small internal tests and revisions before completion. This prototype enables a final user test before the implementation. The user test focuses on interactions, functionalities, the user interface and the visual language.

*Layout and Functionalities of the Template.* A prototype in form of a click dummy was implemented using the authoring tool Adobe Captivate[4]. During the creation process slide designs are used similar to PowerPoint presentations which can additionally be enriched and controlled with complex interactions. Thanks to the HTML5 format, the creation of responsive learning applications is possible independently from an operating system.

The template was created according to the project's layout, defining all colors and shapes. For optimal user orientation, a uniform navigation and information architecture is used. Thereby the page structure of the individual slides is in the form: header, navigation area, content area and footer (see Fig. 8).

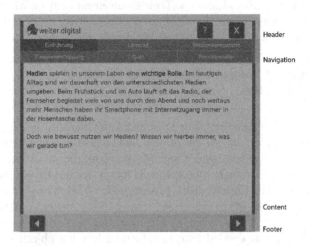

**Fig. 8.** Design of the pages: header, navigation, content and footer.

The header contains the logo and the main control elements like the buttons for closing the application and the help page. Additional options are elements for controlling audio tracks. The navigation area includes buttons which lead through the individual topics. They can be selected individually and are highlighted according to the current position. Structure and naming of the navigation is partly predefined to ensure a standardized look for the project. The content area is the actual heart of the application and contains different functionalities depending on the displayed content. The footer serves navigational purposes and indicates the current position within the learning application.

The navigation through the learning application does not follow a defined sequence or rigid specifications. The user can freely decide whether to work through the microlearning in a linear way with the help of arrows in the footer or via the menu items in the navigation area.

---

[4] Adobe Captivate is a software from Adobe Inc. and enables the creation of interactive learning applications in HTML5 format.

The navigation menu is divided into the learning units: introduction, learning objective, media competence, summary, quiz and outlook (practical transfer). This is emphasized by interactive buttons in the navigation menu. Different interaction types are used throughout the media competence prototype:

- Presentation of texts and images at different positions
- Display of several aspects of a topic in the form of an information slider, providing an additional navigation level within the content area
- Buttons that change in appearance and functionality after selection or initiate complex functions.

*Knowledge Transfer.* The main focus of the prototype is to present media skills information. The entry-level test with underlying complex functionalities does not contain the predefined question types of Adobe Captivate. The goal of the test is to address the user's cognitive abilities and to involve him or her directly in the learning process (see Fig. 9). The test can only be taken once. After the first try the questions are no longer accessible.

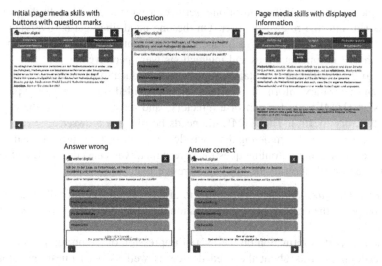

**Fig. 9.** Pages connected to the media skills entry-level test. Top left: starting page with interactive buttons presenting 4 aspects of media skills, top middle: after selecting a button a corresponding question appears, bottom left: pink coloring for incorrect answer, bottom right: green coloring for correct answer, top right: display of further information after giving incorrect answer.

During the entry-level test, the user only has the option to answer the questions or to close the learning application. Navigation elements are inaccessible until a question is answered. In case of an incorrect answer the user must read the information provided before continuing. After the question has been answered, the buttons are renamed with the term of the media skill and only display the corresponding information.

The micro-learning is concluded with an examination using pre-defined question types from Adobe Captivate, relying on the following question types:

- Multiple choice questions
- True or false questions
- Fill-in-the-blank questions
- Matching questions
- Sorting questions.

The user must complete this examination. There is no option to skip it. After completion, the acquired score is displayed and compared to the total points possible. The user can also review the results of the examination, matching his answers to the correct ones.

**Implementation of a Pre-test of the Media Skills Prototype.** The aim of the pre-test is to let the employees of the educational service providers interact with the prototype and thus slip into the role of the user. On the one hand, they get an overview of the possible range of functions of the Adobe Captivate tool and, on the other hand, they evaluate how the functionalities and interactions were perceived.

Prior to the evaluation, the staff will provide the educational installers with a brief tutorial and necessary information to launch the provided files. The prototype is provided as an HTML5 file (as part of a directory) and must be stored on the computer (unzip directory locally). The HTML file needs be run in a browser[5].

After reviewing and completing the micro-learning, the service provider will be able to give feedback using an online questionnaire which was created with LimeSurvey[6]. A pre-test and evaluation of the questionnaire are planned for January 2021.

*Structure of the Questionnaire.* The structure of the questionnaire for the evaluation of the prototype by the employees of the educational service providers is divided into two parts.

In the first part, information on the overall impression of the prototype is collected. The questionnaire asks about the used device as well as open questions about the impression of the prototype in the form:

- Positive things about the prototype are…
- Negative things about the prototype are…
- Suggestions for improvement based on knowledge of the user group…

---

[5] It has been successfully tested on Chrome, Mozilla Firefox and Safari.

[6] LimeSurvey is an online survey tool. For more information see: https://www.limesurvey.org/.

In the second part, specific questions are asked about the interaction as well as the visualization of the information. Here, the questions are structured depending on the answer. Further questions may be asked. The question types are primarily yes/no answers. Only the option for comments are free text areas. The following questions are asked:

- Preference of navigation (using arrows or menu items)
- Visibility of the help functionality
- Recognition of the buttons in the media skills entry test
- Handling and processing of the final quiz.

The goal of the pre-test is to get general feedback on the prototype from education provider staff. Furthermore, the interaction with the prototype is evaluated. The focus is on:

- Use of the end device
- Path control (menu call vs. arrow control)
- Perception of the pre-test and the operation description
- Perception of the final quiz and the process description.

In addition, employees are presented with the functionality of Adobe Captivate using a high-fidelity prototype. The results of the questionnaire will be used in the further development of the template. The template will be used for more modules in the ongoing project.

## 5   Case 3 – Applying Personas and Thinking-Aloud for a User-Centered Evaluation of a Prototypical Application for 3D Image Repositories

### 5.1   Introduction of the Project Urban History 4D

The research group Urban History 4D[7] (www.urbanhistory4D.org) is investigating and developing methods and technologies to improve access to and use of digital image repositories. As a prototypical web application the 4D Browser is developed to present historical images of the city of Dresden in a virtual 3D model (see Fig. 10). A timeline introduces the fourth dimension (4D) and provides information on the development of the city via filtering photos and 3D models according to any selected point in time. The features support image search and filtering, data analysis, data visualization based on acquisition habits and contextualization via linking photos and their spatio-temporal location within the model [19]. The currently accessible collection of 3629 historical images comes from the Deutsche Fotothek[8].

---

[7] The project is funded by the German Federal Ministry of Education and Research (BMBF) running from August 2016 until April 2021.

[8] The Deutsche Fotothek is a picture library and universal archive dedicated to art and cultural history. It is part of the Saxon State and University Library Dresden. See http://www.deutschefotothek.de/.

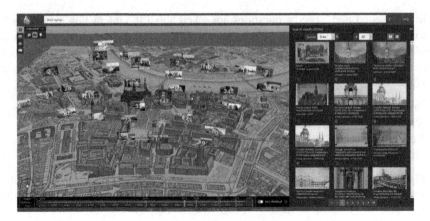

**Fig. 10.** Interface of the 4D Browser web application.

### 5.2 Usability in Digital Humanities

The idea of the 4D Browser is directly connected to research questions for art and architectural heritage. These scholars use images as a main source for analysis and argumentation and therefore turn to (online) digital image repositories [20]. Further data processing may be done with the help of customized applications or conventional software, e.g., Photoshop.

A lot of the existing tools of research platforms and applications stem from computer science and do not necessarily meet the needs of their users from humanities [21] nor consider their behavior and skills. Studies that evaluate the usability of digital humanities tools are clearly underrepresented [22].

For an initial user assessment, Sweetnam et al. provides an overview of the users of digital humanities (DH) collections, which are: professional researchers, apprentice investigators, informed users and the general public [23]. Their heterogeneous backgrounds and demands can be classified by specializations, qualifications, education and information needs [24, 25]. Common requirements of the users in regard to DH collections may be an ease of understanding of the provided data and information, tools for accurate search, research and analysis as well as an intuitive navigation and interface [24]. Scholars emphasize the adherence of scientific standards, transparency concerning workflows within a tool, and thorough documentation through the supply of metadata. Whereas laypersons usually favor a straightforward introduction to the data and topic [25] as well as possibilities to select further material without getting discouraged by an overload of information. The awareness of common issues helps to identify aspects within an application which need to be observed further with the help of suitable test scenarios. However, a challenge is to meet all the needs of the heterogeneous user group. Therefore, user studies were conceived to:

- Collect the information needs of the user groups
- Filter out the challenges that various user groups have when using the tool

- Learn about the requests of the user group
- Identify usability weaknesses
- Adapt the user needs in the developmental process of the web application.

**User Involvement within the Project.** Users were involved from the beginning of the project. In a first stage, the focus was on identification of necessary and useful functions through a literature review but also with the help of actual user inquiry and user studies [26, 27]. A workshop held at the conference *Digital Humanities in the German-speaking Area* (DHd 2018) in February 2018 involved 25 potential users, who were asked to reflect on their own experiences when using image repositories [28]. Amongst a variety of mentioned issues and requirements were:

- Dissatisfaction with insufficient filter options for existing platforms
- Demand for a faceted search functionality
- Wish for labelling buildings within the 3D model
- Need for a feature to compare different images to each other.

With regard to the project's geospatial web application 4D Browser, the participants agreed that it was a sensible addition to the usual language-based search. In general, the reactions were very positive towards the introduced approach, and most reactions mainly concerned the usability of the tool. Therefore, it was decided to develop a design for a user-oriented evaluation of 3D information systems of cultural heritage. The framework supports an evaluation of the 4D Browser, even when the participants do not represent the actual user group. This is particularly useful when a prototype has to be tested concerning initial reactions as well as the placement and general understanding of functions and the interface. The real user group has to be brought in later to ensure the particular consideration of their quality criteria.

### 5.3   Research Design

The overall goal of the usability study is to collect information needs and requests of the users, identify challenges and usability weaknesses that users encounter when using the tool, and adapt the web application according to the user's needs.

The study is part of a workshop and contains different realistic tasks connected to the 4D Browser. The tasks help users to focus on and assess certain functions. They contain scenarios and problems that correspond to the knowledge and skills of an assigned persona that is part of the actual user group of the application. It is very important to properly guide the heterogeneous groups of workshop participants. Hence, the persona approach seemed suitable for this purpose as it provides another level of reason and purpose for participants who come from other academic areas and may not be able to fully envision the genuine intentions of the functions on the spot. Furthermore, thinking-aloud was chosen in order to learn more about the needs and interactions of the users.

**Persona.** Personas serve as a realistic representation of the actual users of a solution. They may include fictitious details in order to provide a more accurate characterization, like demographic and biographical characteristics, imaginary information, and even real names. A representation by an image or picture adds realism [29]. The persona approach may be of value during the development process, because it helps to keep the focus on the user group. However, in this usability study it helps the participants to understand the possibly foreign scenario of the tasks and its objectives more clearly. Additionally, it loosely functions as a boundary object for the participants of the usability tests by indicating expectations and behaviors of one typical user. Boundary objects are concepts which are both plastic enough to adapt to local needs and the constraints of the several parties employing them, yet robust enough to maintain a common identity across sites [30]. They are especially helpful when working in groups.

The personas were developed with the user group described by Sweetnam et al. [23]. In order to keep the personas simple and allow the workshop participants to quickly grasp the idea, only two aspects were chosen as criteria for shaping the personas: their knowledge concerning art history as a topic connected to handling and interpreting historical photographs and their skills regarding digital applications (see Fig. 11). One goal during the persona development was to cover a sufficient range by means of combinations. The developed personas are:

- Professor of art history
- Research associate of art history working on his PhD
- Third semester student of art history
- Teacher representing an informed and interested general public.

**Fig. 11.** Examples of the brief resumes for the student and teacher persona.

**Tasks.** Specific tasks closely connected to the personas serve as user scenarios that guide the participants and focus their actions on certain features of the 4D Browser. The tasks were designed to be realistic and relevant for one of the personas (see Table 1). It was specifically asked to use the think-aloud protocol while working on topics.

**Table 1.** Comprehensive review of the workshop tasks and their intended insights.

| Task | Intention |
|---|---|
| *Task A for the professor:*<br>You are preparing a new scholarly project on the Sophienkirche in Dresden. Compare the 4D Browser as well as the Deutsche Fotothek (www.deutschefotothek.de) and Europeana (www.europeana.eu) websites concerning functions, interface and relevant information | This task aimed at comparing the 4D Browser with platforms that offer similar functions necessary to solve the specific task. The intention is to identify positive and negative aspects of the competing solutions and see which ones are expected and serve the purpose the best |
| *Task B for the research associate:*<br>You want to analyze acquisition habits of photographers. Use the visualization function of the 4D Browser and interpret its displays concerning acquisition angles of buildings based on large numbers of geo-referenced photographs | The goal of this tasks was to see how much and which specific information are necessary to understand the functions for visualizations |
| *Task C for the student:*<br>You have to prepare an assignment on the Sophienkirche in Dresden. Use the 4D Browser to get a first impression of the location, appearance, and changes of the church building over time | This task was designed to find out if the participants can find, understand and make use of the search bar, the time slider, and the image compare functionality |
| *Task D for the teacher*<br>You have come across historic photos of Dresden and want to know what they show. Use the 4D Browser to identify the buildings in the photos and find out if they still exist | This task was intended to see if the participants can find, understand, and make use of the search bar, the time slider, and the functions for combining the 3D model and the photographs |

In order to support the participants when working on the tasks, assistance was provided in form of instructions on how to approach the assignments as well as consecutive steps that helped to guide the participants (see Fig. 12). However, the instructions did not always name the specific tools and functionalities the participants should use. This allowed to observe if they were named and placed in an intuitive manner. In the example shown in Fig. 12, the participants are asked to use information on the back of a photograph to find it in the application, but it does not specifically say to type it into the search bar. According to the task, the participants have to use the virtual city model and the photo to identify depicted buildings. There is a function that allows the user to take the initial spot of the photographer and create an overlay of the slightly transparent photo and the virtual model. There are also several ways to activate this feature and it was important to see if it can be discovered.

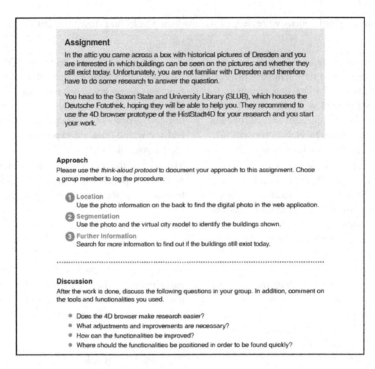

**Assignment**

In the attic you came across a box with historical pictures of Dresden and you are interested in which buildings can be seen on the pictures and whether they still exist today. Unfortunately, you are not familiar with Dresden and therefore have to do some research to answer the question.

You head to the Saxon State and University Library (SLUB), which houses the Deutsche Fotothek, hoping they will be able to help you. They recommend to use the 4D browser prototype of the HistStadt4D for your research and you start your work.

**Approach**

Please use the *think-aloud protocol* to document your approach to this assignment. Chose a group member to log the procedure.

❶ Location
Use the photo information on the back to find the digital photo in the web application.

❷ Segmentation
Use the photo and the virtual city model to identify the buildings shown.

❸ Further Information
Search for more information to find out if the buildings still exist today.

**Discussion**

After the work is done, discuss the following questions in your group. In addition, comment on the tools and functionalities you used.

● Does the 4D browser make research easier?
● What adjustments and improvements are necessary?
● How can the functionalities be improved?
● Where should the functionalities be positioned in order to be found quickly?

**Fig. 12.** Example of instructions for task D for the teacher who represents the general public.

**Thinking-aloud.** Thinking-aloud was proposed to learn more about the user's needs and interactions with the 4D Browser and to initiate a dialog among group members. This data acquisition method is based on introspection methods adopted from cognitive psychology [31] and allows the collect qualitative data. The method is approved and used in professional user experience and usability studies [32]. It states that participants performing a certain task have to verbalize at the same time whatever crosses their mind. This method helps to emphasize interactions between humans and machines and allows insights into users' feelings and thoughts [32]. Audio and screen recording is highly recommended to collect data for a consecutive analysis. The written transcripts of the spoken thoughts are called think-aloud protocols [33].

**Pre-test.** A pre-test of the usability testing was done with five participants. The participants did not know the tasks and methods before, but they were more or less familiar with the web application. The test sample ranged from technically proficient to less proficient to determine challenges of the tasks and interactions with the web application. In addition, the art historical content was checked by a scholar from the field. It was found that usability steps and methods, such as personas and thinking aloud, need to be precisely explained to the workshop participants. Additionally, information on navigation within the 4D Browser needs to be provided. The concept was adapted accordingly.

## 5.4    Implementation of the Workshop

The data for the study was collected during a workshop offered by the research group at the conference *DHd 2019 (Digital Humanities in the German-speaking Area 2019)* in Mainz, Germany. The topic of the workshop was: *Usability Testing for Software Tools in the Digital Humanities* using the example of image repositories. Eight participants (5 women, 3 men) from the academic domain agreed to work in groups of two to three people. The participants of the workshop were students and research associates. The qualification was balanced in terms of general knowledge of art and architectural history and technical skills. Two of the participants were programmers. None of the participants had earlier experience with personas or thinking-aloud.

Due to the low number of participants for the workshop, it was decided to omit one of the prepared tasks as well as the connected persona (cf. Table 2).

**Table 2.** Overview of the workshop groups, their participants as well as the assigned personas and tasks.

| Group | Participants | Assigned Persona | Assigned Task | Audio length |
|---|---|---|---|---|
| 1 | 2 male computer scientists in their 20 s; 1 female researcher from humanities in her 50 s | Research associate | Task B: Testing and interpreting the visualization functionalities | 49 min 41 s |
| 2 | 1 male and 1 female researcher from humanities in their 40 s | Teacher, representing the general public | Task D: Finding a certain photo and identifying the depicted buildings | 36 min 12 s |
| 3 | 3 female students from art history | Student | Task C: Locating a certain building and comparing several images | 36 min 32 s |

**Analysis of Qualitative Data.** All participants agreed to an audio recording of their group work. Afterwards, the audio recordings were transcribed in MAXQDA and coded using thematic analysis—"a method for identifying, analyzing, and reporting patterns (themes) within the data" [34]. Thematic analysis consists of a five-phase process in order to inductively gain insight into the empirical data. It begins with the transcription of the empirical material followed by the generation of initial codes from the verbal data, the searching for themes within the data, and the reviewing of the themes found in the data. The last phase consists of defining and naming themes in this inductive process [34]. Thematic Analysis is related to Grounded Theory [35] and is therefore open towards the empiric material. For the research, it was important to explore which topics were mentioned by the user groups. This will allow to gain insights into the users' personal impressions when interacting with the 4D Browser. Comprehension and solving of the tasks were also part of the observation. The collected data will be valuable for further user-centered studies as it provides facts and figures for comparison.

In several coding rounds, themes were identified and the material was coded accordingly. Re-coding was used to ensure that the coding scheme could be reproduced and that the processes and methods aligned.

**Research Limitations.** The pilot study is limited by the small sample of different, non-comparable user groups. The sample is not representative and randomly selected. A guided case selection did not take place; a theoretical saturation could not be fulfilled. This can be criticized and could be explained by the limited access to the field. For the purpose of obtaining a first impression from different user groups, it is plausible to get first results and to have a data base which can serve as a basis for further large-scale quantitative and qualitative studies.

## 5.5   Results and Discussion

For a thorough data interpretation, besides analyzing the usability weaknesses the execution of the tasks needs to be considered as well. This will also show if any changes of the framework are necessary for future test runs.

**Evaluating the Framework.** Several aspects demonstrate how well the usability testing and the framework itself worked. By means of coding it was revealed how the participants dealt with the personas. It became clear when thinking-aloud was used and if the tasks were understood and solved as intended. The related categories for analysis are:

1. The users' mentioning of the personas and the related skills
2. Use of thinking-aloud
3. Completion of the tasks

In the following passage, these categories are discussed in more detail.

*The User's Mentioning of the Personas and the Related Skills.* For this study, the technical skills are the most important ability of the personas setting them apart from the participants. Art history knowledge was not necessary at all since the participants did not need to interpret any content or findings. Quality criteria connected to art history did not play a role and will be considered in a later study.

The personas only helped to promote the situation for the participants. An actual completion of the tasks could be accomplished without them. In order to see how challenging the interface and functionalities might be for users with different skill sets, the persona approach seemed promising. However, the participants usually try to put themselves in the background, but it is not entirely possible to separate their abilities from themselves as individuals.

The assessment of the data showed that all three groups handled the personas differently. Group 1 consisted of three persons who were assigned the persona of the research associate. The data shows that they did not deal with their persona of a male research associate during the study. The persona was not mentioned during the performance of the tasks, nor was it considered how the persona might proceed or think in specific situations. The only time a group member referred to the persona, he named the wrong one: *"There are much better color scales and let's put it this way, our professor will definitely find it [the heat map]. But that doesn't mean, just because I have a problem with that [the color scale], that it's the same for her." (Group 1).*[9]

In contrast, the second group payed close attention to their persona throughout the whole assignment. Both group members constantly stated how they felt as the persona confronted with the task, what their expectations and challenges were, and how they thought about the progress and performance: *"It's all in English. [...]As a high school music teacher, I do speak English." (Group 2).*

This reflection often occurred. For example, the group members perceived a task as easy, but then separated themselves from the persona and reflected on whether the persona might not have thought this task to be easy. In every step of completing the task, it was considered how they should act as the persona in order to keep the approach realistic: *"Theaterplatz. We found it. We're not going keep filtering because music teachers don't do that. [...] She would scroll through the search results. She would probably click on each one." (Group 2).*

Group 3 was also able to consider their persona of the student during task completion. Similar to group 2, the student's interests and abilities were taken into account before tasks were solved: *"But now from the student's perspective, from Janniks' perspective [note: name of the student persona], he wants to do research and write something about it. Is it enough for him then?" (Group 3).*

An identification with the persona of the student could probably easily occur, since the participants of working group 3 were also students: *"Well, I would look at it from Janniks' perspective as I'm a student, too. Looking at it now, I think this title is much too long." (Group 3).*

Considering the remarks of the participants and their overall engagement, the method was well adopted as a whole. However, it is reasonable to improve the consideration of the persona by involving the participants in the persona development, for example, by completing the personas biography with some of their own ideas or by visualizing the persona with the help of prepared puzzle pieces.

*Use of Thinking-aloud.* Due to the dialog and interactions within the groups, the transcript is not a pure think-aloud protocol. However, the dialog among the fellow group members was just as helpful when it comes to understanding thought processes, ambiguities, and approaches to solutions. All three groups voiced their thoughts and feelings about the application in a way that is useful for further development. The actual thinking-aloud in the way of stating one's own thoughts comprised primarily of commenting on and interpreting of any actions or anything that was seen on the screen:

---

[9] Any interview quotes within this article are direct translations from the German transcripts.

*"Moving Particles. Hm, something is just starting to move, but I am not sure what 'disWeight' means." (Group 1).*

Additional parts relevant for understanding, which do not necessarily count as thinking-aloud were announcements, questions, and answers directed towards the other group members when things were unclear as well as requests to take action. The following examples help to clarify which dialog parts serve a similar purpose to the thinking-aloud:

*"So these are the perspectives, right? The angles at which these photos were taken." (Group 1)*

*"Can you click on it and hold down for a while to get a picture?" (Group 2)*

*"It only says: Find it [the tool for comparing images]. I just assume that we have to create a collection now by adding these three pictures. And then we can compare them." (Group 3)*

It can be said, that the purpose of getting an idea of the participants' thoughts, feelings, and expectations without prompting or explicitly asking was fulfilled and the group work further promoted this. The dialog and input of group members also sparked extended discussion on some topics which introduced new ideas for solutions. It proved very useful when group members agreed or disagreed on opinions or approaches, because it helps to evaluate if individual reactions apply for the whole user group. Unfortunately, there are passages in the transcript where people were interrupted and it was not possible to make sense of the initial idea or thought they wanted to state. Generally speaking, the data which this workshop provided was helpful for the improvement of the application, but in some situations a conventional usability test may be more suitable.

*Completion of the Tasks.* Time spent completing the tasks as well as the connected remarks may show weaknesses of the interface or the functions. Especially issues and dead ends indicate how well the functions are named, placed, and designed. In order to estimate the time which was spend working on a task, it was noted when a task started (usually when group members read and discussed an assignment), how the solution was approached, and when the task was completed. All these aspects are part of the processing time. Table 3 gives an overview of the completion of all (sub-) tasks.

**Table 3.** Overview of the completion of the subtasks including processing time and remarks.

| Group | Task | Processing time | Remarks |
|---|---|---|---|
| 1 | Finding the tool for the visualizations | 1 min 15 s | Perceived as very easy, discussion on the resolution and arrangement of functions |
| 1 | Interpreting visualization | 5 min 35 s 1 min 30 s 10 s | Heat map – correctly identified as accumulation of images (red is more), lengthy discussion on color scales; Vector Field – hiding the map perceived as a very intuitive feature, interpretation of arrows not possible, longer discussion on the image clusters; Radial Fan – correctly identified as Visualization of acquisition angles, correct identification of areas with many and fewer images, questions on the accuracy of the geo-referencing; Radar Chart – correctly identified as Visualization of acquisition angles; Moving Particles – movement is detected but not interpreted, did not understand "disWeight" |
| 1 | Testing out the settings of the visualization | – | Some adjustments to settings had been made during the completion of the previous task, group was satisfied with the approach during the previous subtask and felt the task was completed |
| 2 | Searching for images | 7 min 30 s | Unsuccessful search with search bar because of incorrect search term, unsuccessful attempt to solve with 3D model, unsuccessful attempt to filter with time slider, second try with search bar entering the acquisition date (no filtering of lists by date attempted) and scrolling through results |
| 2 | Combining 3D model and image | 3 min 20 s | No initial idea for solution, did not understand "image opacity" and only found the slider due to prior knowledge, hovering the mouse over a 3D model was discovered by accident but not regarded as intuitive |
| 2 | Exploring the time slider | – | Group encountered solution during the previous subtask when use of time slider was made, group mentioned the need for info boxes, solution was not satisfying for the participants |

(*continued*)

**Table 3.** (*continued*)

| Group | Task | Processing time | Remarks |
|---|---|---|---|
| 3 | Locating a 3D model | 2 min 30 s | Solution cannot be completely confirmed, use of search bar and visual matching of images and 3D model, hovering the mouse over the 3D model to get the name was not applied |
| 3 | Detecting changes | 1 min 10 s | Images of building are sorted by date, changes are detected on the images, no use or mention of time slider which would reveal changes of the 3D model |
| 3 | Comparing images | 7 min 30 s | Correct approach of creating a collection is mentioned right away, use of search bar for image search, several tries to find a suitable search term, search for photographers name and sorting of results by date, prompt use of the image compare button |

All subtasks were completed and no participant called upon the workshop leaders for assistance understanding or completing the tasks. In hindsight a minute to complete an easy task seems long, but it should be regarded that the groups needed time to comprehend the task and exchange ideas on approaching it.

However, the task for group 1 (dealing with the visualizations) needs reworking for a second run. The localization and interpretation of the visualizations are divided into 2 different subtasks. It is more reasonable to have the participants click through the options and comment on them right away. This is actually the way that the group went about to complete the task. Unfortunately, the third subtask was not thoroughly discussed, therefore the assignment should be reworked to make it more concrete and interesting. An idea is to prepare a handout with a visualization the group has to try to recreate. The task has to clearly state the settings which need to be adjusted and also include filtering of the images which also have an effect on the visualization. This would provide an insight into which settings and options the users understand and where they need more information.

The collected data will be useful for comparison with data from a second run. This will demonstrate if improvements helped to speed up the completion of a task or help to avoid dead ends during the completion.

**Analyzing Usability Weaknesses.** Coding helped to identify and understand the challenges the participants had with the 4D Browser. Afterwards, the project team discussed findings and possible adaptations while considering possible impacts for other aspects of the application. In order to approach redesign and adaptations, a list for the developer was compiled and prioritized.

The insights into usability weaknesses of the application which emerged during the workshop were partly expected and partly surprising. The major aspects are discussed in more detail, whereas a few minor ones are listed below.

*Search.* The biggest discovery was that the search function poses quite a few challenges. Group 2 and 3 had to use the search as part of their assignment and struggled with it in a similar way. Participants were not sure which requirements the search terms had to meet, when a search was actually completed and how to get back to the full list of images of the database.

The initial idea of the project team was to use the "sort by" feature or the time slider to help with searching and filtering for certain dates, therefore the metadata entry for date had been omitted for the keyword search. Considering more entries in the metadata as basis for the search will help fix this problem. By transforming entered keywords into interactive tags, it is possible to indicate that a search is complete, that strings of search terms are handled in a certain way and that keywords can be deselected in order to return to the full list of images in the database. Some applications provide clues on why a search did not turn up any results. This is also a suitable approach to improve the success when using the search.

*Linking 3D Model and Image List.* All three groups mentioned that it was not clear if and how the 3D models and the listed images were linked. The users expected some kind of highlighting and zooming when they clicked on a listed image in order to easily locate its georeferenced counterpart in the 3D city model. Additionally, they wanted the keyword search for a building to have an influence on the display of the 3D model and trigger highlighting and zooming to that building in the city model. This indicates that the 'Zoom in' function for images (cube icon in image list or button on info box) was not found or not correctly interpreted and needs to be changed. Highlighting of search results in the 3D model has not been implemented and the new insights will help with the development of a concept for this feature.

*Comparing Images.* It was very surprising that the image comparing which group 3 had to carry out did not cause any issues. Two of the group members stated their approach right away and were able to easily find all the necessary functions. In this case, adding images to a collection in order to compare them seems to have become a standard approach. A second test will reveal if this solution also works for other users.

*Help.* The participants were able to find the help section, but no one bothered to have a look. All stated that they much prefer very short 'tool tips' accessible either through hovering the mouse over a feature icon or by adding a button with a "?"-symbol next to it. Functions and terms which could not be interpreted correctly are: disWeight, opacity, image scale, cluster distance, grid, and selection. They will most likely benefit from added tool tips. Sometimes, a translation of the English terms into German will also be helpful.

*Miscellaneous.* Group 1 preferred the 3D navigation that Google Maps uses, because it is perceived as standard. Although all participants found the button for closing the info box that displays the metadata for images, some stated they would always look for an "X" in the upper right corner first. Group 1 stated several ideas for improving the interface. They noted that collapsibles would be suitable to group and clearly arrange features and settings. They also felt that rearranging the info box for image metadata to cover the 3D model completely made more sense and would allow to directly access the image list and open metadata for another image without having to close the previous box. Groups 2 and 3 very much missed info boxes for 3D models similar to the ones for image metadata.

**Ideas and Wishes for Additions.** Several ideas and wishes were voiced during the workshop that were either not related to any of the implemented functions or bigger add-ons to existing features. Table 4 lists the ideas of the participants.

**Table 4.** List of new ideas mentioned by the workshop participants.

| Function | Description or comments |
|---|---|
| Focal length | Reconstruction of the focal length of the historical images |
| Flagging a false metadata | Flagging of incorrect parts which can later be corrected during a crowdsourcing campaign |
| Further use of clusters | Adding a whole cluster to the collection/selection to allow investigation |
| 2D Overview | Small 2D map to help locate which part is displayed in the 3D window |
| Navigating along a path | Implementing a navigation mode using, e.g., the arrow keys to simulate a tram or carriage ride |
| Shading of 3D models | Projection of the historical image onto the 3D models (previously intended and tests have been made, but not implemented yet); Support to adjust the shading for individual buildings |
| Image overlay | Support to directly display two images on top of each other (extension of Image Compare) |
| Magnifying glass | Feature to spot smaller details without having to constantly zoom in |

The ideas mentioned by the participants are very interesting and may certainly be a valid addition to the 4D Browser. Ideas from the actual user group of art historians will be collected in a different survey.

## 6    Conclusion

By means of the three projects described in this contribution, it is possible to apply different ways to involve users in the development and conduct testing.

The E.V.A. projects puts a lot of emphasize on entertainment with the use of gamification elements to ensure a knowledge transfer. Therefore, the project team heavily relies on an extensive user involvement early on which become clear when looking at the many different methods to inquire information about the user (questionnaire, interview, user context map, user journey map, and empathy map). The paper prototype is mainly used to gather options and feedback on the ideas for the applications before their implementation.

The weiter.digital project has to consider the actual users of the application as well as the provider, who will set up and maintain the application in the future. A key component are the limited resources of the users (primarily time and money). Hence, their solution is kept very simple, intuitive and sleek in order to speed up the time spent with the application. Design and navigational aspects play a big role in this scenario and are tested thoroughly with the help of a high-fidelity prototype.

The project Urban History 4D already has a further developed prototypical web application, where certain features need to be tested to ensure that user can find, understand, and use them as intended calling for a more general and classical usability test. Since the participants of the usability test were not necessarily from the user group, personas and realistic tasks were used to make the test more comprehensible. Thinking-aloud very much helped to understand the participant's thoughts and expectations.

It is important to strengthen and extend the user involvement for (academic) software development projects and this contribution tries to shine a light on the range and possibilities of human-centered design and usability and hopefully inspires others to apply the methods.

**Acknowledgements.** This paper is a collaboration of the projects Urban History 4D, E.F.A. and weiter.digital.

Cindy Kröber who belongs to the Urban History 4D project wrote paragraphs 1, 2, 5 and 6. Leyla Dewitz co-authored paragraph 5. Paragraph 3 was written by Cornelia Schade and Katharina Hammel from the project E.F.A. Nicole Filz wrote paragraph 4 which deals with the project weiter.digital.

Some research, upon which this paper is based, is part of the junior research group Urban History 4D's activities which has received funding from the German Federal Ministry of Education and Research under grant agreement No 01UG1630.

# References

1. Lam, H., et al.: Empirical studies in information visualization: seven scenarios. IEEE Trans. Visual Comput. Graphics **18**(9), 1520–1536 (2012)
2. Nielsen, J.: Mobile Website and Application Usability. Nielsen Norman Group Press, Berkeley (2013)
3. Krug, S.: Don't Make Me Think, Revisited: A common Sense Approach to Web Usability. New Riders, Indianapolis (2014)
4. Shneiderman, B.: The Eight Golden Rules of Interface Design, 27 July 2020 (2016). https://www.cs.umd.edu/users/ben/goldenrules.html
5. Geis, T., Polkehn, K.: Praxiswissen User Requirements: Nutzungsqualität systematisch, nachhaltig und agil in die Produktentwicklung integrieren. Aus-und Weiterbildung zum UXQB® Certified Professional for Usability and User Experience–Advanced Level "User Requirements Engineering". dpunkt. Verlag (2018)
6. Breuer, J.: Spielend lernen? Eine Bestandsaufnahme zum (Digital) Game-Based Learning [Learning by playing? An inventory of (digital) game-based learning]. Landesanstalt Für Medien Nordrhein-Westfalen (LfM), LfM-Dokumente, pp. 1–67 (2010)
7. Ahn, J.: Drawing inspiration for learning experience design (LX) from diverse perspectives. Emerg. Learn. Des. J. **6**(1), 1–6 (2019)

8.  Malamed, C.: Instructional Design Needs A New Name! A Call for Learning Experience Design (2015)
9.  Sailer, M.: Die Wirkung von Gamification auf Motivation und Leistung. Springer, Wiesbaden (2016). https://doi.org/10.1007/978-3-658-14309-1
10. Geis, T., Tesch, G.: Basiswissen Usability und User Experience: Aus-und Weiterbildung zum UXQB® Certified Professional for Usability and User Experience (CPUX)–Foundation Level (CPUX-F). dpunkt. verlag (2019)
11. Snyder, C.: Paper Prototyping: The Fast and Easy Way to Design and Refine User Interfaces. Morgan Kaufmann, Burlington (2003)
12. Schell, J.: Die Kunst des Game Designs: Bessere Games konzipieren und entwickeln. BoD–Books on Demand (2020)
13. Dumas, J.S., Redish, J.: A Practical Guide to Usability Testing. Intellect Books, Exeter (1999)
14. Dumont, E.: Bedarfsanalyse für ein digitales Weiterbildungskonzept im Projekt E.F.A. Westsächsischen Hochschule Zwickau (2019)
15. Berufsbildung, B.F.: Datenreport zum Berufsbildungsbericht 2018. Informationen und Analysen zur Entwicklung der beruflichen Bildung. Bonn (2018)
16. Baacke, D.: Medienkompetenz: Modelle und Projekte. Bundeszentrale für Politische Bildung (1999)
17. Job, M.A., Ogalo, H.S.: Micro learning as innovative process of knowledge strategy. Int. J. Sci. Technol. Res. **1**(11), 92–96 (2012)
18. Jacobsen, J., Meyer, L.: Praxisbuch Usability & UX. Rheinwerk Verlag (2019)
19. Münster, S., et al.: Urban history in 4 dimensions - supporting research and education. Int. Arch. Photogramm. Remote Sens. Spat. Inf. Scie. **42**, 525–530 (2017)
20. Kamposiori, C., Warwick, C., Mahony, S.: Accessing and using digital libraries in art history. In: Münster, S., Friedrichs, K., Niebling, F., Seidel-Grzesinska, A. (eds.) UHDL/DECH -2017. CCIS, vol. 817, pp. 83–101. Springer, Cham (2018). https://doi.org/10.1007/978-3-319-76992-9_6
21. Dudek, I., et al.: How was this done? An attempt at formalising and memorising a digital asset's making-of. In: 2015 Digital Heritage. IEEE (2015)
22. Bulatovic, N., Gnadt, T., Romanello, M., Stiller, J., Thoden, K.: Usability in digital humanities - evaluating user interfaces, infrastructural components and the use of mobile devices during research process. In: Fuhr, N., Kovács, L., Risse, T., Nejdl, W. (eds.) TPDL 2016. LNCS, vol. 9819, pp. 335–346. Springer, Cham (2016). https://doi.org/10.1007/978-3-319-43997-6_26
23. Sweetnam, M.S., et al.: User needs for enhanced engagement with cultural heritage collections. In: Zaphiris, P., Buchanan, G., Rasmussen, E., Loizides, F. (eds.) TPDL 2012. LNCS, vol. 7489, pp. 64–75. Springer, Heidelberg (2012). https://doi.org/10.1007/978-3-642-33290-6_8
24. Barreau, J.-B., et al.: Virtual reality tools for the west digital conservatory of archaeological heritage. In: Proceedings of the 2014 Virtual Reality International Conference. ACM (2014)
25. Maina, J.K., Suleman, H.: Enhancing digital heritage archives using gamified annotations. In: Allen, R.B., Hunter, J., Zeng, M.L. (eds.) ICADL 2015. LNCS, vol. 9469, pp. 169–179. Springer, Cham (2015). https://doi.org/10.1007/978-3-319-27974-9_17
26. Friedrichs, K., Münster, S., Kröber, C., Bruschke, J.: Creating suitable tools for art and architectural research with historic media repositories. In: Münster, S., Friedrichs, K., Niebling, F., Seidel-Grzesińska, A. (eds.) Digital Research and Education in Architectural Heritage. Communications in Computer and Information Science, vol. 817, pp. 117–138. Springer, Cham (2018). https://doi.org/10.1007/978-3-319-76992-9_8

27. Münster, S., Kamposiori, C., Friedrichs, K., Kröber, C.: Image libraries and their scholarly use in the field of art and architectural history. Int. J. Digit. Libr. **19**(4), 367–383 (2018). https://doi.org/10.1007/s00799-018-0250-1

28. Münster, S., et al.: Stadtgeschichtliche Forschung und Vermittlung anhand historischer Fotos als Forschungsgegenstand – Ein Zwischenbericht der Nachwuchsgruppe HistStadt4D, in Digital Humanities im deutschsprachigen Raum (DHd 2018). Cologne (2018)

29. Aquino Junior, P.T.A., Filgueiras, L.V.L.: User modeling with personas. In: Proceedings of the 2005 Latin American Conference on Human-Computer Interaction. ACM (2005)

30. Star, S.L., Griesemer, J.R.: Institutional ecology, translations' and boundary objects: amateurs and professionals in Berkeley's Museum of Vertebrate Zoology, 1907–39. Soc. Stud. Sci. **19**(3), 387–420 (1989)

31. Ericsson, K.A., Simon, H.A.: Protocol Analysis: Verbal Reports as Data. The MIT Press, Cambridge (1984)

32. Ramey, J., et al.: Does think aloud work?: how do we know? In: CHI'06 Extended Abstracts on Human Factors in Computing Systems. ACM (2006)

33. Jääskeläinen, R.: Think-aloud protocol. In: Handbook of Translation Studies, vol. 1, pp. 371–374 (2010)

34. Braun, V., Clarke, V.: Using thematic analysis in psychology. Qual. Res. Psychol. **3**(2), 77–101 (2006)

35. Glaser, B.G., Strauss, A.L., Strutzel, E.: The discovery of grounded theory; strategies for qualitative research. Nurs. Res. **17**(4), 364 (1968)

# Visualization and Presentation

# Visual Representations in Digital 3D Modeling/Simulation for Architectural Heritage

Krzysztof Koszewski[(✉)] [ID]

Faculty of Architecture, Warsaw University of Technology, Warsaw, Poland
krzysztof.koszewski@pw.edu.pl

**Abstract.** The text presents theoretical considerations of the character and role of visual representations in the process of virtual modeling for architectural heritage. These images of the past are analyzed in different contexts, including contemporary culture with its visual character and the modeling process itself, treated as a simulation of the past, with references to modeling and the simulation theory. Terminology aspects regarding the commonly used term "reconstruction" are discussed in the light of the character of virtual models of architectural heritage, their provenance and usage. The role of images as meta-representations of the possible modeled reality visual representations of models is also considered. The need for standards and best practices in the area of visual language and image production for architectural heritage is discussed. The emphasis is put on the methods to neutralize the seductive character of computer-based visualizations. Finally, a postulate for interactivity to be focused more on creating user-based scenarios based on research hypotheses rather than concentrated on the walkability of an immersive environment is formulated.

**Keywords:** Simulation for architectural heritage · Modeling for architectural heritage · Images of architectural heritage · Visual representations in heritage

## 1 Introduction

This text aims to map current problems related to visual aspects in 3D modeling of architectural heritage as well as to identify possible issues influencing the usage of digital methods. These aspects should be subject to further research according to new circumstances related to the societal ways of communication. There are four main areas of interest: contemporary perception of visual messages as an important factor influencing the creation and understanding of heritage-related images; the problem of the relation of a model to represent past reality and its terminological consequences; the epistemological nature of 3D modeling for architectural heritage, and the need for standards for preparing visual messages in the field.

© Springer Nature Switzerland AG 2021
F. Niebling et al. (Eds.): UHDL 2019, CCIS 1501, pp. 87–105, 2021.
https://doi.org/10.1007/978-3-030-93186-5_4

## 2   Images of the Past as a Part of Contemporary Visual Culture

Digitally mediated information has become an indispensable part of our activities in almost all aspects of our lives. This tendency, springing from the concepts of the Internet in the late '60s, through hypertextual world wide web in the late '80s, the creation of information prosumer's Web 2.0 in the mid-2000s and image-based social media in the 2010s, is clearly visible, but at the same time is still treated as a parallel, alternative reality. This digital dualism [1] is still a driver for a special dialectic approach to digital assets and their representations in architectural heritage, even if they have become an inevitable and integral part of research activity in the field. 3D computer models are still seen as an extra, additional tool in the research process. Even if they are already treated not only as mere presentation vehicles but also as important tools of discovery and knowledge production, it is not uncommon to encounter a claim that: "computer-based visualization method should normally be used only when it is the most appropriate available method for that purpose"[1]. Taking into account the proliferation of images which have become the main source of information shaping our vision of the world, we should redefine this somewhat restrained statement. Considering dissemination of the research results we could argue that in some cases we may say: "text-based information should only be used when it is the most appropriate available method". The visual output of 3D modeling for cultural heritage should be treated – in some cases – at least equivalent if not the main means of communication.

Our contemporary culture is visual, and the growing importance of images in cultural practices has been confirmed since the early '90s [3]. However, during the last decade, the meaning and uses, and – first of all – the possibility of sharing and accessing pictures have undergone a significant change. We (and all possible recipients of our visual messages) no longer have to do anything special to see them. They accompany us anytime and everywhere, which is an inalienable characteristic of a networked society [4], pp. 11–12. All images that are or may be produced, including these resulting from our research activity, have become a part of this enormous pictorial flow, and have undergone all its rules. This change cannot be overestimated also due to its scale. We have currently reached almost half (49%) of the Earth population actively using social media[2], which are mainly image-based.

The power of images as facts confirmation is still rooted in the practices and notions derived from traditional photography – even if we are aware of the endless possibilities of modification of the digital assets due to their discreet characteristics. This witnessing ability of contemporary images is perfectly expressed by the networked visual culture founding statement: "pics or it didn't happen". In fact, we provide pics – visual representations of 3D digital modeling of heritage – but we have to find a clear way of

---

[1] This is a preamble of Principle 2 from the London Charter, still the most established and solid common ground for visualization and modeling of cultural heritage [2]. The most up-to-date revision of the charter was issued in 2009, a year before Instagram, the most popular image-based social platform was launched.

[2] Data according to [5]; this percentage is even higher (reaching 70%) in Asia, the US, and Europe.

saying "pics, but it could or could not happen". At the same time pictures that create our visual environment are more and more detached from reality. They become independent entity – simulacra, characteristic for "the age of simulation [which] begins with the liquidation of all referentials"[3]. This puts researchers using images as a tool of experiment and communication in an extremely difficult situation, torn in between their evocative and informative potential.

The pandemic situation has moved most of the communication activities to computer-mediated environments, causing a re-evaluation of societal goals and paradigm shifts associated with the relation of direct personal experience and the virtual one. We interact with avatars – images of people, images of the world. Suddenly, the significant part of our experience has moved to the virtual world, which does not make much difference in interaction with the real, physically existing objects or situations (currently not available directly) and virtual models, including these of the past. In both cases, this contact is mediated by computer interfaces. This fact widens the audience and makes the experience of virtual worlds ubiquitous (everything is virtual in the sense of being mediated), but also makes the distinction between facts and fiction (or hypotheses) even more difficult. We are also still unsure about how the post-pandemic world will look like. Whether the mass tourism of the beginning of the XXI century will be replaced by another form of exploring the world? Will virtual models and interfaces play a more significant role in it? If so, then the number of practically unreachable historical monuments will grow, adding many more cases to these possible to experience only by their virtual representations due to the lack of their physical existence. All these factors make the discussion about the role of visual representations in virtual heritage crucial and needed more than ever.

## 3  Reconstructions or Simulations

The discussion of plausibility, scientific fidelity, and reliability (or even authenticity [7]) of virtual models of architectural heritage objects refers to the term "reconstructions". Its place in professional vocabulary has been well established from the very beginning of their usage [8, 9], but may be discussed in terms of fulfilling the mentioned research requirements. Reconstruction is "the activity of building again something that has been damaged or destroyed" [10], with the explicit presumption of recreating the previous state as it was. This term was transferred to the realm of digital methods used in cultural heritage directly from physical reality[4] only by adding an adjective virtual, which suggests, as Reilly points out in his milestone article on virtual archaeology, "an allusion to a model, a replica, the notion that something can act as a

---

[3] Simulacra and characteristics of simulation cited after Jean Baudrillard [6], p. 4, however, we should carefully distinguish the meaning of "simulation" as term opposed to "representation" – a layer of meaning with no reference to reality, used by Baudrillard, and "simulation" as experimenting method used in M&S (modeling and simulation) theory, which is discussed in the rest of the text.

[4] Which is actually quite justifiable by explicit material roots of archaeology as a discipline, where the first theoretical frameworks for virtual reconstructions emerged.

surrogate or replacement for an original" [8], p. 133. But the difference goes in this case much further. This is not just about translation from physical to digital, intending to create a surrogate of reality. Such transfer results in a fundamental change on both ontological and epistemological levels: a virtual model is subject to the rules of the new media, as defined by Manovich [11], p. 20. Among his well-known five principles[5] the most significant for the term discussed are variability and transcoding. The virtual model may exist in an infinite number of versions (with every single one of them being the original) and is endlessly modifiable, its characteristics and features may be instantly changed by manipulation of input parameters. It is not a stable and solid reflection of reality, and it offers dynamic, variable representation instead. It can be easily transcoded (reshaped and transformed) on both levels: technological (different formats) and cultural (different concepts and meanings). Considering the above one can even argue that virtual reconstruction is a self-contradictory term, denoting a replica of something solid with apparent dynamic features due to its obvious new media nature.

Reconstruction – "building again something that has been damaged or destroyed" – may be also put into question when there are limited sources on which the modeling decisions are based on. In most cases – at best – we create representations of our hypotheses, which do not refer to any unquestionable state of the past, even if they are based on solid sources and rigorous research process[6]. In such circumstances, the term "simulation" may be discussed as more appropriate or at least alternative, since "simulations are our best cognitive representation of complex reality, that is our deepest conception of what reality is" [13]. There is an irrefutable factor of probability in simulation, which is relevant to the character of virtual models of historic structures since their past state is available to our cognition only indirectly. In modeling and simulation theory (M&S) it is used mainly for experimenting and testing purposes when the real system cannot be engaged [14], p. 6. Leaving aside experimental character and projective character of simulation, it is exactly the case when it offers the possibility of insight into the past while offering enough epistemological margin of uncertainty. However, the term simulation is used generally in reference to present or future situations.

It should be noted that the term "virtual reconstruction" is more universal than simulation. It refers to both a process and its subject, while a simulation is rather associated with the process itself, performed on a certain model of reality. This universality may, on the other hand, bring some undesired ambiguity. From the epistemological point of view, the act of creating virtual models of architectural heritage objects and its research background is certainly a simulation, not a reconstruction as such.

Interestingly, in the founding paper of virtual archaeology Reilly mentions simulation, but only as a tool to test the process of planning and carrying out excavations, with nothing to do with interpretative use of the results [8], p. 133. The concept of simulation was discussed again in the light of archaeology by Forte [15] as a part of the

---

[5] Numerical representation, modularity, automation, variability and transcoding.

[6] The matter of adequacy of the term „simulation" is discussed in detail in [12] and goes beyond the scope of this publication.

larger concept of cyber-archaeology. The idea focuses on the interactivity of created virtual environments allowing users to perform their scenarios, and thus enriching their experience and producing knowledge. The same author states that "we do not reconstruct the past anymore; we perform the digital past" [15], p. 299. The point here is that – epistemologically – all the virtual models of the past, including these created at the dawn of the use of computers in heritage related research, bear the potential of simulation, even without postulated interactivity and collaborative features. Calling them "reconstructions" without any further claim immediately brings up a well-known dispute on authenticity, plausibility, and fidelity, in which we actually cannot defend the accuracy of the outcomes [12], p. 69.

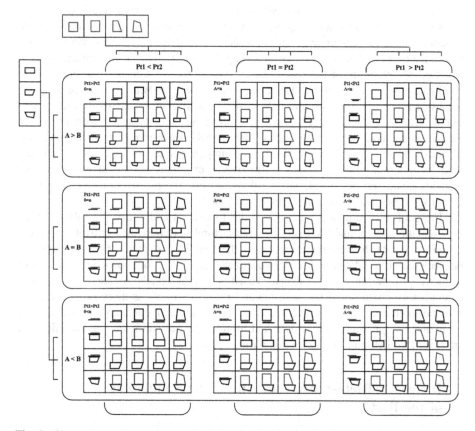

**Fig. 1.** Shape grammars matrix as a basis for the algorithm of parametric creation of different variants of wooden huts in proto-town in Pultusk, Poland. Possible relations between huts (blue) and their vestibules (red) are explored. According to [16]. (Color figure online)

The next step was the introduction of procedural modeling methods, which gave much more variability, allowing easier simulations of different scenarios by simply changing parameters, usually based on shape grammars (see Fig. 1) [16], addressing in this way also problems of uncertainty [17]. Still, this possibility of manipulation was limited to a narrow circle of researchers dealing with the model itself, however, variable results remain an immanent part of this method. On the other hand, some researchers claim that the current state of 3D digital models for architectural heritage cannot be counted as simulations [18], being rather models of the past situations. This is a terminology question related to modeling and the simulation theory, as mentioned before – that simulation is in fact a process performed on a model and cannot be done without it. In a broader meaning, we can call the whole process a simulation as an analogy to the term reconstruction, which also involves the model creation.

This is not my intention to question the already established terminology. Reconstructions were present in research vocabulary related to architectural heritage long before the introduction of computer modeling. Their communicative characteristics in terms of the reliability of the message they convey has always been questionable. In 1973 Adam Miłobędzki wrote: "However, it is necessary to warn against too idealistic reconstructions, isolating the object from the cultural context and its dynamics, presenting architecture "statically", in shapes as clean and orderly as if it were to exist in the past in the conditions of an utopia" [19], p. 483. Even though this statement was obviously related to analog methods, it gained importance regarding virtual models and their presentation, where "clean and orderly" is amazingly compliant with computer methods characteristics. And, noteworthy, the term "reconstruction" is used here, obviously concerning representations of the past.

The goal is to shift the accents in order to discuss and define the role of visual representations in virtual modeling for architectural heritage. Such critical analysis is needed to establish a common ground in the long-lasting debate about the balance between scientific fidelity and seductive attractiveness (level of knowledge and level of iconicity) of representations of the past based on virtual models. Awareness of the self-contradictory character of the term "virtual reconstruction", as discussed concerning new media characteristics, is much needed. Also, features of contemporary practices of using and interpreting pictures, detached from reality but still treated as its reflection, are pivotal in defining the mentioned terminology.

# 4     Images as Meta-representations in the Simulation of the Past

Virtual models are representations of our level of knowledge about a certain object. They are also abstractions taken from reality representing a part of it. In M&S theory one of the goals is to create a model that refers as close as possible to a certain aspect of reality - because this fidelity influences the quality of the simulation applied to this model, and the reliability of the results. Simulation in this case "is the imitation of the operation of the real-world process of the system over time" [14], p. 3. This is the most common understanding and usage of simulation as a research method, however, not the most relevant to architectural heritage modeling[7]. There is a certain category of simulations – stand-alone – for which one of their purposes is to facilitate understanding of the part of reality that our model represents. They serve the purposes of "testing a hypothesis relative to the structure and function of a complex system" [14], p. 16. In fact, this purpose fits in the desired role of virtual models of heritage. Such testing refers to their cognitive role, and it can be performed by assessing and evaluating of the output the of simulation processes. This is not a question of performance explored by changing parameters, but the explorations of the model structure, and thus research on the influence of it on its general features. But whichever the case – we are not able to interact and explore these models directly, since they are pure abstract constructs encoded as a database in information systems. These 3D models are always represented (mediated) by visual means, be it interfaces or images as final results of the process. So, if we treat 3D models as representations of the past (or more precise representations of our idea of what the past could be, based on available evidence and reasoning), then images showing the result are representations of the model, which makes them meta-representation, with all the consequences of this mediation. This two-step relationship is most often overlooked, with the main emphasis on the creation of a model itself, while an image is treated – to some extend – as an automated outcome, defined by the growing capabilities of rendering algorithms. The first stage of this process (research-based model creation) is well standardized [2, 21, 22], the second still lacks commonly agreed ways of imaging and best practices, being mentioned only on a high level of abstraction.

Visualization is defined as an important, almost independent step in M&S theory – "the ability to represent data as a way to interface with the model" [14], p. 3. Such representation is not only a key factor in understanding the simulation process outcome, but a general condition for the process itself which takes place. The visualization pipeline consists of four steps: data analysis, filtering, mapping, and transformation (preparing the structure and visual qualities of communique) and rendering [23]. Complexity and importance of the third step as seen from the M&S theory point of view is even increased when applied to modeling of architectural heritage, where all the societal aspects, including contemporary visual culture constraints mentioned at the beginning, have to be taken into consideration on an equal basis.

What does it mean in practice? 3D models of heritage are cognitive tools, images which are thus knowledge representations serving different purposes on various levels of interpretation, including implicit and explicit representational values and knowledge production and dissemination. All these features influence the way these images are created and how they are perceived (for example in the choice of visualization methods [24]). One of the most significant examples of such an influence is the relation between informative and persuasive (rhetoric) values of images, corresponding to the level of abstraction versus the level of iconicity [25]. This relation is one of the decisions to be made on the third stage of visualization (mapping and transformation), which is

---

[7] There are complex scenarios that include simulation of processes over time in the model of a historic building or city, but then we may speak of simulation within a simulation. Such is the case of "Populating ancient Pompeii with the crowds of virtual Romans" [20], where procedural modeling (which includes probability factors by definition) allowed to create an environment where the behavior of virtual inhabitants was tested.

**Fig. 2.** Realistic rendering showing a high level of iconicity of the results of a parametric simulation of a possible configuration of the proto-town in Pultusk. Most of the huts shown here are the result of the algorithm based on shape grammars shown in Fig. 1, while some of them are based on the actual relics found during excavations (see Fig. 3). According to [26].

strongly influenced by factors related to visual culture, dominated by images with a very high level of iconicity (Fig. 2). The choice here tends to be between reliability and attractiveness and there is still a very limited palette of methods to avoid this trap.

One of the most important factors in scientific visualizations associated with simulation processes is the interactivity. Scientific visual representations (VisRep) "are playing a crucial role in this activity [simulation process – author's note] by enabling the users to monitor and interpret the results in real-time, and to steer the computation (alter the values of the simulation parameter) as needed" [23], p. 106. Moreover, a branch of VisRep research has been defined as visual analytics, "as the science of analytical reasoning supported by the interactive visual interface" [23], p. 107. Interactivity became an implicit feature of visual VisRep in simulation [27]. Taking this into account in the research related to modeling of the past shows the difference in approach – in most cases, interactivity is associated here with walkability of virtual space. This approach refers to monitoring and interpreting the results in real-time, or rather the singular result visualized solution referring to a certain set of parameters corresponding with the posed hypothesis. The only popular interactivity solution not referring to virtual reality walks is the choice of the temporal parameter, allowing to experience changes over time. To fulfill other postulates of scientific visualization in the simulation process on the ground of virtual modeling of the architectural heritage, we would need another kind of inter-action – this mentioned as one which is steering the computation. In other words, this should be possible for a user to manipulate the parameters of the model in terms of these parameters and their range which refers to different hypotheses (possible scenarios) in a certain moment in time on one hand, and the degree of uncertainty on the other one.

A simulation is performed on a model that is created for this purpose, but we can interact and see only the results – an image which is either an interface or a visual result of our manipulations. It is crucial to understand these epistemological differences and their consequences – that the image, which we tend to name as the "model", "recon-struction" or "simulation" is rather the result of a process of modeling or simulation. This result is a meta-representation, since it refers to the created model, while the model features itself represent in turn the possible qualities of the past. This two-step relation brings another new aspect of virtual heritage modeling, which relates to its digital nature[8]. It allows us to treat the model and its representation in a separate way, which was not possible in the analog way where a model was also its representation. Knowledge encoded in a variable way, allowing for creating different outputs, is much easier represented in such a way, allowing easy visualization of probable variants.

## 5    Required Qualities of Visual Representations and the Ways to Encode Them

The need to encode the above-mentioned qualities related to knowledge production and dissemination unambiguously leads to the discussion of visualization standards for architectural heritage, which relate to the decisions affecting created images. Also, the approach presented here, associating virtual modeling of heritage with simulation theory, underlines the importance of visual representations, indicating them as the core aspect of the whole process. The third aspect of these pictorial representations, related to their inevitable context of contemporary visual culture, adds another layer of con-straints to the discussed aspect. All the mentioned aspects have to be taken under consideration when discussing the need and possible importance of standards and best practices related to visual representations in heritage modeling. However, even if there is a lot of research and discussion on the documentation, vocabulary, encoding, and modeling process standards, at the same time there are still no common guidelines on how to visualize uncertainty[9] or even chronology.

---

[8] This can be treated as a very basic level analogy to von Neumann's computer systems architecture design, where processing and memory units are divided from input-output mechanisms. This analogy is strongly justified and actually driven by the numerical nature of virtual models.

[9] "The representation of uncertainty in visualizations is one of the great challenges that face virtual archaeology. Nevertheless, there are few publications and projects that have attempted to address this issue. Generally, the solutions proposed to date have used color, transparency or texture to show levels of uncertainty". [28], p. 22.

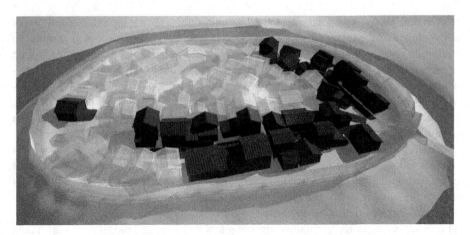

**Fig. 3.** The visualization of the proto-city in Pultusk, showing huts created on the basis of the found relicts, using color-code and replacing feature-rich rendering with the mockup-style one. According to [26].

Various methods of visualization of different non-geometric features of modeled objects, like opacity, color, rendering style (for example wireframe for uncertainty, luminance, or picturing style (from textured full-color to contour) and their mixes were already discussed, but no standards or best practices have been adopted so far. There are interesting research proposals on the topic, including the use of a density-slicing spectrum-based color scale to encode different levels of uncertainty proposed by Apollonio [29] or a more general approach referring to the presentation method itself, based on focusing on the structure of architectural space while introducing a certain level of abstraction and avoiding color to signal hypothetical nature of the model, proposed by Lengyel and Toulouse [30].

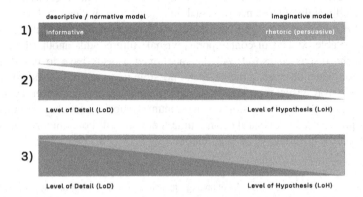

**Fig. 4.** Informative/rhetoric (persuasive) relations of the image in reference to the model character (descriptive/informative) (1). These image features correspond to factors of Level of Detail (LoD) and Level of Hypothesis (LoH), being inversely proportional [31] (2). (3) shows the actual corrected relation taking into account the fact that the LoD never reaches 0 in order to show some information and starts with 1 (we need some details in the situation).

All of these methods require the usage of special pictorial code, superimposed, or sometimes replacing feature-rich rendering with a high level of symbolicity (Fig. 3). This corresponds to constatation that while the level of knowledge encoded in an image is increased, the level of iconicity decreases [25], along with some other features which correspond to this relation (Fig. 4).

While considering a single image as an output of the virtual modeling process, it is clear that maintaining both requirements is impossible, hence the above-discussed methods always sacrifice some pictorial qualities. The constraints are even more complicated and interconnected, possible to represent in a form of the matrix, where production, context and usage aspects of images showing the results of the modeling process relate to their most expected features in a given context (Table 1). The more universal an image usage should be, the more features of that image should be maximized.

**Table 1.** Saturation of features of images (simulation results) in various contexts of their usage in the process of modeling of architectural heritage. Features: Icon – iconicity (persuasive character of images); Pl – plausibility (informative character); InOp – interoperability (flexibility of use in a given context); Sc – semantic capacity (ability to accommodate narratives); Un – uncertainty representation; Chr – chronology representation; InAct – interactivity; Sust – sustainability.

| Feature image context | Icon | Pl | InOp | Sc | Un | Chr | InAct | Sust |
|---|---|---|---|---|---|---|---|---|
| Documentation | + | +++ | +++ | + | + | + | + | +++ |
| Research | + | +++ | ++ | + | +++ | +++ | ++ | ++ |
| Knowledge production | ++ | +++ | ++ | ++ | +++ | +++ | ++ | + |
| Knowledge dissemination | +++ | ++ | + | ++ | ++ | ++ | ++ | ++ |
| VisRep – simulation | ++ | +++ | + | + | +++ | ++ | +++ | + |
| Visual culture | +++ | + | + | +++ | + | + | +++ | + |
| Process pragmatics | ++ | ++ | +++ | ++ | + | + | + | +++ |
| Marketing | +++ | + | + | ++ | + | + | ++ | + |
| Management | + | +++ | ++ | + | + | ++ | + | ++ |

The diversity of requirements expressed by desired features of images, which are in some cases contradictory (for example informative/rhetoric values) leads to the general conclusion that it is impossible to encode and present all of them in a single image. Even if standards of representing different aspects of research and modeling process like chronology or uncertainty are not yet developed, some basic guidelines may be discussed, fostering the process of establishing common ground in the visualization of architectural heritage. Considering the mentioned variety of features to be represented, one of the basic rules of visualization should be to avoid concentrating on a single image, which is, by its nature, relevant only to some spectrum of desired aspects. This relates mostly to images bearing persuasive character, with a high degree of iconicity, shown outside some specified meaningful context (scientific, professional). Such representations have already met with criticism, especially in the early days of pho-torealistic rendering ([32–34] and others), however, their nature fits in the pictorial character of contemporary culture, as discussed earlier, so they cannot be avoided (and they still play an important role in knowledge production and dissemination [35]). If possible, the variety of representations should be made available [36], which is an apparent possibility for electronic media, like in the reconstruction augmentation method developed by Grellert et al. [37], where the stages of interpretation and decision related to considered hypotheses are visualized and made available. Even if we con-sider static, final image which is the result of simulation computation, it can be encoded in electronic transmission systems together with other versions, using different modes of representation. They can be activated either automatically (like animated GIFs) or triggered by the user (like clickable images, but in this case the user has to be aware of their presence). However, this "multi-representation" should be also a desired situation while using computer-created imagery in circumstances, where only analog versions (static images, boards, printouts) can be presented, so in all these environments, which do not allow direct interactivity. This would also refer to the London Charter recom-mendations considering the choice of the most appropriate visualization method[10], that is to be used in a particular case. Rather than making such a choice, we should consider using more than one method – i.e. more than one image (especially considering the addition of more symbolic ones) accompanying those which have strong visual pho-torealistic character. Such concurrent representation would also take off the odium of seductive, non-reliable visual information, which is associated with computer-based renderings. Making it not the only available image would weaken its character as simulacrum and allow for a more nuanced interpretation.

The chance to show variability concerns not only static images, presented either as physical printouts or on electronic displays. One of possible outputs of the digital model, besides images, is the physical mock-up created using 3D-printing technology. The first solution could be to present different possibilities with different physical models, but taking into account the scale of the model (to show some detail, the printout has to be significantly large), the time and the cost – this method has to be optimized. In order to fulfil this requirement, it is possible to design and implement a modular structure of the physical model, allowing certain parts to be replaced to show variations regarding possible versions of the modeled object. It works best in the urban scale, while certain buildings may be replaced with their alternatives. Such a method was developed by Kowal et al. in the course of modeling the proto-city in Pultusk and described in [16] (see Fig. 5 and 6).

---

[10] "...the choice of computer-based visualization method (e.g. more or less photo-realistic, impression-istic or schematic; representation of hypotheses or of the available evidence; dynamic or static) or the decision to develop a new method, should be based on an evaluation of the likely success of each approach in addressing each aim". [2], Principle 2, 2.3. While this recommendation is still actual, it suggests the choice of only one method, hence the one character of produced image(s).

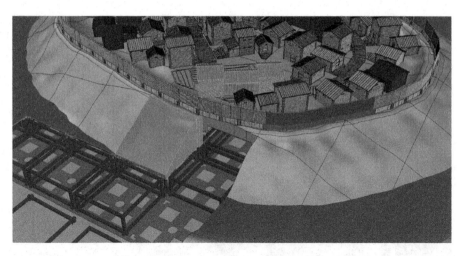

**Fig. 5.** Visualization presenting the modular method of physical model creation, including scaled 10 × 10 m base pattern (blue), supporting grid (yellow), the terrain, the surrounding palisade and huts inside the proto-city. According to [16]. (Color figure online)

Electronic media, by one of its fundamental features – variability – offer the possibility of interaction. As it was already mentioned, this feature in modeling and representation of virtual heritage is associated mostly with the walkability of immersive worlds, with some remarkable exceptions allowing users to experiment with possible scenarios of the modeling process, as presented by Kensek et al. [32]. There is a great potential to be exploited, offering the possibility to not only document choices made during the modeling process, but also to explore hypotheses and scenarios which are plausible in the certain case. This is also one of the postulates of the simulation process – interactivity manifested in the possibility of model alteration to experience the results of these changes. In such light, walkability is just a way to explore a static model[11], which is one of the possible interpretations of the past. However, such an approach results in increased workload, and thus higher cost of the modeling and simulation process, which would significantly reduce the scope of such projects.

Finally, the question of possible guidelines for visualization of modeled architectural heritage regarding these cases where static imagery is involved can be approached also on a different level – not as a discussion referring to the modes of representation and encoding information (and features of produced images), but concerning an expected set of views recommended by available survey standards of drawings and photographs, like these issued by Historic American Buildings Survey [39]. Since the created model is – at its desired state – a representation of some probable historical reality, it can be visualized in an analogous way to that which is dedicated to the existing building; or at least in a way that is informed by these standards.

---

[11] It needs to be noted, that such an interactive model may be effectively used as a research environment – like in [15], p. 307, or [38].

**Fig. 6.** 3D-printed modular model of the proto-city in Pultusk, showing 10 ×10 m grid. The color code is the same as in Fig. 3 and it is used here to distinguish huts based on the found relics from these generated on the basis of the analogy. According to [16]. Photo by R. Rzadkiewicz.

The practice of creating virtual representations of historic structures shows that the chosen model views are mostly driven by the best appearance (resulting from these parts of the model which are best developed and most detailed, or simply the most attractive), not the aspiration to deliver the most complete set of information. Of course, these considerations do not refer to immersive interactive worlds, allowing the user to experience every available point of view, but still, a significant amount of images produced in the realm of architectural heritage is static.

There are also other sets of best practices or established ways of visual encoding of some non-physical features of objects presented as images. One of such examples is chronology, which used to be visualized in the survey drawings with certain color codes (Fig. 7). The practice of such visualization was to use warmer colors for older objects (e.g. red for medieval), while moving to the colder side of the spectrum for the representation of the newer ones. Such an approach may be successfully transferred to different representation modes in the field heritage visualization, like, for example, the map of the Polish listed monuments prepared for the National Heritage Board of

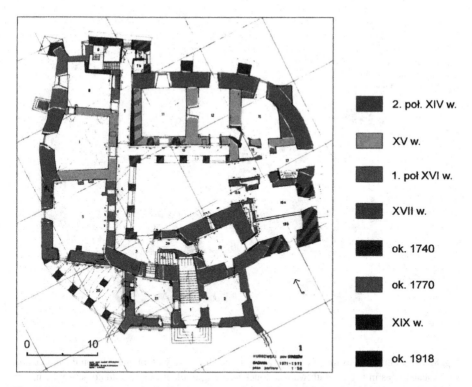

Legend:
- 2. poł. XIV w.
- XV w.
- 1. poł XVI w.
- XVII w.
- ok. 1740
- ok. 1770
- XIX w.
- ok. 1918

**Fig. 7.** Example of the method visual representation of chronology – the drawings resulted from historic-architectural research of the palace in Kurozwęki, Poland. Drawings by M. Brykowska, J. Kubiak, M. Urbanowski 1972, according to [41], p. 88.

Poland, where color codes for chronology were based on the previously mentioned practice [40] (Fig. 8). It has to be taken into consideration while using color for visualizing non-physical features of the modelled objects, but always in relation to the character of the object and the intended use and role of the presented images.

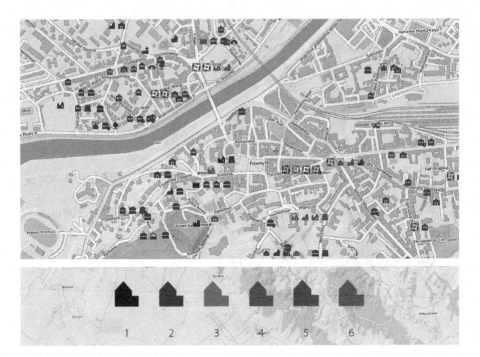

**Fig. 8.** An example of usage of color code for basic chronology of monuments on the map using analogical key as in Fig. 7, with warmer tones referring to older objects and colder to the newer ones (the map legend showing the colors in the example icon: 1 – early medieval, 2 – medieval, 3 – modern times, 4 – XIX century, 5 – contemporary, 6 – no data). According to [40], drawings by K. Koszewski. (Color figure online)

## 6   Conclusion

All the images that are created and disseminated in any area of human activity become a part of the pictorial universe, which adds its characteristics and influences the understanding and the interpretation of them. With no exception this also concerns all the visual output of modeling of architectural heritage. One of the features of contemporary visual culture is that images tend to exist independently from what they represent, significant – being detached from signifié – start to be a separate entity, a *simulacrum*. This causes inevitable consequences for the nature of images produced in the area of architectural heritage. Their informative and semantic capacity has to meet the challenge of being presented and interpreted without any context. A minimum of needed information, corresponding to the nature of these images, being predominantly variations of the possible past, has to be encoded in the way that is clearly understood. This minimum is, at the very basic level, an explicit message about a hypothetical nature of such a visual representation. On the other hand, in some cases when we aim at wide dissemination of knowledge, the pictorial character of feature-rich photorealistic representations has to be taken into account as one of the factors of effectiveness of the communique.

To acknowledge the nature of visual representations of the past and the need to treat them as one of the possible variants of the bygone reality, we need to treat modeling of historical buildings and cities (especially these non-existing) as simulations rather than reconstructions. This will place images as a visual result of the simulation process, an interface and a control tool of the model and the representation of changes invoked by manipulating its parameters. In such circumstances it becomes clear that it is impossible to indicate the one and only outcome, and if it is the case – that it is the only one presented, then it has to be encoded in the way that encompasses this variability.

To achieve all these goals there is a need to define theoretical foundations for establishing the common ground regarding visualization standards for architectural heritage. Such standards and best practices are still to be created, and should include analysis and redefinition of existing guidelines, principles, and standards in the field of digital 3D models as well as possible analogies from related fields. They have to follow basic requirements for the images as the results of the modeling and simulation process: intellectual integrity, reliability, sustainability, and access, while taking into consideration the characteristics of contemporary visual culture, inevitable (and frequently overlooked) factor which is shaping their reception. Applying criteria of M&S theory, especially interpreting these images as visual outcomes of the simulation process implies the need for variability allowing user interaction on the level of altering the model. Yet there are still many cases where it is not possible to introduce interactivity, and the only image available is in fact just the most probable version of the past situation. In these cases, especially when such an image reaches the broader audience, special caution should be applied regarding its credibility as a variant, instead of the unquestionable "reconstructed" past. One of the best practices that should be recommended is to present them along with alternative versions or alternative modes of representation, delivering a message that they are based on assumptions, and they are as close to the reality as we were able to verify our research hypotheses.

# References

1. Jurgenson, N.: The Social Photo: On Photography and Social Media. VERSO Books, London (2020)
2. London Charter. http://www.londoncharter.org/. Accessed 30 Oct 2020
3. Mitchell, W.J.T.: The pictorial turn. In: Picture Theory: Essays on Verbal and Visual Representation, pp. 11–34. University of Chicago Press, Chicago (1994)
4. Mirzoeff, N.: How to See the World: An Introduction to Images, From Self-portraits to Selfies, Maps to Movies, and More. Basic Books, New York (2016)
5. Clement, J.: Social media - Statistics & Facts. https://www.statista.com/topics/1164/social-networks/. Accessed 22 Nov 2020
6. Baudrillard, J.: Simulations. Semiotext(e), New York (1983)
7. Di Giuseppantonio Di Franco, P., Galeazzi, F., Vassallo, V.: Authenticity and Cultural Heritage in the Age of 3D Digital Reproductions. McDonald Institute for Archaeological Research, Cambridge (2018)
8. Reilly, P.: Towards a virtual archaeology. In: CAA90. Computer Applications and Quantitative Methods in Archaeology 1990, pp. 132–139 (1991)

9. Alkhoven, P.: The reconstruction of the past: the application of new techniques for visualisation and research in architectural history. Architectural History, pp. 549–566 (1991)
10. Reconstruction. https://www.oxfordlearnersdictionaries.com
11. Manovich, L.: The Language of New Media. MIT Press, Cambridge (2001)
12. Clark, J.: The fallacy of reconstruction. In: Forte, M. (ed.) Cyber-Archaeology, pp. 63–73. Archaeopress, Oxford (2010)
13. Vallverdú, J.: What are simulations? An epistemological approach. Procedia Technol. **13**, 6–15 (2014). https://doi.org/10.1016/j.protcy.2014.02.003
14. Banks, C.M.: What is modeling and simulation? In: Principles of Modeling and Simulation. pp. 3–24. Wiley, Hoboken (2009). https://doi.org/10.1002/9780470403563
15. Forte, M.: Cyber archaeology: a post-virtual perspective. In: Svensson, P., Goldberg, D.T. (eds.) Between Humanities and the Digital, pp. 295–309. MIT Press, Cambridge (2015)
16. Kowal, S., Koszewski, K., Słyk, J., Wrona, S.: Parametric methods in reconstruction of the medieval Proto-Town in Pultusk, Poland. In: Martens, B., Wurzer, G., Grasl, T., Lorenz, W. E., Schaffranek, R. (eds.) ECAADE 2015: Real Time - Extending the Reach of Computation, pp. 695–700. TU Wien, Vienna (2015)
17. Haegler, S., Müller, P., Van Gool, L.: Procedural modeling for digital cultural heritage. EURASIP J. Image Video Process. **2009**(1), 1 (2009). https://doi.org/10.1155/2009/852392
18. Champion, E.M.: From historical models to virtual heritage simulations. In: Kuroczyński, P., Pfarr-Harfst, M., and Münster, S. (eds.) Digitale 3D-Rekonstruktion als virtueller Raum der architekturhistorischen Forschung, pp. 338–351. Universitätsbibliothek Heidelberg (2019)
19. Miłobędzki, A.: Badania nad historia architektury. In: Skubiszewski, P. (ed.) Przedmiot, metodologia, zawód, pp. 471–494. PWN, Warszawa (1973)
20. Maïm, J., Haegler, S., Yersin, B., Mueller, P., Thalmann, D., Gool, L.V.: Populating ancient pompeii with crowds of virtual romans. In: Proceedings of the 8th International Symposium on Virtual Reality, Archeology and Cultural Heritage - VAST, Brighton (2007)
21. ICOMOS Charter for the interpretation and presentation of cultural heritage sites. Int. J. Cult. Property. **15**, 377–384 (2008)
22. Seville-Principles-IN-ES-FR.pdf. https://icomos.es/wp-content/uploads/2020/06/Seville-Principles-IN-ES-FR.pdf. Accessed 28 Nov 2020
23. Bailey, M.P., Noor, A.K.: Human interaction with simulations. In: Principles of Modeling and Simulation, pp. 91–120. Wiley, Hoboken (2009). https://doi.org/10.1002/9780470403563
24. Karelin, D., Karelina, M.: Methods of reconstructions' presentation and the peculiarities of human perception. In: Kuroczyński, P., Pfarr-Harfst, M., and Münster, S. (eds.) Digitale 3D-Rekonstruktion als virtueller Raum der architekturhistorischen Forschung, pp. 187–201. Universitätsbibliothek Heidelberg (2019)
25. Apollonio, F.I.: Classification schemes and model validation of 3D digital reconstruction process. In: Börner, W., Uhlirz, S. (eds.) Proceedings of the 20th International Conference on Cultural Heritage and New Technologies 2015 (CHNT 20, 2015). Museen der Stadt Wien – Stadtarchäologie, Vienna (2015)
26. Słyk, J., Wrona, S. (eds.): Informacyjne środowisko rekonstrukcji - przedlokacyjna struktura osadnicza w Pułtusku w XIII-XIV wieku. Oficyna Wydawnicza Politechniki Warszawskiej, Warszawa (2015)
27. Fisher, B.: Visual representations and interactions technologies. In: Illuminating the Path: A Research and Development Agenda for Visual Analytics, pp. 69–104. IEEE Computer Society, Los Alamitos (2005)

28. Bendicho, V.M.L.-M., Gutiérrez, M.F., Vincent, M.L., León, A.G.: Digital heritage and virtual archaeology: an approach through the framework of international recommendations. In: Ioannides, M., Magnenat-Thalmann, N., Papagiannakis, G. (eds.) Mixed Reality and Gamification for Cultural Heritage, pp. 3–26. Springer, Cham (2017). https://doi.org/10. 1007/978-3-319-49607-8_1

29. Apollonio, F.I.: Classification schemes for visualization of uncertainty in digital hypothetical reconstruction. In: Münster, S., Pfarr-Harfst, M., Kuroczyński, P., Ioannides, M. (eds.) 3D Research Challenges in Cultural Heritage II. LNCS, vol. 10025, pp. 173–197. Springer, Cham (2016). https://doi.org/10.1007/978-3-319-47647-6_9

30. Lengyel, D., Toulouse, C.: The consecution of uncertain knowledge, hypotheses and the design of abstraction. In: Börner, W., Uhlirz, S. (eds.) Proceedings of the 20th International Conference on Cultural Heritage and New Technologies 2015 (CHNT 20, 2015). Museen der Stadt Wien – Stadtarchäologie, Vienna (2015)

31. Hauck, O., Kuroczynski, P.: How to record and preserve 3D assets of digital reconstruction. Presented at the Proceedings of the 20th International Conference on Cultural Heritage and New Technologies 2015 (CHNT 20, 2015), Vienna (2015)

32. Kensek, K.M., Dodd, L.S., Cipolla, N.: Fantastic reconstructions or reconstructions of the fantastic? Tracking and presenting ambiguity, alternatives, and documentation in virtual worlds. Autom. Constr. 13, 175–186 (2004). https://doi.org/10.1016/j.autcon.2003.09.010

33. Eiteljorg II, H.: The compelling computer image - a double-edged sword. Internet Archaeol. (2000). https://doi.org/10.11141/ia.8.3

34. Bakker, G., Meulenberg, F., de Rode, J.: Truth and credibility as a double ambition: reconstruction of the built past, experiences and dilemmas. J. Vis. Comput. Animat. 14, 159–167 (2003). https://doi.org/10.1002/vis.314

35. Roussou, M., Drettakis, G.: Photorealism and non-photorealism in virtual heritage representation. In: VAST 2003 and 1st Eurographics Workshop on Graphics and Cultural Heritage, pp. 47–56 (2003). https://doi.org/10.2312/VAST/VAST03/051-060

36. Bonde, S., Maines, C., Mylonas, E., Flanders, J.: The virtual monastery: re-presenting time, human movement, and uncertainty at Saint-Jean-des-Vignes. Soissons. null. 25, 363–377 (2009). https://doi.org/10.1080/01973760903331742

37. Grellert, M., Apollonio, F.I., Martens, B., Nussbaum, N., Börner, W., Uhlirz, S.: Working experiences with the reconstruction argumentation method (RAM) – scientific documentation for virtual reconstruction. In: Proceedings of the 23rd International Conference on Cultural Heritage and New Technologies 2018 (CHNT 23, 2018). Museen der Stadt Wien – Stadtarchäologie, Vienna (2018)

38. Kuroczyński, P., Hauck, O., Dworak, D.: 3D models on triple paths - new pathways for documenting and visualizing virtual reconstructions. In: Münster, S., Pfarr-Harfst, M., Kuroczyński, P., Ioannides, M. (eds.) 3D Research Challenges in Cultural Heritage II. LNCS, vol. 10025, pp. 149–172. Springer, Cham (2016). https://doi.org/10.1007/978-3-319-47647-6_8

39. US National Park Service/Historic American Buildings Survey: HABS/HAER/HALS Photography Guidelines (2015). https://www.nps.gov/hdp/standards/PhotoGuidelines.pdf

40. Koszewski, K.: Visualization of heritage related knowledge – case study of graphic representation of Polish national inventory of monuments in spatial information systems. In: Envisioning Architecture: Image, Perception and Communication of Heritage, pp. 377–387 (2015)

41. Brykowska, M.: Metody pomiarów i badań zabytków architektury. Oficyna Wydawnicza Politechniki Warszawskiej, Warszawa (2003)

# Toward an Automated Pipeline for a Browser-Based, City-Scale Mobile 4D VR Application Based on Historical Images

Sander Münster[1]($\boxtimes$) (iD), Christoph Lehmann[2], Taras Lazariv[2],
Ferdinand Maiwald[1], and Susanne Karsten[1]

[1] Digital Humanities, Friedrich-Schiller-Universität Jena, 07743 Jena, Germany
sander.muenster@uni-jena.de
[2] Center for Scalable Data Analytics and Artificial Intelligence (ScaDS.AI),
ZIH TU Dresden, 01062 Dresden, Germany

**Abstract.** The process for automatically creating 3D city models from contemporary photographs and visualizing them on mobile devices is well established. 4D city models that can display a temporal dimension are far more complex to generate automatically. In this article, we focus on major challenges in the process of developing an automated pipeline, starting from content-based image retrieval applied to historical images, via automatic historical image orientation, up to visualization of the 4D data in Virtual Reality (VR). The result is an interactive browser-based device-rendered 4D visualization and information system for mobile devices. This pipeline has been in development since 2015. In this article, we present initial results and early-stage findings in the process of overcoming three major challenges on the way to 4D city models: (1) to identify photographs with corresponding views, (2) to reconstruct the position and orientation of photographs and (3) to design a user-centered, browser-based 4D mobile application.

**Keywords:** Historical architecture · 4D browser interfaces · Content-based image retrieval · Photogrammetry · Virtual reality

## 1 Introduction

The purpose of 4D city models based on historical imagery is to enable virtual heritage tours, which inform tourists about urban history. In this article, we describe how we use an automated VR pipeline based on historical photographs to create an interactive, browser-based, device-rendered 4D visualization and information system for mobile devices. The pipeline shown is currently under development and an initial concept of it was recently published [1]. We present a more advanced version of the pipeline components and its testing.

The article is structured as follows: Sect. 2 contains an introduction of the application scenario and current challenges; Sect. 3 describes three studies to overcome these challenges in the process of developing an automated VR pipeline based on historical photographs; Sect. 4 concludes with a summary and prospects for future work.

© Springer Nature Switzerland AG 2021
F. Niebling et al. (Eds.): UHDL 2019, CCIS 1501, pp. 106–128, 2021.
https://doi.org/10.1007/978-3-030-93186-5_5

## 2 Application Scenario

The main usage scenario of our mobile 4D VR application based on historical images is to support tourists by providing a visual impression of a historic situation at their current location, as well as to provide textual information about single objects on demand [2]. Comparable applications have been researched and reviewed in previous projects [3, 4]. These include "Freiburg Zeitreise" [5], "Streetmuseum" [6], "Zeitfenster Leipzig" [7], and "Zeitfenster Weimar" [8], as well as applications of the Urban Timetravel project [9]. Other applications are more like guided tours or opportunities to explore a city or specific building from distance, e.g., "WDR 360 VR" [10] or "NRW2Go" [11]. Some websites enable users to explore history and travel in time, e.g., "History 360°" [12] or "The Berlin Wall – A multimedia history" [13]. Users of all of these applications can explore history, but only in one of two different times – the user can see a place and its surroundings as they are now, or as they looked like at a particular point in time years ago. Thus, it is not possible to travel in time and see how a place and its buildings or surroundings have looked like in various past years, as should be possible with the 4D application.

Despite the long technological evolution, some fundamental challenges still hinder the large-scale use of 4D VR applications:

1. Typically, AI-based technologies requires large-scale training data to detect corresponding views. Currently, therefore these technologies can only recognize well documented and visually distinctive landmark buildings [1, 14], but fail to deal with less distinctive architecture, e.g., houses of similar style.
2. Current photogrammetric 3D/4D modeling approaches often fail for historical, non-native digital imagery due to sparse samples, missing metadata, incompleteness, and radiometric quality issues [15]. These issues are not only technical but fundamental barriers and despite long periods of research, photogrammetry of historical images [16, 17] still requires a great deal of manual processing.
3. Concerning the design of mobile 4D applications presenting historical content, researchers are currently focusing on visual styling or details [18–20]. Thus there is a lack of research into the bigger picture, or validated design patterns for historical mobile 3D/4D applications [cf. 21].

## 3 Pipeline

The pipeline shown in Fig. 1 consists of two parallel strands. The first strand, comprising steps 1 and 2, involves recognizing similar buildings and views, then the position and orientation of photos. The second strand, based on vectorized maps, involves creating basic geometric shapes of the buildings to enable facade texturing. As a basis for 3D geometry creation, discussed in previous publications [1], we use cadaster plans of the historical city of Dresden. For this, we manually redrew outlines of building footprints as polylines using ArcGIS. From this, we obtained WGS 84-coded point data of the corners of the buildings. Since these polylines currently require manual processing, a future step not realized now will be to automate detection of the building outline using machine learning [22]. Step 3 involves creating a dynamic 3D model and visualizing the basic geometries and projected photo textures in a 4D browser-based mobile VR application.

The following subsections describe steps 1 to 3 in turn, starting with step 1 in Subsect. 3.1, or automatic image retrieval to obtain relevant historical images that contain the object(s) of interest. Step 2, described in Subsect. 3.2, involves feature-based retrieval of orientation information for historical images. Finally, step 3 in Subsect. 3.3 focuses on user experience (UX) development of the mobile 4D browser-based visualization.

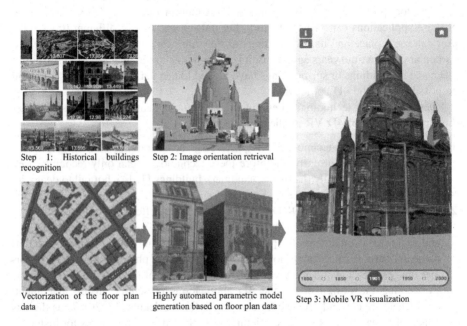

Step 1: Historical buildings recognition

Step 2: Image orientation retrieval

Vectorization of the floor plan data

Highly automated parametric model generation based on floor plan data

Step 3: Mobile VR visualization

**Fig. 1.** Visualization pipeline

### 3.1 Step 1: Historical Buildings Recognition (Content-Based Image Retrieval)

The task in step 1 is the following: given an image with an object of interest (OI), to find historical images that contain the same OI. As mentioned earlier, the process of identifying historical images with relevant objects is still manual. This is mainly due to incomplete, incorrect, inconsistent, or misleading metadata in image repositories. Thus, developers/researchers need to review search results that contain hundreds or even thousands of images. The following approach is to automate or at least to support the retrieval process based on deep neural networks. Image retrieval is a well-known task in computer vision that is approached in quite different ways. Approaches based on deep neural networks show good or at least promising performance in comparison to standard approaches, e.g., VLAD, Bag-of-Words, or improved Fisher (IFV) [cf. 23, Sect. 4, Table 7, 24]. The approach [25, p. 255] based on a convolutional neural network (CNN) even outperformed common image representations such as VLAD and IFV. It is worth mentioning that in [25] the Oxford5k dataset is used, which consists of modern images and does not include historical ones. For all our experiments, the chosen parameters are motivated from [25] and it is of interest, whether these parameters are appropriate for using historical images.

**Data**

All experiments are based on 847 images that were downloaded via the Sächsische Landesbibliothek – Staats- und Universitätsbibliothek Dresden (SLUB) from Deutsche Fotothek and contain historic photographs and a few drawings of buildings. Examples of the images are shown in Fig. 4. All images were annotated manually and assigned to seven different OI. These OI are seven sights in and around Dresden (percentage in brackets is the proportion of the OI within dataset): 1) Frauenkirche (20%), 2) Hofkirche (22%), 3) Moritzburg (2%), 4) Semperoper (9%), 5) Sophienkirche (6%), 6) Stallhof (4%), and 7) Zwinger (37%). As some buildings are located very close to each other in the inner city, several OI may appear simultaneously on one image. Thus, some images are assigned to many OI. The data contains different file formats (jpg, tif, and gif) and color spaces, as well as varying resolutions, with the smallest images of size $257 \times 400$ and the largest of size $3547 \times 2847$. During a pre-processing step all images were converted into jpg format with RGB color channels, without changing the resolution.

**Method and Experiments**

The image retrieval was implemented according to [25], and the basic idea is as follows: for every retrieval there are two types of images: 1) the query image with the instance/OI; 2) the reference images that are compared. This approach is based on a pretrained CNN (here: VGG16 [26]), where one of the upper convolutional layers (here: the last convolutional layer) is used as a vector-based image representation for every single image. The output of the last convolutional layer is 512 feature maps, each with the dimensions $7 \times 7$ (feature maps should contain the main characteristics of an image, such as edges, shapes etc.). These feature maps are reduced in dimension by using global max pooling (spatial pooling) [25, p. 253]. This standard operation of max pooling [cf. 27, Sect. 5.1.2] can be done with different parameters, mainly kernel size and stride. The resulting set of feature maps is flattened to a vector whose length depends on the parameters used. Within the experiments, three different max pooling parameter settings are used:

1. kernel size $7 \times 7$ with stride 0, leading to resulting feature maps of size $1 \times 1$ each (i.e., maximum reduction); flattened to vector of size $512 \times 1 \times 1 = 512$
2. kernel size $4 \times 4$ with stride 3, leading to resulting feature maps of size $2 \times 2$ each; flattened to vector of size $512 \times 2 \times 2 = 2048$
3. kernel size $1 \times 1$ with stride 1, equivalent to no reduction; flattened to vector of size $512 \times 7 \times 7 = 25088$.

The resulting vector representations within each setting have the same size for every image and they are used to calculate the distance between the query image and every reference image. Here, we used the Euclidean distance (denoted as $L_2$ normalized distance in [25, p. 254, Eqs. (1), (2)]). In the final step, a ranked list is created based on the calculated distances.

For every OI, 10–12 different query images are defined, in total 76 query images for seven categories. Finally, all query images are compared against the total 847 reference images. Each query image contains only a single OI, while the reference images may contain several OI. The result of a single image retrieval based on one query image is a sorted list (ranked list) of 847 images, containing the distance between the query image and every reference image, with best matches on top.

In order to improve the retrieval results, the reference images are divided into sub-patches according to [25, p. 254, Eqs. (1), (2)]. The level of division is characterized by the order parameter L. The number of resulting sub-patches is determined by $\sum_{i=1}^{L} i^2$, e.g., an order of L = 4 leads to 30 sub-patches. Within the experiments in [25] a reference order of L = 3 and L = 4 led to good results. Note that the query images can be divided into sub-patches. This is called "jittering" [25] and it follows the same procedure as for the reference images. For the application at hand, we use a fixed query order of L = 3, i.e., 14 sub-patches for the query images. Using sub-patches of query and/or reference images, the same procedure of distance calculation (see above) is applied for every single pair of sub-patches. These distances need to be aggregated into one final distance number, which is done here following [25, p. 255, Eqs. (3), (4)].

**Results and Evaluation**

The following results are based on the data as described above: 847 reference images, 76 query images over seven OI. To represent the features, the last convolutional layer from the CNN VGG16 was used. The recent prototype was implemented in Python 3.7 based on Pytorch 1.3 for feature extraction from the VGG16 net. All experiments were performed on IBM Power9 nodes with an Nvidia V100 GPU. A single retrieval result is a ranked list of the 847 reference images, ordered by the minimum distance between query image and reference image. The absolute distances are not of main interest, but the relations between the distances for all reference images under consideration. Based on the manual image annotation, the ground truth is created: every reference image can be categorized as relevant or irrelevant referring the query image (and herewith the OI). A ranked list of minimum distances (in ascending order) can be evaluated for every position:

- relevant image before or at the considered position is a true positive (TP or a hit)
- irrelevant image that occurs after the considered position, is a true negative (TN)
- relevant image that occurs after the considered position, is a false negative (FN)
- irrelevant image that occurs before or at the considered position is a false positive (FP or a miss)

From these numbers, the following evaluation measures can be calculated [cf. 28, 29]:

$$TPR = \frac{TP}{TP + TN} \text{ (true positive rate, hit rate, or recall)}$$

$$FPR = \frac{FP}{FP + FN} \text{ (false positive rate)}$$

$$PPV = \frac{TP}{TP + FP} \text{ (precision or positive predictive value)}$$

Combinations of these measures are used to evaluate the quality of a retrieval result from different perspectives. In the following, we mainly take two approaches to evaluation, receiver operating characteristics (ROC) and precision-recall (PR) curves.

Calculation of the ROC curve is based on the ranked list of the results in descending order of relevance (or ascending by minimum distance). A ROC curve can be seen as moving along the ranked list through every single position, starting from the top. For every position in a list, the true positive rate (TPR) and the false positive rate (FPR) are calculated: together, they constitute a point on the ROC curve. Note that with increasing quality of retrieval results the ROC curve tends to the upper left corner. Low quality results show ROC curves around the bisectrix. We would like to have a steep increase in the ROC curve, as this means that along the ranked list we see relevant images quite early without getting too many irrelevant images. Figure 2 shows the top three and the worst three ROC curves over all 76 queries for the seven different OI. Note that all the other ROC curves are located somewhere between the top three and worst three. For instance, the interpretation for OI "Zwinger" (Fig. 2, bottom right), could be as follows: roughly 60%–75% (=TPR) are of the OI Zwinger, approximately 25% (=FPR) of the images are non-OI. Here, the problem becomes obvious: these 25% non-OI can be a large absolute number, especially if the total amount of non-OI is large. This is the case with skewed data, i.e., the relation between OI and non-OI is rather small (e.g., 0.05, 0.01).

When the data is skewed, ROC curves tend to be overly optimistic about the quality of the retrieval. Therefore, a second step of evaluation is the PR curve. The concept is quite similar to that of the ROC curve, but with slightly different measures. For every single position in the ranked list, the precision and the recall (=TPR) are calculated: together, they constitute a point on the PR curve. The perfect PR curve is a horizontal line at one, which describes a situation where all hits directly follow one another. More practically, a good PR curve tends to the upper right corner. Figure 3 shows the top three and the worst three PR curves over all 76 queries for the seven different OI. Note that all the other PR curves are located somewhere in between the top three and worst three. The interpretation for OI Zwinger (Fig. 2, bottom right) could be as follows: finding roughly 50%–75% (=TPR) of the OI Zwinger means that approximately 70% (precision) of all images in the result list belong to OI Zwinger. In contrast to the ROC curve, a PR curve is a non-monotonous function, e.g., OI Stallhof at Fig. 3. Note that there is a one-to-one-correspondence between ROC and PR curves [see 30, Theorem 3.1]. Thus, they both contain the same information, but from a slightly different perspective.

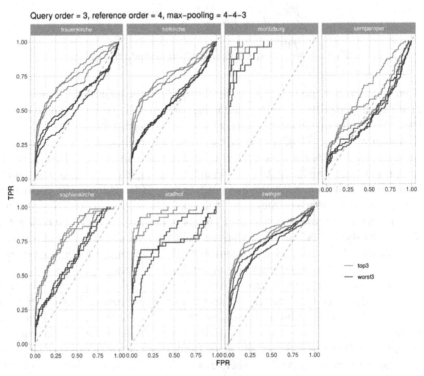

**Fig. 2.** Top three and worst three ROC curves over all 76 queries for all seven OI

Figures 2 and 3 show that there are large differences within the seven OI, as these are different types of buildings. Nevertheless, the order of overall quality for the OI is mainly the same for the ROC and PR curves. The OI Zwinger and Moritzburg are quite distinctive buildings (within these seven OI) and provide the best results. Furthermore, most of these images in the dataset are of high quality. The OI Frauenkirche, Hofkirche, and Stallhof provide mixed results and there is a large variation in the quality of the single retrievals. Probably, this is because images of these OI were taken from quite different perspectives. By far the worst performing retrievals are for two OI: the Semperoper and Sophienkirche. The reason might be that the appearance of these buildings has changed over time and from different perspectives, the characteristic attributes seem very different.

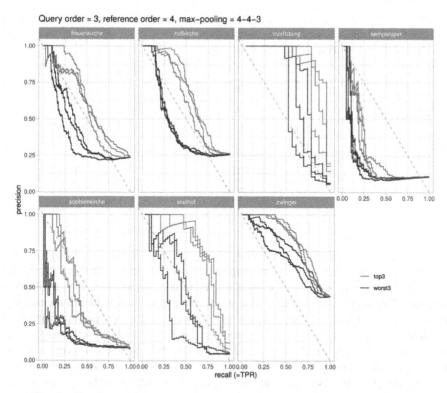

**Fig. 3.** Top three and worst three PR curves over all 76 queries for all seven OI

The last step in the evaluation is to provide an overview of the influence of retrieval parameters, such as reference order and dimension reduction by max pooling. Therefore, the ROC and PR curves are further aggregated. To aggregate a ROC curve into one single number, the area under the ROC curve (AUROC) is used, which takes values in the unit interval [0, 1]. To aggregate a PR curve into one single number, the average of all single precision values along one PR curve is used; this value is also in the unit interval 0, 1] and is simply called average precision (AP). The closer a value of AUROC or AP is to 1, the better the retrieval result. For further reduction, the mean overall AUROC and AP values for every OI is calculated. Table 1 shows these values for different settings of retrieval parameters. Table 1 indicates that a reference order of 4 mostly outperforms a reference order of 3. For max pooling, the settings 1-1-1 (i.e., no reduction of the feature maps) is the worst and the settings 4-4-3 (kernel size 4 × 4 with stride 3) and 7-7-0 (kernel size 7 × 7 with stride 0) are to be preferred. This result is consistent with previous findings [25, Table 1] that a reference order 4 yielded the best results and dimension reduction (global max pooling) of the description vectors further improved the results.

**Table 1.** Mean average precision and mean area under the ROC curve for all queries for different OI over different parameters, referring to sub-patch division of reference images and reduction with max pooling

| reference_order | maxpod | | frauenkirche | hofkirche | moritzburg | semperoper | sophienkirche | stallhof | zwinger | frauenkirche | hofkirche | moritzburg | semperoper | sophienkirche | stallhof | zwinger |
|---|---|---|---|---|---|---|---|---|---|---|---|---|---|---|---|---|
| | | mAP | | | | | | | | mAUROC | | | | | | |
| 3 | 1-1-1 | | 0.41 | 0.41 | 0.62 | 0.21 | 0.20 | 0.46 | 0.75 | 0.56 | 0.55 | 0.86 | 0.48 | 0.66 | 0.86 | 0.74 |
| 3 | 4-4-3 | | 0.49 | 0.50 | 0.72 | 0.20 | 0.25 | 0.48 | 0.78 | 0.62 | 0.62 | 0.87 | 0.49 | 0.71 | 0.83 | 0.77 |
| 3 | 7-7-0 | | 0.51 | 0.50 | 0.72 | 0.18 | 0.26 | 0.50 | 0.77 | 0.64 | 0.62 | 0.88 | 0.49 | 0.73 | 0.82 | 0.76 |
| 4 | 1-1-1 | | 0.45 | 0.47 | 0.69 | 0.24 | 0.22 | 0.49 | 0.76 | 0.59 | 0.59 | 0.88 | 0.50 | 0.68 | 0.86 | 0.74 |
| 4 | 4-4-3 | | 0.52 | 0.56 | 0.75 | 0.22 | 0.27 | 0.51 | 0.78 | 0.65 | 0.66 | 0.88 | 0.51 | 0.73 | 0.84 | 0.76 |
| 4 | 7-7-0 | | 0.53 | 0.56 | 0.74 | 0.20 | 0.27 | 0.53 | 0.77 | 0.66 | 0.67 | 0.89 | 0.52 | 0.73 | 0.83 | 0.75 |

It is important to emphasize that the results presented in Table 1 are based not on a benchmark dataset, but on real, heterogeneous use-case data. This influences the results, which are not as good as those achieved in previous research [25] in absolute numbers. This is probably due to the large difference in the data used and the fact that our data was pre-processed less. Nevertheless, we found that the parameter settings that previous researchers used [25] are appropriate for retrieving historical images. Our application deals with a real dataset, which is highly heterogenous in terms of color, resolution, and image type. In that sense, the setting here is realistic and provides insights about what is possible under real-world conditions without data-specific optimization.

Finally, Fig. 4 gives a rough insight into concrete retrieval results for the images in the dataset. Figure 4(a) shows the relevant reference images with the largest distance to the query image. Figure 4(b) shows the irrelevant reference images, with the smallest distance to the query image.

(a) relevant reference images with the largest distance to the query image (leftmost)

(b) irrelevant reference images with the smallest distance to the query image (leftmost)

**Fig. 4.** Distances for relevant and irrelevant images of different OI: (from top to bottom) the Hofkirche, Stallhof, Sophienkirche, and Sophienkirche (sic!)

All experiments had a runtime of 5–30 min, depending on the concrete parameters, i.e., retrieving a single query image within approximately 1000 reference images takes 10–30 s.

In conclusion, image retrieval offers valuable support enabling researchers or developers to find images of interest in hundreds or thousands of instances. It is likely that results can be further improved by a metadata search that pre-filters the image data before retrieval. If this strategy does not produce satisfactory results, the retrieval can also be performed directly in a database without a metadata search. This is more time-consuming, but can lead to more relevant hits and can be performed automatically.

### 3.2   Step 2: Retrieving Image Orientation

**Related Work**
Different approaches can be used to retrieve 3D spatial information from diverse historical images. But, the accurate orientation of historical image data is still an issue and images are often oriented manually [31–33] or (if the building is still standing) with the help of additional recent images [34] or terrestrial laser scanner data [35] of the depicted structure. Conventional Structure-from-Motion (SfM) workflows provided in e.g., Agisoft Metashape [36], Meshroom [37], or COLMAP [38] often fail when calculating the orientation of historical images for two main reasons:

1. Missing or incorrect estimation of camera parameters
2. Large (radiometrical and geometrical) differences between pairs of images, leading to wrong feature matches.

In addition, the usage of historical data material for a photogrammetric reconstruction of buildings and structures relies heavily on archive browsing and manually selecting appropriate sources [33, 34, 39].

**Methods**
After automatically detecting appropriate images from a large database, the second step is to adapt the conventional SfM workflow to orient historical images automatically. The exact image orientation and position is required to map the image texture accurately onto 3D city models in Web, augmented reality (AR) and VR applications. In the following, we show how the proposed workflow addresses these issues (Fig. 5).

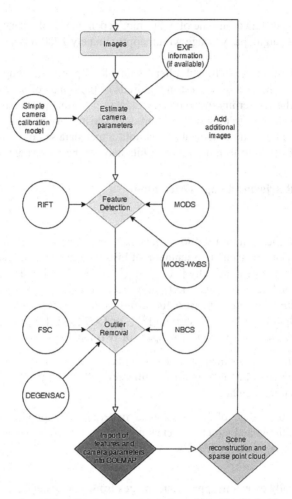

**Fig. 5.** Proposed workflow for the automatic orientation of multiple historical images

Due to autocalibration it is not strictly necessary to provide values for the camera parameters. Still, if the initial approximation values for the SfM pipeline are not sufficiently accurate, the orientation of the cameras is likely to fail. We attempted to solve this by extracting initial camera parameters automatically, and show here what assumptions have to be made to do this.

Firstly, most of the available SfM software packages try to extract camera parameters from the EXIF metadata of every single image, which is mainly possible for digital photographs. Sometimes, analog images provide values, e.g., from the scanning device. After extraction, all fields of EXIF data should be deleted.

Secondly, we made the following common assumptions. Pixels are square, the center of projection is coincident with the image center [40], and a simple camera calibration model (only modeling radial distortion parameters k1, k2) is used for the historical images. The initial values of k1 and k2 are set to 0. For the camera constant we follow the recommendation of COLMAP [38] and use $f = 1.25 * \max(Width_{px}, Height_{px})$.

The quality of historical redigitized images varies for several reasons, e.g., digitization artifacts or varying camera models [41]. These differences affect the process of feature matching and conventional widely-used approaches like SIFT (and its variations) [42], AKAZE [43] or SURF [44] usually find a lot of keypoints in the images. Often, however, the matching of these features fails, mainly because only a small number of all putative matches are correct. Also, complete end-to-end SfM pipelines – like Agisoft Metashape, Meshroom [45], COLMAP [38] or VisualSFM [46] – have been extensively tested on different historical datasets, but these approaches mostly fail at the image orientation step [47].

Other recent methods which have been developed for special feature matching tasks are meant to perform better on historical images. These combine radiation-invariant feature matching (RIFT) with a method that is successful especially on image pairs with a wide baseline, Matching with On-Demand Synthesis (MODS). The proposed set of features consists of RIFT features [48] filtered with Fast Sample Consensus (FSC) [49], RIFT features filtered based on the normalized barycentric coordinate system (NBCS) [50], MODS [51] and MODS-WxBS [52]. MODS and MODS-WxBS use DEGENSAC [53] for outlier removal.

Using these four methods ensures that there is an overall higher number of putative features with a more heterogeneous distribution on the historical images since the single algorithms only produce few features. The feature points are calculated for every possible image pair combination of the dataset and are matched using the four methods. This ensures a high number of distinctive feature points to describe the historical images.

Additionally, all these methods in combination with the selected filtering algorithms yield only a very small number of outliers, which can then be filtered by geometric verification in COLMAP. A disadvantage of the proposed method is the large amount of time needed to compute all four feature sets. The camera parameters, images and feature matches are imported into COLMAP [38] where the scene is reconstructed and the positions of the cameras are optimized globally. For feature points, which are tracked in a minimum of three images, the equivalent 3D points in object space are calculated in a sparse point cloud.

## Data

In the proposed workflow, currently the images are selected interactively. At first, the feature matching methods were tested on a benchmark dataset of 24 images [41]. The proposed combination of RIFT + MODS achieved the best results on real historical photographs [47]. The benchmark dataset is extended to make it suitable for the SfM approach. This new dataset consists of 26 images showing the Semperoper in Dresden and is meant to be evaluated with the RIFT + MODS method as a proof-of-concept (Fig. 6).

**Fig. 6.** 19 images of the Semperoper dataset showing the diversity of historical photographs

## Results

For the Semperoper dataset the RIFT+MODS method is able to register 19 out of 26 images (Fig. 7).

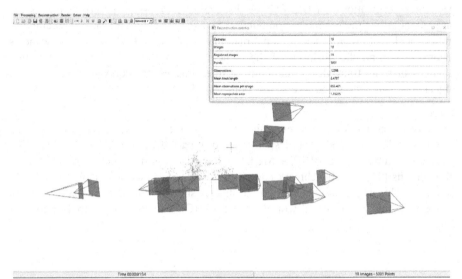

**Fig. 7.** The 19 images from Fig. 6 registered with the RIFT+MODS method in COLMAP

Global bundle adjustment is used to create 5001 3D points with a mean reprojection error of 1.13 pixels.

Combining the four methods allows reliable matching of historical images and enables the creation of a sparse point cloud to provide orientation information for most of the historical images. Further feature matching methods based on neural nets like D2-Net [54] or DELF [55] will be tested in the future.

Since this combined method was only evaluated on a small benchmark dataset and just one SfM dataset, it will be necessary to generate further historical image datasets to prove the effectiveness and robustness of the proposed workflow.

### 3.3    Step 3: Mobile VR Visualization

**Related Work**

Well established on desktop systems for a long time, 3D visualization based on WebGL for browsers is also supported on most mobile devices. WebGL-based frameworks for 3D graphics such as X3DOM [56] or Three.js [57] are well supported by mobile browsers. Specific pipelines for browser-based 3D content visualization of cultural heritage objects have been developed in numerous projects. Smithsonian [58] developed a 3D pipeline that covers workflow, metadata, repositories, and a viewer especially for museum artifacts. 3D HOP [59] and HexaLab [60] by ISTI-CRM are highly versatile viewers that are frequently used in various cultural heritage projects [15–18]. The INCEPTION project developed a workflow particularly for monument data [61]. Since these viewers are primarily focused on desktop systems, various browser-based viewers for cultural heritage 3D objects on mobile devices are already available [62, 63].

These current applications did not meet our requirements for various reasons. As already offered by virtual globes [64], one requirement for our application is to enable worldwide coverage and rely on established standards such as the WGS 84 geo-coordinate system [65]. Another requirement is to enable parametric modeling to create buildings from polylines. These features are already offered by various city modelers, such as ESRI CityEngine, but rarely for mobile browsers. Finally, we wanted to make it possible for visitors to populate and share location-based content, as realized in many projects [66]. Since there are no solutions available yet to cover all these requirements, we decided to develop a browser-based application capable of running on both iOS/WebKit and Android/Chrome browsers.

**Application Design**

The technological framework is based on a Linux/Apache/MySQL/PHP (LAMP) web server and the JavaScript 3D framework Three.js [57]. Within our pipeline, a PHP script queries a MySQL database to retrieve 3D models and additional information like text and images connected to specific scenery.

While Three.js by default requires local Cartesian coordinates, geo-related data is usually stored in polar coordinate systems such as WGS 84. Therefore, we developed a simple WGS 84 to XYZ converter, which converts latitude and longitude information of geometries into Cartesian coordinates. As it does not calculate the bending of polar coordinates, it produces a systematic deviance of 78 mm per km. When viewing an area as large as a city center, this deviance is negligible. To minimize it, we use this conversion in dependency on the coordinates of the city center.

In the next step, a HTML file is constructed containing both a Three.js JavaScript part with links to the models in the media file repository and HTML content with textual information about the buildings. Within the media file repository, geometry information is either stored as point information of the ground plot outline for geometries with a simple level of detail (LoD 1,5), or as Collada files for complex geometries. Point information is linked to a path and extruded to the assumed height of the building. Since previous studies have shown the importance of roof-like structures in helping observers recognize buildings [20], the extrusion is beveled to create a roof-like look.

A central functionality of this design is dynamic rendering of textured buildings. To support the automatic texturing of the geometry with images dynamically loaded from the media file repository, we use perspective projection mapping. This is the process of projecting the images by pointing a virtual camera toward the geometry, which maps the image onto the surface of the model. To achieve this, in step 1 a virtual projection camera for each image used as a texture is instantiated, and then the image is loaded into a texture which is then bound to its camera. The necessary metadata about the orientation and position of the photos are created in step 2 and loaded from the SQL database to be fed into the projection- and camera-matrices of the cameras. From those the view matrix is computed and the model with the associated textures is drawn.

Another important user interface (UI) element is a timeline which enables filtering of 3D geometries and textures by year and position/orientation – the latter filter is required due to the inability of mobile OS, especially iOS, to cope with more than eight texture projections at the same time. In the current version, the framework is capable of showing content depending on GPS location information and sensor-based orientation. Additionally, split-window stereo views for Google Cardboard-based VR can be generated. Another main functionality is to add points of interest (POI) to the 3D model interactively. If a user points on the 3D viewport, a ray is traced to the 3D model to retrieve the point of intersection with the 3D geometry. At this point, a new POI can be created and the user can add textual information. This data can be saved to the database and is available as 3D clickable spheres for all other users.

**User Testing of the Graphical User Interface of the Mobile 4D VR Application**
To develop an appropriate graphical user interface (GUI) for the mobile 4D VR application, the development team first generated and implemented initial ideas. Then, an expert evaluated them according to usability and user experience (UX) criteria, as well as UI guidelines and patterns [67, 68]. Using the results of the expert evaluation and the knowledge of the literature research, we conceptualized a new design for the GUI of the mobile 4D application (see Fig. 8).

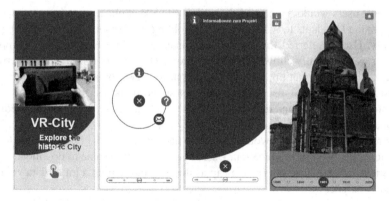

**Fig. 8.** Design concept (left, middle) and implementation (right) of the UX redesign

## Methodology

The new UI design concept of the mobile 4D VR application was tested by means of a small user study. The main goal was to find out if the concept works and meets the desired objectives. The additional aim was to find out what users think about the application and the idea behind it. The user studies were conducted from November 1 to 11, 2020 via Skype meetings, each with a duration from 15 to 60 min. During each meeting, the test coordinator first explained the test to the participants. Then they received a link for the mockup prototype application, which had been realized in Adobe XD.

For the user studies, we compiled a questionnaire including item batteries from Attrakdiff [69] and UEQ [70, 71]. It contains open and closed questions about different parts and aspects of the 4D application, e.g., the cover and introductory pages, the home and submenu and their buttons, the timeline, and animations. It asks for example about the first impression of the prototype application, if it is easy to use and learn, if the functionality of the timeline is clear, whether users understand the tutorials and animations, what users liked the most, and what they did not like at all.

## Results

A total of six test users (3 female, 3 male) took part in the study. On average, they were 36 years old (the youngest was 25 and the oldest, 63). Five of the test users had a university degree and one an extended secondary school certificate. Their self-assessed general technical affinity was just above average, at 3 on a scale from 1 (very technology-savvy) to 7 (not at all technology-savvy).

It was stated positively by test users that, in general and especially when traveling, people can use the application to get interesting knowledge or background information about certain buildings and sights, particularly with the AR function. However, some symbols on the home menu and submenu should be improved or reconsidered, since users did not always understand the meanings or know what they linked to (e.g., the camera button on the main screen). Moreover, we noted that the placement of the buttons on the main screen should be reconsidered to enable both, right and left-handed users to reach most relevant buttons easily.

The test users would have liked the mobile 4D VR application to have a responsive design, so the UI adapts to whether a user is holding their mobile device horizontally or vertically. Users preferred the landscape format for looking at a group of houses or buildings as it generally allows them to see more. The portrait format was preferred for reading texts or information, and for looking at a single house or sight.

Besides that, the test users made various suggestions for improving the current application. They suggested that there could be something like a quiz or knowledge test and small comments about a building or city, such as "did you know that...". Furthermore, some stated that it would be nice to have videos of the POIs, be able to listen to music while using the application. Users also wanted to be able to download data for a specific location before going on a trip as these would require a lot of data volume to download on site.

**Discussion**

Overall, the test users received and rated the new UI design concept and the whole current application positively.

From the UX study, we got positive feedback on integrating playful interaction and navigation techniques (e.g., a timeline with a slider), and animations of screen elements. These aspects apparently contribute a lot to making such an application appealing, fun to use, and engaging, and have a positive effect on the UX and user acceptance [cf. 72, 73]. Additionally, we recommend that even a mobile-first application is produced in a responsive design, and support both, portrait and landscape formats on mobile devices.

One of the main problems that emerged during the user studies was that the test users could not interpret the buttons or their symbols correctly, so we recommend that future developers pay particular attention to this aspect. Buttons or their icons should be chosen wisely – users need to understand their meaning to increase the likelihood of using them [74].

The placement of icons on smartphones is a well-researched topic and several suggestions regarding icon arrangement by function or frequency of use have been empirically validated [75, 76]. On mobile devices, the most important criterion is that users must be able to reach icons easily, ideally with the thumb of the preferred hand [cf. 77]. That is, an application should support users who are left- or right-handed. Another issue is age: larger button size and spacing is preferred for older people [78]. In the best case, it should be possible to adjust this in the settings of an application.

# 4    Conclusion and Future Work

In this article, we have presented the basic parts of an automated pipeline for a browser-based mobile 4D VR application that utilizes historical images. Since this prototype pipeline is generally functional, our ongoing task is to assess and improve the steps involved.

Concerning step 1, retrieval of historical images works and automation of this could assist developers/researchers within a manual working process. To be effectively implemented in practice, this approach requires a GPU, especially for feature extraction based on a CNN for image retrieval. Transfer learning (i.e., using a pretrained CNN) is very advantageous and drastically reduces preparation time. All our experiments had a runtime of 5–30 min, depending on the concrete parameterization, i.e., retrieving a single query image within approximately 1000 reference images takes 10–30 s. It should be emphasized that these results here are based not on a benchmark dataset, but on real, heterogeneous use-case data.

In future, we plan to identify the main success drivers for retrieving historical images. In this context, we intend to apply the promising results from approaches such as the DELF algorithm [cf. 79] or the ONE algorithm [cf. 80]. In technical terms, this means interconnecting an image retrieval backend with large repositories like Europeana (www.europeana.eu) that provide a REST API, which enables stronger automation of the retrieval process. This should improve the retrieval results presented here, as the data is pre-selected by a metadata search, which is common in such image repositories. Therefore, future experiments should be performed on data that has been pre-selected from a metadata search.

Step 2 shows as a proof-of-concept that completely automatic image orientation is possible for specific datasets using specialized feature detectors and matchers like RIFT and MODS. Importing the derived feature matches into COLMAP enables accurate scene reconstruction, which can be used to determine the camera orientation parameters. While we tested this workflow on a small benchmark dataset and only one larger dataset, it yielded promising results. In future, we plan to test further features derived by neural networks on additional historical datasets with a predefined ground truth. Contemporary images may help to improve the orientation of historical images with large radiometric differences. The position and orientation of the images will be imported into the mobile 4D viewer application.

Within step 3, the 4D Browser application is currently at the beta stage and is functioning on many devices. The next step is to develop its compatibility and robustness to ensure stability on a variety of mobile devices. Since the UX tests indicated that the design is promising, further testing via an onscreen survey is currently in progress to validate the reported initial findings. Finally, there are some extended functionality priorities for the mobile 4D viewer application. Since the technical feature for enabling users to generate and populate POIs is already included in the system, the next stage is to develop and test redactional workflows and UX. After that, we aim to test the interplay of the single steps and to scale the testing up with larger datasets.

**Acknowledgments.** The research for this paper was carried out in the projects TMPC (Sächsische Aufbaubank, 100377090), TMPCJ (Thüringische Aufbaubank, 220FGI0045), and Denkmalschutz4D (Deutsche Bundesstiftung Umwelt, 35654) as well as the junior research group UrbanHistory4D (German Federal Ministry of Education and Research, 01UG1630). Furthermore, this work was supported by the German Federal Ministry of Education and Research (BMBF, 01/S18026A-F) by funding the competence center for Big Data and AI "ScaDS.AI Dresden/Leipzig." The authors gratefully acknowledge the Gemeinsame Wissenschaftkonferenz's support for this project by providing computing time through the Center for Information Services and HPC (ZIH) at TU Dresden on HRSK-II.

# References

1. Münster, S., Maiwald, F., Lehmann, C., Lazariv, T., Hofmann, M., Niebling, F.: Introducing an automated pipeline for a browser-based, city-scale mobile 4D VR application based on historical images. Paper Presented at the ACM Multimedia - SUMAC Workshop, Seattle (2020)
2. Ceconello, M., Spagnoli, A., Spallazzo, D., Tolino, U.: Playing design- mobile serious games to valorize design culture in the urban space. Paper Presented at the Digital Heritage 2015, Granada, Spain (2015)
3. Breitenstein, M., Münster, S., Niebling, F.: Gamifizierte augmented reality-anwendungen im tourismuskontext: ein literaturreview zu Gestaltungsansätzen, Chancen und Risiken. In: Köhler, T. (ed.) Communities in New Media. Researching the Digital Transformation in Science, Business, Education & Public Administration, pp 197–209. TUDPress, Dresden (2019)
4. ViMM WG 2.2: Meaningful Content connected to the Real World (Report) (2017)
5. Mathis, R.: Freiburg Zeitreise - die Stadtjubiläum 2020 app (version 1.1.0) (2020). https://play.google.com/store/apps/details?id=com.extendedvision.futurehistory.freiburg2020&hl=de. Accessed 21 Dec 2020
6. Youssef, M.: Museum of London: streetmuseum app (version 2.03) (2016). https://apkpure.com/de/museum-of-london-streetmuseum/com.streetmuseum. Accessed 21 Dec 2020
7. Schücking, B.A.: Zeitfenster app - friedliche revolution leipzig (version 1.1.1) (2018). https://zeitfenster.uni-leipzig.de/. Accessed 21 Dec 2020
8. Burkert, P., Straubinger, S., Schaufler, B.: Zeitfenster app (2018). https://www.zeitfenster-app.de/. Accessed 21 Dec 2020
9. Berdin, J., Helder, M., Fridhi, A.: Applications of the urban timetravel project (2019). https://www.urbantimetravel.com/project. Accessed 21 Dec 2020
10. Buhrow, T.: WDR 360° VR app (2017). https://play.google.com/store/apps/details?id=de.WDR.VR&hl=de. Accessed 10 Oct 2020
11. Buhrow, T.: NRW2go app (version 1.0.3) (2019). https://play.google.com/store/apps/details?id=de.WDR.NRW2go&hl=de. Accessed 10 Oct 2020
12. Bellut, T.: History 360° (2019). https://history360.zdf.de/. Accessed 10 Oct 2020
13. Schulte-Kellinghaus, J.: The Berlin wall – a multimedia history (2013). https://www.the-berlin-wall.com/. Accessed 10 Oct 2020
14. Mager, T., Hein, C.: Digital excavation of mediatized urban heritage: automated recognition of buildings in image sources. Urban Plann. 5(2), 24–34 (2020)
15. Maiwald, F., Schneider, D., Henze, F., Münster, S., Niebling, F.: Feature matching of historical images based on geometry of quadrilaterals. Int. Arch. Photogramm. Remote Sens. Spatial Inf. Sci. **XLII-2**, 643–650 (2018). https://doi.org/10.5194/isprs-archives-XLII-2-643-2018
16. Pomaska, G.: Zur Dokumentation und 3D-modellierung von denkmalen mit digitalen fotografischen verfahren. In: Heine, K., Rheidt, K., Henze, F., Riedel, A. (eds.) Von Handaufmaß bis High Tech III - 3D in der historischen Bauforschung, pp. 26–32. Verlag Philipp von Zabern, Mainz (2011)
17. Maiwald, F., Vietze, T., Schneider, D., Henze, F., Münster, S., Niebling, F.: Photogrammetric analysis of historical image repositories for virtual reconstruction in the field of digital humanities. Int. Arch. Photogr. Remote Sens. Spat. Inf. Sci. **42**, 447 (2017). https://doi.org/10.5194/isprs-archives-XLII-2-W3-447-2017
18. Wood, J., Isenberg, P., Isenberg, T., Dykes, J., Boukhelifa, N., Slingsby, A.: Sketchy rendering for information visualization. IEEE Trans. Vis. Comput. Graphics **18**(12), 2749–2758 (2012). https://doi.org/10.1109/TVCG.2012.262

19. Glaser, M., Lengyel, D., Toulouse, C., Schwan, S.: Designing computer-based learning contents: influence of digital zoom on attention. Educ. Tech. Res. Dev. **65**(5), 1135–1151 (2016). https://doi.org/10.1007/s11423-016-9495-9
20. Münster, S.: Cultural heritage at a glance. Four case studies about the perception of digital architectural 3D models. In: Alonso, F. (ed.) 2018 3rd Digital Heritage International Congress (DigitalHERITAGE) held jointly with 2018 24th International Conference on Virtual Systems & Multimedia (VSMM 2018). IEEE, San Francisco (2018)
21. Burmester, M., et al.: Lost in space? 3D-interaction-patterns für einfache und positive nutzung von 3D interfaces. In: Hess, S., Fischer, H. (eds.) Mensch und Computer 2018 – Usability Professionals (Electronic Book). Gesellschaft für Informatik e.V. und German UPA e.V., Bonn (2018)
22. Oliveira, S.A., Lenardo, I.D., Kaplan, F.: Machine vision algorithms on cadaster plans. In: Conference of the International Alliance of Digital Humanities Organizations (DH 2017), Montreal, Canada, 8–11 August 2017 (2017)
23. Razavian, A.S.: CNN features off-the-shelf: an astounding baseline for recognition. Paper Presented at the Proceedings of the IEEE Conference on Computer Vision and Pattern Recognition (CVPR) Workshops (2014)
24. Wan, J., et al.: Deep learning for content-based image retrieval: a comprehensive study. Proceedings of the 22nd ACM International Conference on Multimedia, pp. 157–166 (2014)
25. Razavian, A.S., et al.: Visual instance retrieval with deep convolutional networks. ITE Trans. Media Technol. Appl. **4**(3), 251–258 (2016)
26. Simonyan, K., Zisserman, A.: Very deep convolutional networks for largescale image recognition. arXiv preprint arXiv:1409.1556 (2014)
27. Chollet, F.: Deep Learning with Python. Manning, Shelter Island (2018)
28. Ting, K.M.: Confusion matrix. In: Sammut, C., Webb, G.I. (eds.) Encyclopedia of Machine Learning and Data Mining. Springer, Boston (2016). https://doi.org/10.1007/978-1-4899-7502-7_50-1
29. Ting, K.M.: Precision and recall. In: Sammut, C., Webb, G.I. (eds.) Encyclopedia of Machine Learning and Data Mining. Springer, Boston (2016). https://doi.org/10.1007/978-1-4899-7502-7_659-1
30. Davis, J., Goadrich, M.: The relationship between precision-recall and ROC curves. In: Proceedings of the 23rd International Conference on Machine Learning, pp. 233–240 (2006)
31. Schindler, G., Dellaert, F.: 4D cities: analyzing, visualizing, and interacting with historical urban photo collections. J. Multimed. **7**(2), 124–131 (2012). https://doi.org/10.4304/jmm.7.2.124-131
32. Zawieska, D., Markiewicz, J.: Development of photogrammetric documentation of the borough at biskupin based on archival photographs - first results. In: Ioannides, M., et al. (eds.) EuroMed 2016. LNCS, vol. 10059, pp. 3–9. Springer, Cham (2016). https://doi.org/10.1007/978-3-319-48974-2_1
33. Bevilacqua, M.G., Caroti, G., Piemonte, A., Ulivieri, D.: Reconstruction of lost architectural volumes by integration of photogrammetry from archive imagery with 3-D models of the status quo. Int. Arch. Photogr. Remote Sens. Spat. Inf. Sci. **XLII-2/W9**, 119–125 (2019). https://doi.org/10.5194/isprs-archives-XLII-2-W9-119-2019
34. Maiwald, F., Vietze, T., Schneider, D., Henze, F., Münster, S., Niebling, F.: Photogrammetric analysis of historical image repositories for virtual reconstruction in the field of digital humanities. ISPRS Int. Arch. Photogr. Remote Sens. Spat. Inf. Sci. WG V/5 447–452 (2017). 3D-Arch 2017 – 3D Virtual Reconstruction and Visualization of Complex Architectures (XL-5/W5)

35. Bitelli, G., Dellapasqua, M., Girelli, V.A., Sbaraglia, S., Tinia, M.A.: Historical photogrammetry and terrestrial laser scanning for the 3D virtual reconstruction of destroyed structures: a case study in Italy. ISPRS – Inte. Arch. Photogr. Remote Sens. Spat. Inf. Sci. **XLII-5/W1**, 113–119 (2017). https://doi.org/10.5194/isprs-archives-XLII-5-W1-113-2017
36. n.b.: Agisoft Metashape (2020). www.agisoft.com. Accessed 10 Oct 2020
37. AliceVision: Meshroom: a 3D reconstruction software (2018)
38. Schönberger, J.L., Frahm, J.-M.: Structure-from-motion revisited. In: Conference on Computer Vision and Pattern Recognition (CVPR) (2016)
39. Condorelli, F., Rinaudo, F.: Cultural heritage reconstruction from historical photographs and videos. Int. Arch. Photogr. Remote Sens. Spat. Inf. Sci. **XLII-2**, 259–265 (2018)
40. Snavely, N., Seitz, S.M., Szeliski, R.: Photo tourism: exploring photo collections in 3D. ACM Trans. Graph. (TOG) **25**, 835–846 (2006)
41. Maiwald, F.: Generation of a benchmark dataset using historical photographs for an automated evaluation of different feature matching methods. Int. Arch. Photogr. Remote Sens. Spat. Inf. Sci. **XLII-2/W13**, 87–94 (2019). https://doi.org/10.5194/isprs-archives-XLII-2-W13-87-2019
42. Lowe, D.G.: Distinctive image features from scale-invariant keypoints. Int. J. Comput. Vis. **60**(2), 91–110 (2004)
43. Alcantarilla, P.F., Solutions, T.: Fast explicit diffusion for accelerated features in nonlinear scale spaces. IEEE Trans. Pattern Anal. Mach. Intell. **34**(7), 1281–1298 (2011)
44. Bay, H., Tuytelaars, T., Van Gool, L.: Surf: Speeded up robust features. In: Leonardis, A., Bischof, H., Pinz, A. (eds.) ECCV 2006. LNCS, vol. 3951, pp. 404–417. Springer, Heidelberg (2006). https://doi.org/10.1007/11744023_32
45. Moulon, P., Monasse, P., Marlet, R.: Adaptive structure from motion with a contrario model estimation. In: Lee, K.M., Matsushita, Y., Rehg, J.M., Hu, Z. (eds.) ACCV 2012. LNCS, vol. 7727, pp. 257–270. Springer, Heidelberg (2013). https://doi.org/10.1007/978-3-642-37447-0_20
46. Wu, C.: Towards linear-time incremental structure from motion. In: 2013 International conference on 3D Vision-3DV, pp 127–134. IEEE (2013)
47. Maiwald, F., Bruschke, J., Lehmann, C., Niebling, F.: A 4D information system for the exploration of multitemporal images and maps using photogrammetry, web technologies and VR/AR. Virtual Archaeol. Rev. **10**(21), 1–13 (2019)
48. Li, J., Hu, Q., Ai, M.: RIFT: multi-modal image matching based on radiation-invariant feature transform. arXiv preprint arXiv:180409493 (2018)
49. Wu, Y., Ma, W., Gong, M., Su, L., Jiao, L.: A novel point-matching algorithm based on fast sample consensus for image registration. IEEE Geosci. Remote Sens. Lett. **12**(1), 43–47 (2015). https://doi.org/10.1109/LGRS.2014.2325970
50. Li, J., Hu, Q., Ai, M.: Robust feature matching for geospatial images via an affine-invariant coordinate system. Photogram. Rec. **32**(159), 317–331 (2017)
51. Mishkin, D., Matas, J., Perdoch, M.: MODS: fast and robust method for two-view matching. Comput. Vis. Image Underst. **141**, 81–93 (2015). https://doi.org/10.1016/j.cviu.2015.08.005
52. Mishkin, D., Matas, J., Perdoch, M., Lenc, K.: WxBS: wide baseline stereo generalizations. arXiv preprint arXiv:150406603 (2015)
53. Chum, O., Matas, J.: Matching with PROSAC-progressive sample consensus. In: 2005 IEEE Computer Society Conference on Computer Vision and Pattern Recognition, CVPR 2005, pp 220–226. IEEE (2005). https://doi.org/10.1109/CVPR.2005.221
54. Dusmanu, M., et al.: D2-Net: a trainable CNN for joint description and detection of local features. In: 2019 Proceedings of the IEEE Conference on Computer Vision and Pattern Recognition, pp. 8092–8101 (2019)

55. Noh, H., Araujo, A., Sim, J., Weyand, T., Han, B.: Large-scale image retrieval with attentive deep local features. In: Proceedings of the IEEE International Conference on Computer Vision, pp 3456–3465 (2017)
56. X3DOM (2018). https://x3dom.org/
57. Three.js (2019). https://threejs.org/
58. Smithsonian 3D Labs (2019). https://3d.si.edu/labs
59. 3D HOP (2019). http://vcg.isti.cnr.it/3dhop/
60. Hexalab (2019). https://www.hexalab.net/
61. INCEPTION (2018). https://www.inception-project.eu/en. https://www.inception-project.eu/en
62. Champion, E., Rahaman, H.: Survey of 3D digital heritage repositories and platforms. Virtual Archaeol. Rev. **11**(23) (2020). https://doi.org/10.4995/var.2020.13226
63. Fernie, K., et al.: 3D content in Europeana task force. The Hague (2020)
64. Prechtel, N., Münster, S., Kröber, C., Schubert, C., Schietzold, S.: Presenting cultural heritage landscapes – from gis via 3D models to interactive presentation frameworks. ISPRS Ann. Photogr. Remote Sens. Spat. Inf. Sci. **II-5/W1**, 2013 (2013)
65. NIMA – National Imagery and Mapping Agency: Department of Defense World Geodetic System. Technical report, TR 8350.2 (1984)
66. Borda, A., Bowen, J.P.: Smart cities and digital culture: models of innovation. In: Giannini, T., Bowen, J.P. (eds.) Museums and Digital Culture. SSCC, pp. 523–549. Springer, Cham (2019). https://doi.org/10.1007/978-3-319-97457-6_27
67. Nielsen, J., Budiu, R.: Mobile Usability. Academic Press, Salt Lake City (2013)
68. Harrison, R., Flood, D., Duce, D.: Usability of mobile applications: literature review and rationale for a new usability model. J. Interact. Sci. **1**(1), 1 (2013). https://doi.org/10.1186/2194-0827-1-1
69. Hassenzahl, M., Burmester, M., Koller, F.: AttrakDiff: Ein Fragebogen zur Messung wahrgenommener hedonischer und pragmatischer Qualität. In: Ziegler, J., Szwillus (eds.) Mensch & Computer 2003. Interaktion in Bewegung, pp 187–196. B.G. Teubner., Leipzig (2003)
70. Schrepp, M., Hinderks, A., Thomaschewski, J.: Design and evaluation of a short version of the user experience questionnaire (UEQ-S). IJIMAI **4**(6), 103–108 (2017)
71. Laugwitz, B., Held, T., Schrepp, M.: Construction and evaluation of a user experience questionnaire. In: Holzinger, A. (ed.) USAB 2008. LNCS, vol. 5298, pp. 63–76. Springer, Heidelberg (2008). https://doi.org/10.1007/978-3-540-89350-9_6
72. Klamert, K., Münster, S.: Child's play - A literature based survey on gamified tools and methods for fostering public participation in urban planning. In: Parycek, P., et al. (eds.) Electronic Participation. LNCS, pp. 24-33. Springer, Heidelberg (2017). https://doi.org/10.1007/978-3-319-64322-9_3
73. Niebling, F., Maiwald, F., Barthel, K., Latoschik, M.E.: 4D augmented city models, photogrammetric creation and dissemination. In: Münster, S., Friedrichs, K., Niebling, F., Seidel-Grzesinska, A. (eds.) UHDL/DECH -2017. CCIS, vol. 817, pp. 196–212. Springer, Cham (2018). https://doi.org/10.1007/978-3-319-76992-9_12
74. Jylhä, H., Hamari, J.: An icon that everyone wants to click: how perceived aesthetic qualities predict app icon successfulness. Int. J. Hum Comput Stud. **130**, 73–85 (2019)
75. Böhmer, M., Krüger, A.: A study on icon arrangement by smartphone users. In: Proceedings of the SIGCHI Conference on Human Factors in Computing Systems, pp 2137–2146. Association for Computing Machinery (2013). https://doi.org/10.1145/2470654.2481294
76. Lavid Ben Lulu, D., Kuflik, T.: Wise mobile icons organization: apps taxonomy classification using functionality mining to ease apps finding. Mob. Inf. Syst. **2016**, 3083450 (2016). https://doi.org/10.1155/2016/3083450

77. Colley, A., Häkkilä, J.: Exploring finger specific touch screen interaction for mobile phone user interfaces. Paper Presented at the Proceedings of the 26th Australian Computer-Human Interaction Conference on Designing Futures: the Future of Design, Sydney, New South Wales, Australia (2014)

78. Gao, Q., Sun, Q.: Examining the usability of touch screen gestures for older and younger adults. Hum. Factors **57**(5), 835–863 (2015). https://doi.org/10.1177/0018720815581293

79. Noh, H., et al.: Large-scale image retrieval with attentive deep local features. In: IEEE International Conference on Computer Vision, pp. 3456–3465 (2017)

80. Xie, L., et al.: Image classification and retrieval are one. In: Proceedings of the 5th ACM on International Conference on Multimedia Retrieval, pp. 3–10 (2015)

# Comparing Methods to Visualize Orientation of Photographs: A User Study

Jonas Bruschke[1(✉)], Markus Wacker[2], and Florian Niebling[1]

[1] Human-Computer Interaction, University of Würzburg, Würzburg, Germany
{jonas.bruschke,florian.niebling}@uni-wuerzburg.de
[2] University of Applied Sciences Dresden, Dresden, Germany
wacker@informatik.htw-dresden.de
https://www.hci.uni-wuerzburg.de/, https://www.htw-dresden.de/

**Abstract.** We present methods to visualize characteristics in collections of historical photographs, especially focusing on the presentation of spatial position and orientation of photographs in relation to the buildings they depict. The developed methods were evaluated and compared in a user study focusing on their appropriateness to gain insight into specific research questions of art historians: 1) which buildings have been depicted most often in a collection of images, 2) which positions have been preferred by photographers to take pictures of a given building, 3) what is the main perspective of photographers regarding a specific building. To analyze spatial datasets of photographs, we have adapted related methods used in the visualization of fluid dynamics. As these existing visualization methods are not suitable in all photographic situations—especially when a multitude of photographs are pointing into diverging directions—we have developed additional cluster-based approaches that aim to overcome these issues. Our user study shows that the introduced cluster-based visualizations can elicit a better understanding of large photographic datasets concerning real-world research questions in certain situations, while performing comparably well in situations where existing methods are already adequate.

**Keywords:** Spatial browsing · Visualization methods · Architectural history

## 1 Introduction

Photographs of city architecture are an essential source and key objects for historical research in the Digital Humanities (DH) [2]. In the last decades, numerous digital image archives have been set up within digitization projects, making vast numbers of photographs of historical buildings available for research. Previously, studies in Cultural Heritage (CH) often have out of necessity only considered limited time spans and very confined spaces, due to the massive amount of manual labor involved in retrieving and localizing image sources.

Traditional analytic photogrammetry has since increasingly been complemented by digital image processing and analysis. Nowadays, the elaborate process of manual image analysis can be largely automated, resulting in large image collections from

© Springer Nature Switzerland AG 2021
F. Niebling et al. (Eds.): UHDL 2019, CCIS 1501, pp. 129–151, 2021.
https://doi.org/10.1007/978-3-030-93186-5_6

**Fig. 1.** Visualizing distribution of position and orientation of historical photographs in relation to 3D models of architecture.

which geometric information, i.e. 3D models, as well as the spatial position and orientation of photographs can be generated and extracted [25]. This allows for wider research focuses and makes multi-focus analysis of urban development possible [8].

Historians in CH research are now enabled to explore new research directions through statistical analysis due to the availability of multitudes of digitized historical photographs in image repositories. They follow research questions like: Which buildings have been depicted most often in a collection of images? Which positions have been preferred by photographers to take photos of a given building? What is the main perspective of photographers regarding a specific building?

While these research interests have been identified among historians [8], conventional repositories of historical photographs lack features in supporting those specific research. Subsequently, domain experts approach this research manually. With this regard, we develop a browser application that aims to support historians in their research (Fig. 1) [4,5]. To this end, we deal with visualizations of spatial properties of large numbers of images. Such methods have mainly addressed the display of positional data, e.g. using heat maps, that allow users to easily perceive the density of a conglomeration of images on a city map. These existing methods in general omit the orientation of images, and are thus—a result of our research presented in this paper—not beneficial towards exploring research topics targeting photographic perspective. In this work, we present visualization methods that allow for the exploration of positions and orientations of large datasets containing photographic depictions of buildings, enabling historians to investigate spatial research questions such as the ones outlined above.

The remainder of this paper is organized as follows. Section 2 surveys related methods to visualize spatial properties. Visualization methods that are used in the study are described in Sect. 3. Section 4 details characteristics and creation of our (synthetic) dataset. Sections 5 and 6 give an overview of the approach and implementation of our user study. Analysis and discussion of our results are presented in Sect. 7.

## 2    Related Work

Photographs are projective mappings of 3D scenery onto image planes. Image formation can be approximated with a pinhole camera where the position of 3D scene points within the image is given by a simple projective transformation, and the distance between the image plane and the projective point is called focal length. From a visualization view, possible parameters to visualize in an aggregation of photographs are, e.g., the position, rotation, focal length, aperture angle, as well as the 3D scene points that are depicted by the respective photographs.

While each spatialized photograph can be visualized by a camera glyph [25], this quickly results in an incomprehensible clutter on big amounts of data (cf. Fig. 2a). Visualization methods can help to retain an overview of the data and extract characteristics that would have remained concealed otherwise. Many methods already exist that visualize large collections of images with regard to diverse criteria [18,31].

### 2.1 Heat Maps

A very simple and basic visualization method for collections of spatial data is a conventional heat map, also known as attention map. It eases the identification of aggregations of positions [7,14] and provides semantics that are familiar to most users. However, we point out that by using conventional heat maps, only positions, but no orientations are visualized. Whereas most heat maps are two-dimensional on a plane—in spatialized photography often used to visualize aggregations of positions from where photographs have been taken—a special type of heat map is applied to 3D surfaces by projecting spatialized photos onto the 3D geometry [6]. This approach reveals which parts of the geometry occur most often in the photos and thus have been preferably photographed. A more common application domain of this kind of heat map are virtual reality environments to analyze the distribution of visual attention [20]. The main disadvantage of this visualization is that the positions of the photographers are not visualized. Hence, a combination with a conventional heat map may be possible. However, we established in pre-studies that this approach lacks of clear relationships between the hot spots on ground and buildings and was therefore not investigated further.

### 2.2 Vector and Flow Fields

Visualization methods for vector fields and fluid dynamics are capable to visualize both positions and orientations and have already been widely explored for a broad range of applications [3,12,13,26]. They range from simple representations of vectors by glyphs over streamlines to dense texture-based approaches. Particle-based techniques are mostly used to visualize the advection of massless particles along the vector field. Animated representations of flow offer some benefits over static views, since the user can better trace the various directions towards a target and thus, the orientation information can be interpreted more easily [29,30].

A structured vector field is basically a grid of positions each having a vector with a direction. An aggregation of spatialized photographs can be reduced to a vector field by summing all photographs that fall into a common grid cell, where the vector will point to the average direction of photos of the cell and its length correlates to the number of photos.

The main characteristic of visualizations based on vector fields is that only one direction can be represented at each point in the field. In our use case however, there can be multiple photographs at one point (or close to each other) pointing in different directions. This violates the basic assumption of a vector field visualization. Reducing multiple directions to a single vector by averaging them, basically eliminates the variety of photographs pointing in different directions. For example, considering two main perspectives of an collection of photographs, the vectors tend to point in the more dominant direction (cf. Fig. 2d). If the photos are unfortunately distributed, this can even result in vector fields that partly point inwards (cf. Fig. 2e). An approach by Urness et al. [28] aims to solve this issue by layering multiple vector field visualizations. However, their approach is limited to a very small number of different vector fields making this approach inappropriate to visualize a potentially large number of directions as in our case.

### 2.3  Cluster-Based Approaches

Our aim is to visualize multiple directions of an aggregation of photographs, which is challenging utilizing vector field and flow visualization methods due to the reasons described above. Sometimes, if the space the data originates from is not sufficient to visualize all parameters, additional dimensions might be introduced. For example, to visualize the movement of geospatial 2D positions on a map, the data can be presented in a 3D space, where the trajectory of movement raises above the map according to the time component [11, 17]. While this is a suitable option for time series, layering multiple directions often is not easily comprehensible.

Another option is the clustering of data. When visualizing geo-referenced images or other data on maps, clustering is a common approach to display data without cluttering [10, 22]. The clusters are often represented by a marker visualizing the number of objects in the cluster. The markers may vary in color and size or may incorporate a representative image or tag.

Directional data, i.e. trajectories with origins and destinations that implicitly have directions, can also be clustered in multiple ways such as edge-bundling [1, 32, 33]. However, photographs may not have a destination in terms of movement, only an origin and a direction. Instead of using an image or tag, a cluster can also be represented by a more complex glyph, i.e. a chart that is able to visualize characteristics of the data that is part of the cluster [3]. In addition, the clustering leads to an adequate placement of these glyphs leaving space in between to prevent overlapping. Hyougo et al. present an approach to visualize aggregated directional movement data as cluster glyphs [9]. The glyph is divided into several segments by direction of movement and the extends of the segments depend on the distances of the movements.

## 3  Rationale and Proposed Visualization Methods

For datasets of spatialized photographs, the parameters to be visualized are both position and orientation of the camera with respect to the depicted buildings and the part of the photographed scene. In city photography, the orientation of a photograph is primarily defined by the pan angle of the respective camera. The tilt angle plays a rather small role, since most often the camera will be aligned close to the horizontal plane. For the same reason, the roll angle also has only a minimal influence. For reasons of simplicity and since in our real-world dataset of historical photographs we did not encounter any significant variance, the respective visualization methods only consider the pan angles. Tilt and roll angles are omitted. The focal length can only be approximated from historical photographs, is only of little interest and, therefore, omitted as well. Simple methods for visualizing aggregations of image data, such as e.g. heat maps, only consider the projection points of an image, i.e. the position of the respective photographers. Since positions and orientations can be represented by 3D vectors, methods for vector field and flow visualization are reasonable candidates as starting points for the visualization of aggregations of photographs.

Hence, our first step was the adaption of existing methods, namely heat maps as well as existing flow visualization methods such as glyph- and particle-based vector field visualization techniques. In addition, we have introduced three cluster-based visualization methods that allow the simultaneous aggregated display of both position and orientation for a large number of spatialized photographs. In a user study, these new approaches are compared with four of the existing methods on how they perform in various use cases derived from research questions of historians. Although heat maps are not able to visualize orientation, they are part of the study as a baseline tool, since it is the only method that has been occasionally used by the target group. As a common basis, a color scale is applied to all methods to visualize the number of photographs at respective positions. In the employed scale, bluish/cold colors represent low and reddish/warm colors represent high values. Of course, these values can also be changed and investigated further [24], which is not a subject of the presented research.

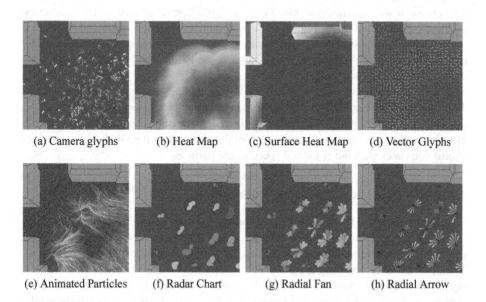

(a) Camera glyphs    (b) Heat Map    (c) Surface Heat Map    (d) Vector Glyphs

(e) Animated Particles    (f) Radar Chart    (g) Radial Fan    (h) Radial Arrow

**Fig. 2.** Proposed visualization methods, which have been applied to the exact same set of photographs pointing towards points of interest at the top and the lower left building.

### 3.1 Heat Map and Surface Heat Map

As a first method, we adopted a conventional *Heat Map* (Fig. 2b). Though it can only be used to communicate aggregations of positions, this is a useful visualization method regarding some of our experts application domain use cases. We included this method as a baseline comparison for the efficiency of other method's abilities to convey positional information.

We also implemented the *Surface Heat Map* (Fig. 2c) due to its ability to reveal points of interest directly on buildings. To compute the map as a texture to the geometry, we take into account position and orientation of the photographs, as well as the view frustum of the respective cameras and surrounding building geometry. The latter leads to shadows on the map when geometry occludes other buildings or parts of buildings.

### 3.2 Vector Glyphs and Animated Particles

Methods for vector field and flow visualization are sufficient and suitable in many of our use cases. The aim of our study is not to test a wide variety of visualizations, since this has already been done extensively [12,16]. Hence, two representatives of vector field and flow visualization have been chosen to compete with the others in this user study.

Our *Vector Glyphs* visualization method (Fig. 2d) is based on a jittered grid. For each grid point, the average orientation of all photographs in its vicinity is computed (keeping in mind the disadvantages described in Sect. 2.2). The vector is represented by a glyph, i.e. a wedge. The appearance of this glyph depends on additional parameters: (a) the color correlates to the number of photos contributing to the vector and (b) the size is affected by the distance of the grid point to the nearest photo in relation to the vicinity radius. The larger the number of photos around the specific grid point, the higher we depict the color intensity of the glyph.

As a second representation, we have chosen an animated, particle-based technique. The *Animated Particles* (Fig. 2e) is based upon a vector field computed similar as above, this time on a regular grid. This is required, since the vector field is encoded as a normal map that is used to compute the animation of the particles on the GPU. The number of photos correlates with the color and speed of the particles.

### 3.3 Radar Chart, Radial Fan, and Radial Arrow

Finally, we introduce three cluster-based methods. In our approach, a cluster is represented by a chart with the aim to make the dominant direction of the respective cameras easily recognizable without neglecting the whole spectrum of different directions. Thus, two possibly opposing main perspectives should be distinguishable. For clustering the photographs, we used the hierarchical single-linkage clustering algorithm [21]. Depending on the user's view on the scene, the clusters of a higher level of the hierarchy tree are shown with increasing distance. For each cluster, the full 360° circle around the center of the cluster is divided into 16 discrete, equally distributed direction vectors. The direction vectors of the photographs that are part of the cluster are then mapped to these discrete direction vectors proportionately, resulting in discretized vectors of different length.

Our first proposal for visualizing the resulting vectors is the *Radar Chart* (Fig. 2f), where discrete direction vectors are interpolated to form a bubble shape. The biggest deflection of the bubble shape corresponds to the main direction, with the variance of the photographers' directions indicated by its width. The color of the chart correlates with the number of images within the cluster.

The *Radial Fan* (Fig. 2g) visualization method is similar to the *Radar Chart*. Here, each discrete direction vector is represented by a segment, with the longest segment indicating the main direction. The color coding as well as the size of the segments correspond to the number of photographs contributing to each particular segment.

The *Radial Arrow* (Fig. 2h) is basically the same as the *Radial Fan*, apart from the shape of the fans, which are arrow-shaped in this case. This hopefully enables a better recognition of orientation, as in a pretest it was found that a small subset of users were interpreting *Radial Fan* glyphs to point in the opposite direction.

## 4  Dataset Synthesis

An empirical user study that compares our seven selected methods of visualization requires hundreds of stimuli with a great variety to obtain valid results. Our prototype application containing real-world historical photographs features only a relatively small number of spatialized photos at the moment. More extensive real-world datasets could be used, such as the YFCC100M dataset [27]. However, real-world datasets, especially publicly available ones, have major drawbacks: The metadata for spatialized photos often contains only the position, but no orientation which is a key parameter for our visualization methods. Another prohibitive drawback is that there is insufficient ground truth concerning the points of interest in a photo, which also would have to be generated and corrected manually. Finally, a specific dataset has to be analyzed carefully with respect to user bias, i.e. real-world datasets often do not contain sufficient variability in the depicted building situations. While selecting and extracting possible stimuli, it has to be ensured that they do not feature only similar or even identical patterns.

In order to meet the requirements of a proper user study, a generative data model [23] has been developed to synthesize a huge amount of unbiased stimuli. This approach ensures the generality of the data, since we want to test these visualization methods on all possible situations of photographs including those that do not occur in our current real-world dataset. An additional benefit of this approach is the exact knowledge of the ground truth for the evaluation process.

### 4.1  Imaging Situations and Phenomena

As a first step, we identified *imaging situations* in photographic datasets. We define an imaging situation as "specific positions, shapes and surrounding of buildings, and a collection of associated photographic images, which are spatialized, i.e. the exact

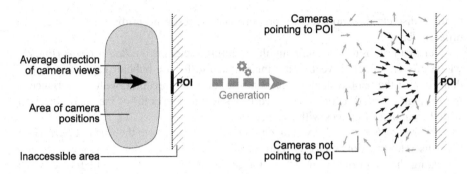

**Fig. 3.** An imaging phenomenon (left) is used as template to generate virtual imaging situations (right).

position and orientation of the camera are known" [19]. Many of them show recurring patterns that were broken down to distinctive features including a recognizable position and orientation of the photographs and the arrangement of building geometries. By these features, the imaging situations could be classified and transferred to *imaging phenomena* that we refer to as abstract formulations of imaging situations [19].

An imaging phenomenon consists of a small number of **phenomenon primitives** (cf. Fig. 3):

- *Areas of Camera Positions* (AoCP), i.e. polygons to describe the areas where photographers were standing when taking photos,
- *Points of Interest* (POI), i.e. areas of varying extent that the photographers were trying to capture and are usually located at buildings,
- *Inaccessible Areas* where additional building geometry and other items are located that potentially blocked the photographer's way or view.

We point out that AoCPs are related to one or more POIs. This relationship is visualized by an arrow that acts as a representation for the cameras looking at the corresponding POI.

The identified phenomena have been grouped into six primary categories:

| | |
|---|---|
| *Detached* | Single, freestanding buildings or monuments |
| *Facade* | POIs at one side of a building |
| *Corner* | POIs at two sides of a building |
| *Square* | Town square or surrounding buildings |
| *Gallery* | Street-like situations, POIs down the road |
| *Bridge* | More distant spots photographed from a bridge |

A secondary categorization criterion considers the number of AoCPs as well as the number and arrangement of POIs:

| | |
|---|---|
| *Simple* | One AoCP and one POI |
| *Similar POIs* | One AoCP, multiple POIs close to each other |
| *Similar AoCPs* | One POI photographed from multiple AoCPs |
| *Corresponding* | Multiple AoCPs with corresponding POIs |
| *Opposite* | One AoCP with multiple opposite POIs |
| *Fuzzy* | Broad or fuzzy POI, e.g. a skyline |

Combinations of the categories result in a set of 32 imaging phenomena [19]. Figure 4 shows a selection of these. While this list of phenomena covers observed and deduced imaging situations, few and uncommon scenarios might be missing, but should have little influence on the study results.

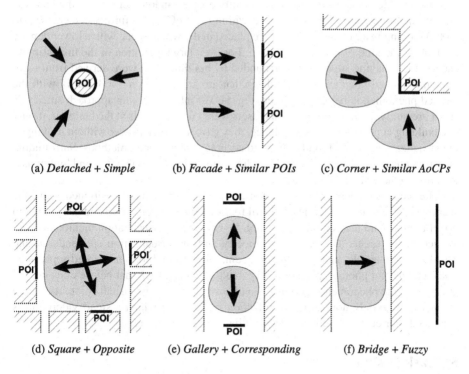

(a) *Detached + Simple*      (b) *Facade + Similar POIs*      (c) *Corner + Similar AoCPs*

(d) *Square + Opposite*      (e) *Gallery + Corresponding*      (f) *Bridge + Fuzzy*

**Fig. 4.** Some imaging phenomena of 32 phenomena in total [19].

## 4.2 Stimuli Generator

In order to use the imaging phenomena as templates for the automatic generation of stimuli, the phenomena have been transferred into SVG files. A command line tool has

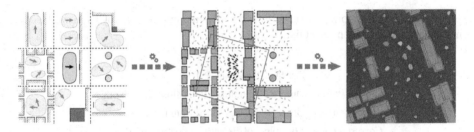

**Fig. 5.** 3 × 3 matrix of phenomena used to generate additional, contextual building geometry. The render camera looks down onto the virtual imaging situation with random position and angle (red). Finally, a visualization method is applied and the scene gets rendered. (Color figure online)

been specially developed for the generation process. It reads a template SVG file and produces a variety of virtual imaging situations (Fig. 3), i.e. 3D scenes of very abstract city models. To achieve a good variance and to reduce repetition to a minimum, several parameters are randomized: (a) multiple building blocks are randomly positioned within the inaccessible area, (b) the AoCPs are shifted by a random degree, (c) the cameras (several hundreds) are randomly placed within the AoCPs, (d) further cameras (up to 2,000) looking in a random direction are placed in the whole scene with a lower density to create some kind of background noise. For even larger variation of the final stimuli, each virtual imaging situation is surrounded by buildings that were derived from eight randomly picked phenomenon templates that are arranged in a 3 × 3 matrix with the queried phenomenon being the center (Fig. 5). We introduced this approach since in a small pre-study, we have observed that users were guessing POIs at the building, if only one building appears in the scene. Hence, they gave a correct answer without looking at the visualization, i.e. we found only good accuracy values for all methods. Surrounding buildings ensure the lack of isolated buildings indicating the (right) POI and higher user attention to the visualization method.

The scene is rendered by a top-down camera that is randomly positioned above the scene (within certain boundaries, but still focusing the relevant areas) and has a random orientation around the depth axis (cf. Fig. 5). One of our visualization methods is then applied to the scene. The building geometry and the visualization are rendered and saved as a bitmap file, meta information containing ground truth are stored separately. The cameras and photographs are not visible to the user, such that he/she does not get any hints to the phenomenon primitives and has to focus on the visualization. *Animated Particles* is the only non-static visualization method, for which a small video clip is generated. For our user study, 6,195 stimuli have been generated.

## 5   Task Design

With regard to the use cases and research questions, we have derived three tasks for the user study. During the execution of the study, users are presented with static or animated renderings shown in Fig. 5 right, without the possibility to adjust the viewpoint of the scene. Users then have to interactively insert the phenomenon primitives, AoCP, POI and perspective, by drawing into the presented renderings, according to the task. In the analysis phase, user input is compared to the ground truth elements to determine accuracy measures. The following tasks presented to the users are taken from real-world research questions of the target group of architectural historians.

## 5.1  User Instructions

*Task 1: Identifying Points of Interest.* An important information to know when browsing photographs is what are the pictured objects and which of them have been photographed the most. In the first task, the user has to identify these points of interest (POI) regardless from where they have been photographed. Since the POIs can vary in size, we have decided that the user should not just click points, but draw one or more lines where he/she thinks the POIs are situated in the scene. Since we have a top-down view and are interested in surfaces, we can limit the interaction to lines. *Gallery* is the only phenomenon where the POIs are not located on buildings, but somewhere down the street that can even be outside the generated image. In this case, the user is supposed to draw a line near the edge of the scene image to indicate the direction the photographers were looking at, which is later also explained during the training phase of the user study.

*Task 2: Locating Preferred Photographers' Positions.* The second task consists of extracting those areas where the majority of photographers stood to take photos (AoCP). For this information, only the positions of photographs are relevant, but no orientations of the photographs. The user is instructed to roughly outline those areas by drawing one or more polygons.

*Task 3: Finding the Main Perspectives.* The final task combines Task 1 and Task 2. For finding the main perspectives, the POIs and the corresponding AoCPs need to be identified. To this end, we want the user to draw one or more arrows from AoCPs towards the respective POIs.

## 5.2  Measure and Accuracy

To gain an accuracy measure for the analysis, the recorded user inputs are compared to the ground truth elements. This measure is either based on the distance of pixel sets (lines or polygons) or on the angle between vectors of an user input and a ground truth element. Both, distance and angle, are mapped to a weighting value $\omega_d$ or $\omega_\alpha$, resp. in $[0, 1]$, for further computation steps. Each of the three tasks has a different computation process to meet the requirements for the accuracy measure with respect to the aggregation of multiple user inputs and ground truth elements.

The requirements to the design of the weighting values are: If a user input exactly matches the ground truth, the measure (distance or angle) results in 0 and is considered as most accurate, i.e. $\omega_d(0), \omega_\alpha(0) = 1$. If the distance or the angle is above a certain threshold, the input is considered to be completely wrong, i.e. $\omega_d(d_{threshold}), \omega_\alpha(\alpha_{threshold}) = 0$. Usually, user inputs will not match the ground truth exactly. But if they are close enough, they should still be considered as accurate. To this end, we have chosen a slight exponential (1.7) instead of a linear falloff, where a measured distance below a specified tipping point distance results in a better accuracy than in the linear case (cf. Fig. 6). This leads to the distance measure in Eq. (1). We set

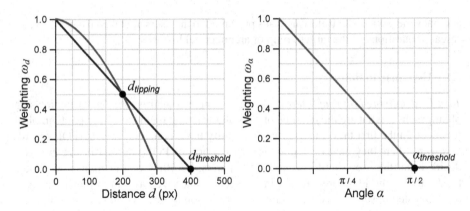

**Fig. 6.** Left: Mapping of distance $d$ to weighting measure $\omega_d$ with an exponential falloff (red) compared to a linear falloff (blue), with $d_{tipping} = 200$ and $d_{threshold} = 400$. Right: Linear mapping of angle $\alpha$ to weighting $\omega_\alpha$, with $\alpha_{threshold} = \pi/2$. (Color figure online)

$d_{tipping} = 200$, $d_{threshold} = 400$ for Task 1 and 3 and $d_{tipping} = 250$, $d_{threshold} = 600$ for Task 2.

$$\omega_d(d) = 1 - \min\left\{ \frac{(d/d_{tipping})^{1.7}}{d_{threshold}/d_{tipping}}, 1 \right\} \tag{1}$$

The weighting value of an angle $\alpha$ between two vectors $\mathbf{v}$ and $\mathbf{w}$ is determined by Eq. (2). In our user study, we set $\alpha_{threshold} = \pi/2$.

$$\omega_\alpha(\mathbf{v}, \mathbf{w}) = 1 - \min\left\{ \frac{\arccos(\hat{\mathbf{v}} \cdot \hat{\mathbf{w}})}{\alpha_{threshold}}, 1 \right\} \tag{2}$$

**Task 1: Identifying Points of Interest.** For Task 1, two sets of lines (user input and ground truth) are compared. As a first step to measure the accuracy, we calculate the Hausdorff distance $d_H$ between each drawn user input $P_{user}$ to the ground truth POIs $P_{truth}$. If $\omega_d(d_H) > 0$, we assign the line sets to each other. For the special phenomenon *Gallery* we construct two vectors: each starting from the centroid $C_{aocp}$ of the associated AoCP of the ground truth data and ending at the midpoint $M_{poi}$ of the ground truth POI or the midpoint $M_{user}$ of the user input, respectively. From these two vectors we calculate $\omega_\alpha$. If $\omega_\alpha > 0$, the line sets are assigned to each other.

For further accuracy calculations, we have to take into account possible user inputs which differ from the ground truth elements but are drawn with the right intention and are considered to be correct, e.g. staggered inputs instead of continuous ones. Hence in a second step, from the assigned user input lines to each ground truth POI a list of all possible combinations of merged user lines $P_{comb}$ is calculated. Two lines are merged by connecting their closest endpoints. From this list, again the Hausdorff distance to the ground truth line is calculated and the minimum is used to calculate the distance measure $\omega_i$ of the i-th ground truth POI $p_i$ according to Eq. (1):

$$\omega_i = \omega_d\big( \min\{d_H(x, p_i) \mid x \in P_{comb}\} \big).$$

For the *Gallery* phenomenon, the user lines are not merged. Instead the weighting measures of the angles of the assigned user lines computed in the first step are averaged to obtain a single accuracy measure for the respective ground truth POI.

$$\omega_i = \frac{1}{|K|} \sum_{k \in K} \omega_\alpha (\overrightarrow{C_{aocp}M_{poi}}, \overrightarrow{C_{aocp}M_k})$$

where $K$ is the set of assigned user input lines ($K \subseteq P_{user}$).

The last step to an accuracy value averages the weighting measures of all ground truth POIs (Eq. (3)). If there are some user inputs that could not be assigned to any ground truth POI ($P_{nonassigned} \subseteq P_{user}$), i.e. completely wrong, they impact the final result negatively.

$$Accuracy = \frac{|P_{user}| - |P_{nonassigned}|}{|P_{user}|} \cdot \frac{1}{|P_{truth}|} \sum_{i=1}^{|P_{truth}|} \omega_i \qquad (3)$$

**Task 2: Locating Preferred Photographers' Positions.** At this task, the user is requested to draw one or multiple polygons to indicate the AoCPs. In contrast to Task 1, the user inputs and ground truth elements are not assigned to each other in the first instance. Sometimes, if two AoCPs are close to each other, they are sometimes not always clearly distinguishable in the final visualization. Hence, the user might draw only one big polygon which is considered to be correct in this case. To this end, we first generate two lists of possible combinations of merged user polygons $B_{user}$ as well as ground truth polygons $A_{truth}$, respectively. Two polygons are merged by computing their convex hull. Second, we compare these lists of polygons using the formula of the Hausdorff distance, where the distance function for a pair of polygons is again the Hausdorff distance:

$$f_d(X,Y) = \max \left\{ \sup_{x \in X} \inf_{y \in Y} d_H(x,y), \sup_{y \in Y} \inf_{x \in X} d_H(x,y) \right\}.$$

From the generated list of distances, we take the minimum distance. Finally, the minimum distance is mapped to the accuracy value according to Eq. (1):

$$Accuracy = \omega_d \left( \min \left\{ f_d(A_i, B_j) \mid A_i \in A_{truth}, B_j \in B_{user} \right\} \right).$$

**Task 3: Finding the Main Perspectives.** At Task 3, the user is asked to draw arrows from AoCPs towards associated POIs. The accuracy is again computed in several steps: We start by assigning each user arrow to one (or more) ground truth set(s), i.e. AoCP and corresponding POI. If the user arrow starts inside a ground truth AoCP, a corresponding ground truth arrow is generated as the vector from the start point $A_{user}$ of the user arrow to the midpoint $M_{poi}$ of the respective ground truth POI. Otherwise, if the user arrow does not start inside any AoCP, it will be compared to vectors that start at the centroid $C_{aocp}$ of each ground truth AoCP to the midpoint of the respective POI.

$$\vec{AB}_{user} = B_{user} - A_{user},$$

$$\vec{AB}_{truth} = \begin{cases} M_{poi} - A_{user}, & \text{if } A_{user} \in aocp, \\ M_{poi} - C_{aocp}, & \text{otherwise}, \end{cases}$$

where $B_{user}$ the end point of the user arrow and $aocp$ is the polygon of the ground truth set. The assignment also depends on the angle between $\vec{AB}_{user}$ and $\vec{AB}_{truth}$. A user arrow is assigned to a ground truth set, if the $A_{user}$ starts inside the ground truth AoCP and $\vec{AB}_{user} \cdot \vec{AB}_{truth} > 0.5$. If a user arrow could not be assigned to any ground truth set yet, it will be compared again against the ground truth sets and gets assigned, if $\vec{AB}_{user} \cdot \vec{AB}_{truth} > 0$. This two-step check is necessary to prevent user arrows bleeding into neighboring ground truth sets with similar directions.

In the next step, for each ground truth set a weighting measure $\omega_i$ is computed by averaging the weights of all assigned user arrows, each composed of an angle measure $\omega_\alpha$ and an additional distance measure $\omega_d$. If the start point of the user arrow is outside the AoCP polygon, the closest distance to the polygon is computed ($f_d(A_{user_k}, aocp_i)$) and used to calculate $\omega_d$. Otherwise, if the point is inside, the distance is 0, ergo $\omega_d = 1$.

$$\omega_i = \frac{1}{|K|} \sum_{k \in K} \omega_\alpha(k, \vec{AB}_{truth}) \cdot \omega_d\left(f_d\left(A_{user_k}, aocp_i\right)\right),$$

where $K$ is the set of assigned user arrows ($K \subseteq \vec{AB}_{user}$) to the i-th ground truth set.

In the last step, the weighting measures of all ground truth sets are averaged to compute the overall accuracy while also considering user arrows that could not be assigned to any ground truth arrow in the first step (cf. Eq. (3)).

## 6    Study Implementation

### 6.1    Participant Pool

In total, 62 university students enrolled in Human-Computer-Interaction BSc and MSc degree programmes participated in an online experiment and received course credits in return. Domain experts were queried in qualitative pre-studies, but the group of art historians specializing in architectural history is in general too small to generate meaningful quantitative results. Historians thus aided in the preparation of the user study to ensure participants where instructed appropriately in a training phase to generate meaningful results even from a user group consisting of non-experts. The participants (45 female, 17 male) were aged between 18 and 40 ($\varnothing = 21.4$) and had no uncorrected visual impairments.

### 6.2    Timing and Training

An application has been written specifically for our experiment using web technologies to be used as an online study during the contact restrictions caused by the COVID-19 pandemic. This has also the advantage to address more users than in a study conducted on site in the future. Before the actual test starts, the user gets a general introduction to the context of this study and the seven visualization methods. In a following tutorial section, the user learns about all three tasks and should get familiar with the input modes for POIs and AoCPs. Each task is explained in two steps: In the first step, the very basics of the tasks are covered. The ground truth is visible in a stimulus that the user has to redraw to get familiar with the interaction pattern. The user can evaluate his/her inputs by unveiling the accuracy on the spot. In the second step, the user has to test his/her skills on a stimulus, where no ground truth is visible this time. The user is also taught that there can potentially be multiple POIs or AoCPs to be identified. After auditing the inputs for accuracy, the user can retry, before he/she continues with the tutorial for the next task.

After completing the tutorial, the real user test starts. The test is carried out in three chunks, one for each task, in random order. Each chunk has 28 stimuli that are randomly picked from the generated dataset. However, it is guaranteed that the visualization methods are equally distributed, i.e. each chunk has four stimuli of each method, and no stimulus occurs twice. For each stimulus, the time is logged when the data gets presented and when the user proceeds to the next one. In total, the study takes about 20–30 min. One user will go through 84 stimuli in total.

# 7   Results and Discussion

In total, 5,208 stimuli were tested by the participants, 1,736 of each task. The statistical difference in mean between two sets of samples has been obtained utilizing the Student's $t$-test. Values of $p < 0.05$ are considered as significant (*) and $p < 0.01$ as very significant (***) as marked in the respective figures accordingly. For each task, all visualization methods have been compared to each other by their measures and checked for significant differences.

The general outcome of this study is that both cluster-based methods *Radial Fan* and *Radial Arrow* outscore the other visualization methods in some situations, while not being significantly worse otherwise. As expected, both heat map visualizations have mostly bad results due to their inabilities to visualize orientations.

## 7.1   Outliers and Obstacles

However, we observed some problems that required a filtering of the data: (a) The time the users needed to complete the study (without tutorial section) varied quite a lot ranging from 5–31 min. This is also reflected in the recorded times of each stimulus, i.e. the time a user needed to perceive the stimulus and make some inputs. We observed that especially those, who were rushing through the user study, e.g. only very few seconds per stimulus, often made arbitrary inputs taking the study not seriously enough. This especially applies to two participants, who have been removed completely from the results. Others took quite a long time to go through the study, sometimes up to a minute per stimulus, and were obviously not very focused and probably distracted by other things. This is certainly one of the disadvantages of an unsupervised online study. However, the advantages described in Sect. 6.2 outperform these shortcomings. For the latter however, we could not observe a negative impact on the results. (b) Some users misunderstood the tasks they had to accomplish. Although the respective task description was present all the time, some users tried to draw polygons around AoCPs in Task 1 and, vice versa, lines for POIs in Task 2 resulting in bad accuracy values. In those cases, we had to reject the whole chunk of the misunderstood task (8 chunks in total).

Another observation is that users had difficulties to match the amount of requested POIs or AoCPs. This is especially the case if there are multiple POIs, in particular *Similar POIs*, *Corresponding*, and *Opposite* phenomena. *Square* phenomena can even have up to four POIs. Indicating the wrong number of POIs affects the accuracy negatively. Such effects are reflected in the results of the respective phenomena in Task 1 and 3. This is a general conflict between having precise user instructions versus granting the user some freedom of choice. On the one hand, the task description asks the user to identify the most dominant POIs. How many of them are considered as dominant is, however, up to the user. On the other hand, asking the user to indicate a specific number of POIs would have made the methods less comparable to each other. If a method is not capable to visualize hints to multiple POIs, the user should not be forced to do more inputs as he/she thinks are suitable.

### 7.2    Task 1: Identifying Points of Interest

The expected outcomes of Task 1 are that the *Heat Map* will show bad results, while *Surface Heat Map* should be amongst the best, since it clearly indicates the POIs. At this task, some users misunderstood the task as described above. After eliminating those, 1,595 of 1,736 stimuli remained.

The results of the *Heat Map* confirms our expectation (Fig. 7 left). However, the *Surface Heat Map* is significantly better than only the *Vector Glyphs*. The *Radial Arrow* performs best, being very significantly better than all other methods, except the *Radial Fan* that is second being (very) significantly better than *Vector Glyphs* and *Radar Chart*.

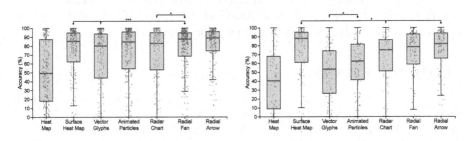

**Fig. 7.** Task 1, identifying POIs: Accuracy results grouped by visualization method unfiltered (left) and filtered by *Similar POIs* and *Opposite* phenomena (right) showing selected significance values. *Heat Map* is very significantly worst, as expected. Analyzed over all phenomena, *Radial Arrow is very significantly better than most of the other methods*, *Surface Heat Map* and *Radial Fan* are very significantly better than *Vector Glyphs*, *Radial Fan* is significantly better than *Radar Chart* (left). In *Similar POIs* and *Opposite* phenomena, *Surface Heat Map*, *Radial Fan*, and *Radial Arrow* are very significantly better than *Vector Glyphs* and *Animated Particles* (right).

Looking at the characteristics of POIs and AoCPs, the results are more diverse. *Simple* and *Similar AoCPs* phenomena have in general quite good results, since there is only one POI to indicate. User inputs for phenomena with *Fuzzy* POIs are not very accurate by default. Significant differences between the visualization methods occur within *Similar POIs* and *Opposite* phenomena (Fig. 7 right). Here, the cluster-based methods outstand: *Surface Heat Map*, *Radial Fan*, and *Radial Arrow* are very significantly better than *Vector Glyphs* and *Animated Particles*. Also, the *Radar Chart* is very significantly better than the *Vector Glyphs*, but significantly worse than *Surface Heat Map* and *Radial Arrow*. The *Vector Glyphs* being significantly worse than the *Animated Particles* are actually as bad as the *Heat Map*, i.e. no significant difference. This is due to the fact that *Vector Glyphs* and *Animated Particles* often lead to confusion in these cases, since the averaging of diverging directions can result in odd vectors that are the basis for these two methods.

A peculiarity of the cluster-based methods is that the distribution and size of the clusters depend on the distribution of the photos and the viewing distance of the user, i.e. the virtual camera looking at it. When generating the stimuli, the amount of photos in neighboring AoCPs and the amount of photos looking at different POIs are equally distributed. However, the positioning within the AoCPs is random. Hence, if the photos are unfortunately distributed, an aggregation of photos might be represented by, e.g., three clusters, while another aggregation with the same amount of photos is represented by only one cluster (cf. Fig. 8). Consequently, the three clusters are less pronounced and many users made their inputs only at the apparently more dominant POIs. Here lie still some aspects for future research to find even better visualization methods.

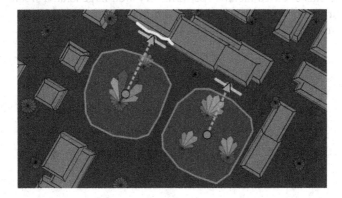

**Fig. 8.** Example of *Radial Fan* visualization with distinctly different clusters including user input (yellow) and ground truth for area of camera positions (blue area) and positions of interest (green lines). (Color figure online)

### 7.3   Task 2: Locating Preferred Photographers' Positions

In Task 2, only the position of the photographs (instead of orientation) is relevant. Hence, the *Heat Map* is supposed to show its strengths, while the *Surface Heat Map* should perform poorly, since it should give no real hints from where the POIs have been photographed. After filtering out the outliers, 1,652 stimuli remain.

As presumed, the *Surface Heat Map* has very bad accuracy results (Fig. 9), as users could only guess where respective AoCPs are located. In contrast, all other methods perform pretty well. Still, there are significant differences between them: The *Heat Map* has the most accurate results, as it is significantly better than all other methods, even very significantly better than the cluster-based methods. The *Radar Chart* is (very) significantly worse than the *Vector Glyphs*, *Animated Particles*, and *Radial Fan*. There are no notable differences throughout the various phenomena categories. The few bad results are mainly due to users who indicated not only the queried AoCPs with a big number of photos, but sometimes also tiny hot spots that randomly occur in the background noise.

There is, however, a notable difference in the user behavior regarding the cluster-based methods: some users tend to outline only single clusters instead of the whole AoCP, which is usually represented by multiple clusters (depending on viewing distance). This reveals that these users see neighboring clusters as not related to each other, which leads to slightly worse results compared to the other methods. In general, different aggregation radii of clusters might be interpreted differently. Since the degree of clustering is controlled by the distance of the camera rendering the scene and stimuli have been generated with random distances, clusters feature various sizes and radii. However, the cluster-based methods perform very well in general, a significant difference in accuracy between stimuli of small and big cluster sizes can not be identified. Yet, optimizing clustering might enhance them further.

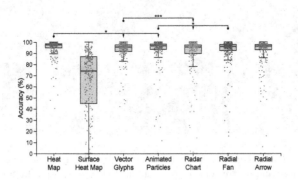

**Fig. 9.** Task 2, locating preferred photographers' positions: Accuracy results grouped by visualization method showing selected significance values. *Heat Map* is (very) significantly best, as expected, and only presented for comparison. *Radar Chart* is very significantly worse than *Vector Glyphs* and significantly worse than *Animated Particles*. The other clustered methods *Radial Fan* and *Radial Arrow* are comparable to *Vector Glyphs*.

## 7.4   Task 3: Finding the Main Perspectives

To accomplish this task, it is important to identify the AoCPs and their related POIs. Hence, both *Heat Map* and *Surface Heat Map* are expected to score badly, while the other methods may feature similar results as for Task 1. In total, 1,652 out of 1,736 stimuli remain after removing the outliers.

The results show indeed bad scores for *Heat Map* and *Surface Heat Map* (Fig. 10 left). *Surface Heat Map* is very significantly better than *Heat Map*, since hot spots at building facades give at least some hints from where they might have been photographed, whereas guessing the main direction from a heat map is less often correct. However, both are very significantly worse than the other methods. Their results show similar patterns as in Task 1. *Radial Arrow* is significantly better than *Animated Particles* and very significantly better than *Vector Glyphs* and *Radar Chart*. Again, *Radial Fan* also shows good results scoring (very) significantly better than *Vector Glyphs* and *Radar Chart*. When looking only at *Similar POIs* and *Opposite* phenomena (Fig. 10 right), *Radial Fan* and *Radial Arrow* are showing their strengths both being very significantly better than *Vector Glyphs* and *Animated Particles*. The *Vector Glyphs* are even significantly worse than the *Surface Heat Map*. While for the other phenomena, there are no significant differences between *Animated Particles*, *Radial Fan*, and *Radial Arrow*.

Regarding the cluster-based methods, a similar observation is made as in Task 2: some users understand the cluster as not related to each other. The result is that these users drew arrows from each cluster towards the respective POIs. Though, this does not particularly impact the final accuracy value, since all user arrows that have been assigned to a ground truth arrow are averaged.

We have also noticed that a few users interpreted the main directions indicated by the visualization methods in the very opposite direction. This specifically occurs at

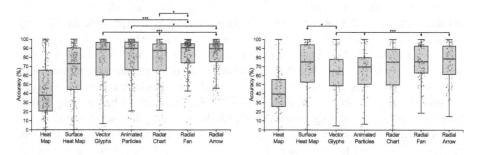

**Fig. 10.** Task 3, finding the main perspectives: Accuracy results grouped by visualization method unfiltered (left) and filtered by *Similar POIs* and *Opposite* phenomena (right) showing selected significance values. *Heat Map* is very significantly worst, as expected. Analyzed over all phenomena, *Surface Heat Map* is very significantly worse than the other methods, excluding *Heat Map*. *Radial Arrow* is very significantly better than both *Radar Chart* and *Vector Glyphs*, *Radial Fan* is very significantly better than *Vector Glyphs* and still significantly better than *Radar Chart* (left). In *Similar POIs* and *Opposite* phenomena, *Radial Fan* and *Radial Arrow* are both very significantly better than *Vector Glyphs* and *Animated Particles* (right).

visualizations of the *Vector Glyphs*. Obviously, the chosen type of vector glyph was not always clear enough for these users. But also a very few visualizations of *Animated Particles* as well as *Radial Fan* have been interpreted incorrectly with opposite directions. This behavior also happened to a smaller extent at Task 1. But interestingly, these users have mistaken not all, but only a few visualizations of the respective type within their session.

# 8 Conclusion

In Cultural Heritage research, photographs play an important role especially in understanding the urban development and the photographic culture of past times. The spatial information of these photographs can be used to answer specific research questions of historians. Visualizations can help to better extract this information in particular from aggregations of photographs and to get statistical insights. Existing visualization methods can visualize the positions and orientations, but none of them were satisfying in all situations. Conventional heat maps only visualize aggregations of positions, and methods from vector field visualization and flow dynamics are not able to visualize the variance of multiple directions at a certain position. Hence, we developed two cluster-based methods capable of communicating this information to the user.

In order to generate a huge amount of stimuli for a user comparison of visualization methods, we analyzed real-world datasets for recurring imaging situations, derived imaging phenomena from those, and constructed randomized, synthetic imaging situations to generate an unbiased broad and scalable dataset. The participants of our study had to perform three different tasks that were designed in accordance with the historians' research questions. The recorded inputs were measured and compared to ground truth data to compute accuracy values.

Our results show that especially two of the cluster-based methods, *Radial Fan* and *Radial Arrow*, can compete with *Vector Glyphs* and *Animated Particles* and even overtop them in situations with diverging directions. *Radar Chart* also shows good results, but does not outstand, probably due to directions not being interpretable as precisely as with the other cluster-based methods. As expected, *Heat Map* scores well only in tasks where directional information is largely irrelevant. *Surface Heat Map* performs well only in Task 1, identifying POIs. However, it is not significantly better here than most of the other methods. Although there is no direct significant difference between the static *Vector Glyphs* and *Animated Particles*, the latter scores better compared to the other methods, validating the results of [29]. In our study, the users were performing an unsupervised online study, which resulted in a huge variance in task duration. As this makes it hard to assess timing of any sort, it is still open to future research if one visualization method is significantly faster to read with respect to the accuracy than others.

In a next step, when our real-world dataset reaches a greater extent, we will analyze how these methods perform on real-world data by conducting more qualitative studies paying special attention on the bias of real-world datasets. Additionally, we will increase interactivity, so that users are enabled to actively take measures at their points of interest to extract data beneath the visualization, e.g. precise numbers of photos. To apply these methods to more general use cases, positions and orientations of cameras can be computed for existing image databases with Structure-from-Motion techniques [25]. Though, points of interest would not be part of the outcome, they were merely important for defining the ground truth and measuring accuracy as part of this study. In this regard, approaches in saliency detection [15] in combination with photographs of architecture could fill this gap and add useful information. The computational analysis of the content-related focus, i.e. what are the objects that were important for the photographer to capture, could further enhance the visualization methods. Although we deal with historical photographs that cover several decades, time dependency, i.e. the date the photo was taken, has not been considered yet. Hence, future work may extend the presented visualizations to show changes of distributions of photographs over time.

**Acknowledgments.** The work presented in this paper has been funded by the German Federal Ministry of Education and Research (BMBF) as part of the research project "HistStadt4D—Multimodale Zugänge zu historischen Bildrepositorien zur Unterstützung stadt- und baugeschichtlicher Forschung und Vermittlung", grant identifier 01UG1630A/B.

# References

1. Andrienko, N., Andrienko, G.: Spatial generalization and aggregation of massive movement data. IEEE Trans. Vis. Comput. Graph. **17**(2), 205–219 (2011). https://doi.org/10.1109/TVCG.2010.44
2. Beaudoin, J.E., Brady, J.E.: Finding visual information: a study of image resources used by archaeologists, architects, art historians, and artists. Art Documentation J. Art Libr. Soc. North Am. **30**(2), 24–36 (2011). https://doi.org/10.1086/adx.30.2.41244062
3. Borgo, R., et al.: Glyph-based visualization: foundations, design guidelines, techniques and applications. In: Sbert, M., Szirmay-Kalos, L. (eds.) Eurographics (STARs), pp. 39–63 (2013). https://doi.org/10.2312/conf/EG2013/stars/039-063
4. Bruschke, J., Maiwald, F., Münster, S., Niebling, F.: Browsing and experiencing repositories of spatially oriented historic photographic images. Stud. Digit. Heritage **2**(2), 138–149 (2018). https://doi.org/10.14434/sdh.v2i2.24460
5. Bruschke, J., Niebling, F., Maiwald, F., Friedrichs, K., Wacker, M., Latoschik, M.E.: Towards browsing repositories of spatially oriented historic photographic images in 3D web environments. In: Proceedings of the Web3D. ACM, New York (2017). https://doi.org/10.1145/3055624.3075947
6. Chippendale, P., Zanin, M., Andreatta, C.: Spatial and temporal attractiveness analysis through geo-referenced photo alignment. In: Proceedings of the IGARSS, vol. 2, pp. II-1116–II-1119. IEEE (2008). https://doi.org/10.1109/IGARSS.2008.4779195
7. Fisher, D.: Hotmap: looking at geographic attention. IEEE Trans. Vis. Comput. Graph. **13**(6), 1184–1191 (2007). https://doi.org/10.1109/TVCG.2007.70561
8. Friedrichs, K., Münster, S., Kröber, C., Bruschke, J.: Creating suitable tools for art and architectural research with historic media repositories. In: Münster, S., Friedrichs, K., Niebling, F., Seidel-Grzesinska, A. (eds.) UHDL/DECH -2017. CCIS, vol. 817, pp. 117–138. Springer, Cham (2018). https://doi.org/10.1007/978-3-319-76992-9_8
9. Hyougo, Y., Misue, K., Tanaka, J.: Directional aggregate visualization of large scale movement data. In: Proceedings of the IV, pp. 196–201. IEEE (2014). https://doi.org/10.1109/IV.2014.34

10. Jaffe, A., Naaman, M., Tassa, T., Davis, M.: Generating summaries and visualization for large collections of geo-referenced photographs. In: Proceedings of the MIR, pp. 89–98. ACM, New York (2006). https://doi.org/10.1145/1178677.1178692
11. Kapler, T., Wright, W.: GeoTime information visualization. Inf. Vis. 4(2), 136–146 (2005). https://doi.org/10.1057/palgrave.ivs.9500097
12. Laidlaw, D.H., et al.: Comparing 2D vector field visualization methods: a user study. IEEE Trans. Vis. Comput. Graph. 11(1), 59–70 (2005). https://doi.org/10.1109/TVCG.2005.4
13. Laramee, R.S., Hauser, H., Doleisch, H., Vrolijk, B., Post, F.H., Weiskopf, D.: The state of the art in flow visualization: dense and texture-based techniques. Comput. Graph. Forum 23(2), 203–221 (2004). https://doi.org/10.1111/j.1467-8659.2004.00753.x
14. Li, C., Baciu, G., Han, Y.: Interactive visualization of high density streaming points with heat-map. In: Proceedings of the SMARTCOMP, pp. 145–149. IEEE (2014). https://doi.org/10.1109/SMARTCOMP.2014.7043852
15. Liu, N., Han, J., Yang, M.H.: PiCANet: pixel-wise contextual attention learning for accurate saliency detection. IEEE Trans. Image Process. 29, 6438–6451 (2020). https://doi.org/10.1109/TIP.2020.2988568
16. Liu, Z., Cai, S., Swan, J.E., Moorhead, R.J., Martin, J.P., Jankun-Kelly, T.J.: A 2D flow visualization user study using explicit flow synthesis and implicit task design. IEEE Trans. Vis. Comput. Graph. 18(5), 783–796 (2012). https://doi.org/10.1109/TVCG.2011.110
17. Mayr, E., et al.: Visualizing biographical trajectories by historical artifacts: a case study based on the photography collection of Charles W. Cushman. In: Proceedings of the BD (2019). https://doi.org/10.17605/OSF.IO/E62X4
18. Nguyen, D.Q., Schumann, H.: Web-based exploration of photos with time and geospace. In: Cordeiro, J., Krempels, K.-H. (eds.) WEBIST 2012. LNBIP, vol. 140, pp. 153–166. Springer, Heidelberg (2013). https://doi.org/10.1007/978-3-642-36608-6_10
19. Niebling, F., Bruschke, J., Messemer, H., Wacker, M., von Mammen, S.: Analyzing spatial distribution of photographs in cultural heritage applications. In: Liarokapis, F., Vouolodimos, A., Doulamis, N., Doulamis, A. (eds.) Visual Computing for Cultural Heritage. SSCC, pp. 391–408. Springer, Cham (2020). https://doi.org/10.1007/978-3-030-37191-3_20
20. Pfeiffer, T., Memili, C.: Model-based real-time visualization of realistic three-dimensional heat maps for mobile eye tracking and eye tracking in virtual reality. In: Proceedings of the ETRA, pp. 95–102. ACM, New York (2016). https://doi.org/10.1145/2857491.2857541
21. Reddy, C.K., Vinzamuri, B.: A survey of partitional and hierarchical clustering algorithms. In: Aggarwal, C.C., Reddy, C.K. (eds.) Data Clustering: Algorithms and Applications. Data Mining and Knowledge Discovery Series, pp. 87–110. Chapman and Hall/CRC, New York (2014). https://doi.org/10.1201/9781315373515
22. Rezaei, M., Franti, P.: Real-time clustering of large geo-referenced data for visualizing on map. Adv. Electr. Comput. Eng. 18(4), 63–74 (2018). https://doi.org/10.4316/AECE.2018.04008
23. Schulz, C., et al.: Generative data models for validation and evaluation of visualization techniques. In: Proceedings of the BELIV, pp. 112–124. ACM, New York (2016). https://doi.org/10.1145/2993901.2993907
24. Silva, S., Sousa Santos, B., Madeira, J.: Using color in visualization: a survey. Comput. Graph. 35(2), 320–333 (2011). https://doi.org/10.1016/j.cag.2010.11.015
25. Snavely, N., Seitz, S.M., Szeliski, R.: Photo tourism: exploring photo collections in 3D. ACM Trans. Graph. 25(3), 835–846 (2006). https://doi.org/10.1145/1141911.1141964
26. Telea, A., van Wijk, J.J.: Simplified representation of vector fields. In: Proceedings of the Visualization, pp. 35–42. IEEE (1999). https://doi.org/10.1109/VISUAL.1999.809865
27. Thomee, B., et al.: YFCC100M: the new data in multimedia research. Commun. ACM 59(2), 64–73 (2016). https://doi.org/10.1145/2812802

28. Urness, T., Interrante, V., Longmire, E., Marusic, I., O'Neill, S., Jones, T.W.: Strategies for the visualization of multiple 2D vector fields. IEEE Comput. Graph. Appl. **26**(4), 74–82 (2006). https://doi.org/10.1109/MCG.2006.88

29. Ware, C., Bolan, D., Miller, R., Rogers, D.H., Ahrens, J.P.: Animated versus static views of steady flow patterns. In: Proceedings of the SAP, pp. 77–84. ACM, New York (2016). https://doi.org/10.1145/2931002.2931012

30. Wegenkittl, R., Groller, E., Purgathofer, W.: Animating flow fields: rendering of oriented line integral convolution. In: Proceedings of the CA, pp. 15–21. IEEE (1997). https://doi.org/10.1109/CA.1997.601035

31. Windhager, F., et al.: Visualization of cultural heritage collection data: state of the art and future challenges. IEEE Trans. Vis. Comput. Graph. **25**(6), 2311–2330 (2019). https://doi.org/10.1109/TVCG.2018.2830759

32. Zhou, Z., et al.: Visual abstraction of large scale geospatial origin-destination movement data. IEEE Trans. Vis. Comput. Graph. **25**(1), 43–53 (2019). https://doi.org/10.1109/TVCG.2018.2864503

33. Zhu, X., Guo, D.: Mapping large spatial flow data with hierarchical clustering. Trans. GIS **18**(3), 421–435 (2014). https://doi.org/10.1111/tgis.12100

# In Which Images Does This Corner Appears?
# A Novel Approach for Three-Dimensional
# Query of Historical Photographs Collections
# in Urban Heritage Research

Antonio Suazo[✉][iD]

Centro Nacional de Conservación y Restauración,
683 Recoleta St, Santiago, Chile
asuazol@uc.cl

**Abstract.** In order to improve the cataloging and search of historical photographs available in public online archives, recent advances support for spatially orienting images in a three-dimensional environment to freely explore these collections, thus addressing navigation issues. However, common search tasks still depend on the traditional approach based on text descriptions and keywords. To overcome this, a novel approach is proposed for querying images based on recovered 3d spatial data. By projecting image pixels over the surface of reconstructed geometry from depicted objects, a resulting point cloud is stored and queried by a search volume, retrieving 3d points and so the associated images. The proposal and its potential are validated through a specific case study from the field of urban history, a dilapidated building located in Santiago of Chile, and its associated photographic collections. Finally, the results obtained are discussed, the types of queries that the system allows, and some limitations identified. The conclusion shows that a new set of possibilities emerges, which allows interrogating images with specific tools and functions derived from a 3d spatial database, improving the access and use of collections for historical research with three-dimensional interest.

**Keywords:** Spatial query · Historical photograph · Point cloud

## 1 Introduction

In addition to the value that historical photographs have as an object of cultural interest in itself, it is well known the potential they offer as a record of a moment for their use in research. According to that, for art historians, scholars, and professionals in the cultural heritage field, the expected practice is to go beyond the notion of image as a secondary source of information and get to utilize them as a primary source of information, directly feeding heritage studies. Therefore, for the administrators of these collections, it is important not only to preserve all the information associated with the images but to recover the greatest amount of data embedded in them that allows their use as primary research sources. In this context, it is said that spatial searching and retrieving of media repositories will certainly become increasingly valuable and relevant in research topics

© Springer Nature Switzerland AG 2021
F. Niebling et al. (Eds.): UHDL 2019, CCIS 1501, pp. 152–170, 2021.
https://doi.org/10.1007/978-3-030-93186-5_7

associated with urban history, disappeared urban and architectural heritage, and on the history of photography itself.

Following that observation, some of that potential has been exploited due to recent advances in the last years that allows extracting the position and spatial orientation of the camera by photogrammetric means. Nevertheless, and despite the progress that these advances represent, search and retrieval challenges remain bound to the usage of metadata, text descriptions, and keywords for describing image content, which presents serious limitations to carry out spatial queries. Given that scenario, until now is not simple for a researcher to determine which photos depict certain areas he or she is interested in.

The work introduces the topic listing the main advances available for the recovery of spatial and temporal acquisition data associated with historical photographs. The second part delves into the challenges of defining a dedicated spatial image search functionality, by critically reviewing current approaches and describing the require-ments for an effective search and retrieval system based on the recovered data. In the third part, a new approach is proposed to carry out three-dimensional queries of image collections, developing and describing the workflow in which it would be inserted, and outlining the main applications and expected benefits. In the fourth part, the proposal is put to the test in a case study -a ruined building and the associated photographic collections- and evaluation criteria are defined in the form of key tests to be performed. In the fifth part, the results obtained are displayed and commented on. Finally, in the sixth part, the main conclusions are offered, discussing specific evaluation criteria results and providing a reflection on wider implications as well as founded further research topics.

## 2    Search and Retrieval Challenges

The principle behind describing image content through words presents some inherent limitations, well documented in the literature. First of all, despite efforts for having standardized vocabularies and thesaurus, image metadata is usually found to be using incomplete, imprecise, and non-standardized textual descriptions [1]. In this sense, a search system is tightly bound to the quality and completeness of the descriptions used by archivists in the first place. Additionally, in the context of a complete and extensive collection of photographs, manually describing annotations with text and/or keywords can become a task prone to the emergence of numerous obstacles. Human error, higher costs and time involved, and imprecision and subjectivity of keywords used -which may not reflect or describe in full complexity the information present in the images- are some of the most recurring topics [2]. But even with complete, accurate and stan-dardized descriptions, useful metadata must address an even deeper problem: since the content is expressed in the photograph through non-written language, an intrinsic information representation problem raises. As a result, when trying to represent a still image through text, a translation or transcoding obstacle is added, which introduces distortions and subjective associations [3] that ultimately makes it difficult to trace back to the original content.

Spatial queries, on the opposite, aims for overcoming these issues by addressing the main challenge of search and retrieval in a way that does not introduce distortions or subjective associations but using instead the image content itself. What it is intended with a spatial search, therefore, is to diminish importance from the act of 'naming' or labeling the 'things' depicted in images: it is not so relevant to determine what it is or how the thing is called, but where it is and what it has around it.

## 2.1  Current Approaches

The approaches available today for search in historical photographs repositories can be considered to be poor or too naive for allowing proper spatial queries, and so far doesn't allow for retrieving images associated with certain areas under study. Nevertheless, they constitute the current state of the art, and considering the approach they take can be divided into three categories:

- In the simplest case, images are represented by a point in a 2d space, which denotes only the position of the camera within an urban setting. This approach is too naive for performing spatial queries and lacks representing the camera orientation, which is mandatory considering that a query made on the position of the cameras does not necessarily return information about the objects that appear in them. This is to the fact that photographs with the same position but different orientations show very different objects [4].
- In a second group, images are represented on a 2d map by cones, where the pivot point represents the position of the camera and the angle represents the field of view. However, the finite nature of the cone geometry description contrasts with the infinite behavior of the pinhole camera model and perspective projection [5], which in turn presents serious problems to be used directly for searching associated images. As can be seen, in both approaches the limitation of the system has to do with the inherent simplification of using a 2d representation, and with the fact that so far they don't leverage any mechanism for associating images with objects depicted in them.
- In contrast, the third group of systems addresses image visualization problems through a three-dimensional representation, in which pictures appear spatially aligned and oriented, allowing navigation and free exploration of the collections [1, 6, 7, 20]. Despite the progress that these advances represent, this approach privileges visual inference over actual spatial querying, thus none of these applications implements proper search and retrieval mechanisms. On top of that, since they are based on the visual identification of the images by the user, they may present visualization issues with a high volume of photographs being consulted simultaneously.

## 2.2  Requirements for Effective Spatial Search of Images

To be able to address the main functionality of an effective search and retrieval system based on the recovered data on associated images, critical requirements for a spatial query mechanism are listed and described, as well as the principal aspects that the underlying solution should provide under the hood:

- As a first point to note, a decision has to be made to take full advantage of the three-dimensional data effectively recovered as a result of the photogrammetric analysis. For instance, it is found that many historical photographs are vertically tilted or have height inclinations (i.e. taken from balconies and roofs) and other spatial considerations that are noted to affect the relationship between the photograph and the objects depicted in them. That relationship, in turn, is mainly responsible for driving correct image searching according to spatial queries on retrieval time. For that reason, it seems relevant that the system should use a full 3d data model to describe both the image and objects representation, avoiding falling into 2d representations that would cause information misusing and potentially leading to retrieval errors.
- A second important point, following the first one described, is that the query mechanism should avoid using a rectangle to determine the search area, as it has been seen in 2d maps representations. This has to do with many circumstances in which the surface being studied is not laying on the XY plane, but on a vertical or oblique surface, like while studying facades ornamentation, roof structures and so on. For that reason, it is noted that the spatial query should use a volume - an auxiliary parallelepiped, cuboid, or sphere - for defining the sector on which it is desired to search for images from the collection. That volume should act as a proxy geometry that could be exposed to affine transformations -like moving, rotating, and scaling- that the end-user could manipulate at will to better reflect the search region that fits the surfaces under study.
- Finally, with the intention of step aside from textual descriptions of image content, the system should look for information that is already present in the photographs. This is closely related to the so-called "Content-based image retrieval" approach, which seeks to base image searching not in concepts but in image content -color, shape, texture- or "any other information that derives from the image itself" [8]. What it means for a spatial query mechanism is that both the data model and the underlying database of the system should be fed with information directly extracted from images. In the best scenario, these references would be the actual pixels of the image, which in turn would model associations between the images and the search volume the system would use.

## 3   A Novel Approach

Based on the observations and definitions established, a new technical approach is proposed for spatial search on historic visual media. The key observation is that every image pixel can be projected and located at the spatial position over the surface of reconstructed geometry from depicted objects. The resulting 3D point cloud is stored and can be queried by a search volume (i.e. a sphere). Hence, a spatial query on the sector under study will retrieve 3D points within the area of interest and so the associated images. As a result, by enabling a mechanism for performing proper search and retrieval of images based on spatial criteria a new set of possibilities emerges, which allows us to interrogate images with specific tools and functions derived from a spatial database, and to perform queries of the type "In which images of the collection does this surface appears?.

To conceive an approach like this, inspiration was drawn from the following technical references:

- In the first place, considering the image as the actual in-view from the camera sensor is a manner of taking into account camera frustum as well as intrinsic and extrinsic parameters for the line of sight calculation, which in turn is the base for extending *Viewshed* analysis to a three-dimensional environment. Two-dimensional line of sight calculation is a functionality very common in most geographic information system (GIS) software and is concerned with using location and geometric properties in determining visibility from points of interest.
- Secondly, three-dimensional matches between photographs in Structure-from-Motion workflows allow filtering images by selecting a group of points in space, which is a common feature in many photogrammetry packages like *Agisoft Photoscan* and *Alicevision Meshroom*. Sparse point cloud representation of images is what partially inspired the need for a new method of representing the information contained in historical photographs, and ultimately to take advantage over the already existent relationship between images and the corresponding objects depicted in them.
- Lastly, the idea of converting images into a point cloud by projecting actual pixels in 3d space was largely inspired by Patricio González work "Skylines III - City point cloud" [9], which in turn inspired Marco Cavallo for his paper "3D City Reconstruction From Google Street View" [10]. In parallel, Maiwald et al. [11] implement raycasting to project pixels on the surface of the building's geometry. None of these techniques, though, take advantage of storing the point cloud for a later purpose, and neither of them is being used for providing spatial query functionality, so the proposed approach seems to be fairly new to address the main challenge.

### 3.1 Workflow Definition and Implementation

The new approach is presented in the context of a wider workflow, distributed along a sequence of four processing steps (Fig. 1). These steps involve generating consistent spatial data with the help of already available contributions in the field of study, upon which a new processing step generates new data that model spatial representation of photographs -point cloud generation. This information, in turn, is formatted to fit a 3d spatial database, establishing a link between points and images, which ultimately can feed a search and retrieval system.

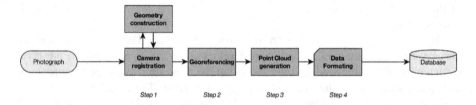

**Fig. 1.** Proposed workflow (Image: author).

The **first** of these steps consists of the alignment and registration of cameras, that feedback each other with the process of geometry estimation (of what is going to be analyzed, present in the image). In this way, both cameras representation and objects depicted in them get determined in local 3d coordinates. This is calculated with the contributions of [12–14]. Implementation details on this step propose to focus on the main intrinsic camera properties (only sensor size, focal distance, and central point shifting), thus other parameters are left outside this formulation on purpose (i.e. horizontal and vertical skew, radial distortions, etc.) for considering that they impact less on the final result. Also, the level of detail for the geometry to be considered enough for calculation is established in terms of general volumetric consistency; in that sense, it is proposed to use CityGML -an OGC compliant format- as a standard reference, and the LoD N° 2 as the ideal geometry definition for enabling following steps in the workflow [15].

The **second** step, taking into account that these are urban photographs that coexist in a space-time reality, consists of the conversion of local positions and orientations obtained to a geographical coordinate system, with absolute values. This can be done with the aid of ground control points of known points already present in images, 3d objects, or both, by resection according to [1]. Implementation details on this step suggest using historical urban and/or architectural records for determining ground control points and their precision and accuracy. It is strongly noted that, whenever possible, consider using topographic surveys, or even better urban planning drawings that incorporate height values, to be able to give the overall model the sufficient redundancy in Z-axis measures.

The **third** step, where the new approach takes place, consists of the projection of the pixels over the volume obtained in the first step. It is proposed to carry out this by means of 2 simple calculations, acting on each pixel:

1. First measuring the real physical distance ($d$) from the position of the camera to the first surface, point at which a vertex is generated ($x, y, z$), and
2. Second, by transferring the color values ($r, g, b$) from the image to the newly created vertex.

By doing both calculations through all the pixels of the photograph, you get a set of points associated with the surfaces that were originally registered with the photographic capture. For the purpose of this work, a simple implementation was done using a custom routine code in python language, raycasting visible surfaces from camera position and orientation. An optional parameter in the main function sets the resolution of the computed point cloud, in other words, controlling the number of real pixels considered in the loop.

In the **fourth** step, the results are prepared to be saved. The preparation contemplates assigning a structure to the obtained values $(x, y, z, r, g, b, d)$, which preserves the integrity of the retrieved information and at the same time allows for compactness and quick access from the database during search time. The actual database's sole function is to keep track of the relationship between points and images associated with them, so its implementation details are mostly related to the chosen prototyping environment. During the implementation made for this specific work, values were formatted and stored using Point Cloud Library (PCL) library [16]. This decision was made intending to use native PCL functionality at a later point for performing actual spatial queries since it allows searching through a sphere out of the box.

### 3.2    Expected Applications and Benefits

As mentioned, the main expected application has to do with being able to make spatial queries that allow knowing in which images a certain surface is represented. Since the query is made from a volume, the approach is agnostic regarding its size, being able to potentially search from small areas (at the scale of walls or smaller) to larger urban areas (at the scale of blocks or greater), so it is interesting to know these scopes.

As a result of these applications, it is expected that a search system of this type will allow to identify differences in the spatial distribution of the photographs, in order to spot well-documented sectors, or those that are not fully documented at all, or even compare collections with each other to estimate and statistically study biases, gaps and other relevant aspects.

Finally, with the new spatial information generated for each photograph, it is expected that it will be possible to evaluate the images (individually and as a collection) in relation to criteria used in visual documentation (such as quality and resolution of images) and criteria used in cultural artifacts photography (like distance and orientation of the surface of interest with camera sensor). This type of inputs could be used to filter and sort the records already retrieved, allowing for example not only to know the photographs associated with a facade, but to sort them according to the distance or to filter those that do not exceed a specific orientation with respect to the plane, etc.

## 4    Application and Evaluation

Having established an overall workflow for the proposed method, it is now the turn for defining precise experiments that seek to evaluate main functionality, trying them out in a real case scenario, and ultimately collecting resulting data for running specific evaluation exercises.

## 4.1 A Case Study

The proposed approach is put to the test with a specific case: a set of buildings built between 1905 and 1909 in an extensive lot in Santiago of Chile, intended to house the facilities of the Institute of Hygiene [17] (see Fig. 2). In the last 60 years, the fate of the buildings underwent successive changes of occupants, use and significant architectural adjustments to each of the pavilions. As a result, the sequence of interventions constitutes the cornerstone for the urban and architectural study of the buildings, their evolution and spatial understanding from a historical perspective. Also, the set was photographed on various occasions throughout its years, the main one being the registration made by the Architecture Department of the Ministry of Public Works [18].

**Fig. 2.** Images of the different pavilions to the year of inauguration of the Hygiene Institute. a) General view of the 5 pavilions; b) Hygiene and Demography; c) Chemistry and Toxicology; d) Microscopy and Bacteriology; e) Serotherapy; f) Public Disin-fector (Photographs: Chilean Memory - National Library).

The case was selected for meeting the main requirements to carry out the study. Foremost, it is about disappeared architecture works that can only be revisited through its photographic records. Also, available photographs exhibit good enough resolution and are relatively few, which will be useful for checking evaluation tests manually (one by one). Lastly, being this the entire collection makes it interesting for observing decisions at a collection level.

160    A. Suazo

**Fig. 3.** Some of the photographs considered for the case study. The associated metadata only consign 'Institute of Hygiene' as the unique spatial reference (Photographs: Photo Archives Architecture Direction, Ministry of Public Works).

Initially, images were filtered by year and photographic process, resulting in 20 views from exterior and 3 views from interior (see Fig. 3). Then, photographs were processed with the proposed approach. During step 1 of the workflow, intrinsic properties of the camera (sensor size, focal distance, and central point position) and extrinsic properties (relative position and orientation) were obtained, data that was used to recover the general volumetry of the buildings (up to LoD N° 2 of the CityGML specification) (see Fig. 4). In step 2, available historical cartography was used [19], identifying points in the images that had their equivalent in map locations, and solving the set by resection (see Fig. 5). In step 3, the point cloud was generated for a set of chosen photographs, according to the proposed calculation method, using custom code in python language (see Fig. 6). In step 4, point clouds were formatted and stored using the Point Cloud Library (PCL) library.

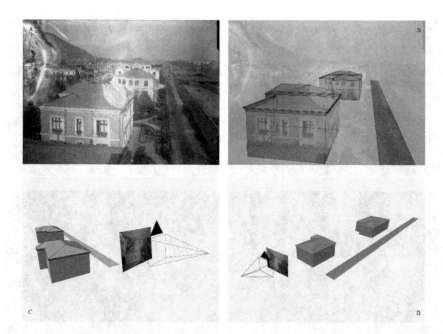

**Fig. 4.** Preliminary results of step 1 (left to right, top to bottom). a) Original photograph; b) General volumetry recovered; c) and d) bird's eye views where the position and orientation of the camera is observed at the moment when the photograph was captured. (Images: a) Photo Archive Architecture Department, Ministry of Public Works; b, c, d) author).

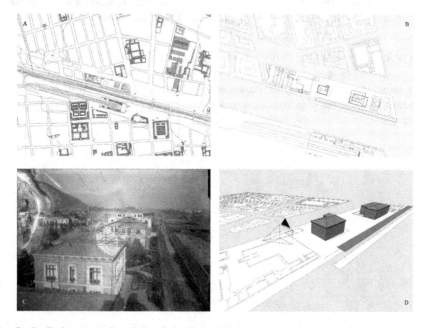

**Fig. 5.** Preliminary results of step 2 (left to right, top to bottom). a) Map of Santiago 1910 (detail); b) global alignment of the volumes and the camera; c) geographical tracks represented in the original photograph; d) integrated geographical clues in three-dimensional space (Images: a) Rosas et al., 2011; b, c, d) author).

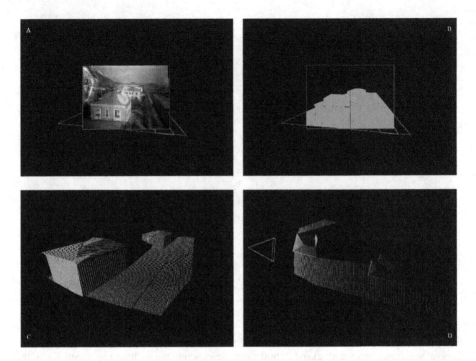

**Fig. 6.** Preliminary results of step 3 (left to right, top to bottom). a) View from the original position of the camera; b) view of the projected pixels on the surface, from the same point of view; c) point cloud obtained, from a different point of view; d) overhead view, distribution of the points and position of the camera on the left side is observed (Images: a, b, c, d) author).

In order to carry out the defined spatial queries tests, native PCL functionality was used, which allows searching through a sphere (a 3d point and a radius). As a result, it was possible to perform three-dimensional queries directly on the set of point clouds, and return the necessary information to know the images associated with them (see Fig. 7).

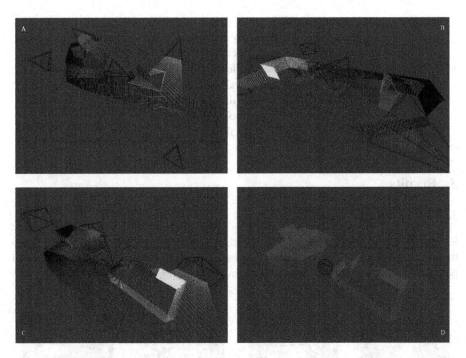

**Fig. 7.** Multiple preliminary test results (left to right, top to bottom). a) Overhead view showing 5 photographs and their respective point clouds, projected in space. Unique colorization was carried out for displaying purposes; b) view at street level, there is concentration of points in vertical walls; c) a sphere representing a "query volume" is located at the center of the image; d) the isolated points in the volume are used to identify the corresponding photographs (Images: a, b, c, d) author).

## 4.2    Testing Methodology

With a case study already set up, expected benefits were articulated as evaluation goals to be tested on the case and its internal structure. In that regard, two main criteria were established to gain a better understanding of the new approach behavior and limitations: image to point cloud conversion, and spatial querying functionality and performance.

On image to point cloud conversion, it is relevant to determine if there are obstacles for performing the point cloud generation and/or colorization and to spot differences between images that may produce different point clouds. On spatial querying functionality and performance, it becomes relevant to estimate how well the system behaves at different three-dimensional search scales, and if it supports identifying trends in the spatial distribution of photographs, as well as calculating performance and storage curves at different point cloud resolutions. As a result, these two general criteria were translated into simple metrics and exercises that could generate resulting data to be evaluated.

- Image to point cloud conversion:
  - Number of photographs successfully converted
  - Table with total amount of points generated per image
- Spatial Querying Functionality and Performance:
  - Search exercises at three scales (window, facade, and building)
  - Search exercise looking for images distribution (buildings)
  - Average retrieval time at different point cloud resolution
  - File size at different point cloud resolution

## 5   Results

### 5.1   Point Cloud Generation

Regarding image to point cloud conversion, it is noted that the complete set of photographs was successfully processed, generating 23 fully colorized and geo-registered point clouds, as can be seen with 4 of them on Fig. 8 and in detail on Fig. 9.

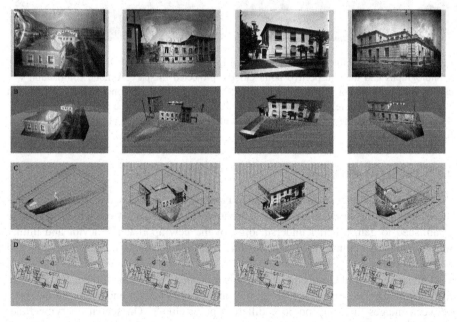

**Fig. 8.**  Image to point cloud conversion results - extract of 4 photography examples in columns (left to right) on which can be seen the following views (top to bottom). a) original photograph; b) perspective view of generated point cloud; c) isometric view of point cloud main statics, amount of points, bounding box dimensions and global orientation; d) top view showing point clouds within geo-referenced coordinate system (Images: a, b, c, d) author).

**Fig. 9.** Pixel projection is limited in self-occlusion situations where volumetry is partially covered. If enough data is available the covering object could be also recovered -a) electric pole- or discarded -b) this trees should be masked out (Images: a, b) author).

**Table 1.** Image to point cloud conversion rates.

| Image ID | Pixels total | Number of points | Coverage (%) | Image ID | Pixels total | Number of points | Coverage (%) |
|---|---|---|---|---|---|---|---|
| PL-0950 | 1471680 | 751805 | 0,511 | PL-0963 | 1512000 | 917274 | 0,607 |
| PL-0951 | 1496160 | 333864 | 0,223 | PL-0981 | 1514880 | 898501 | 0,593 |
| PL-0953 | 1517760 | 834924 | 0,550 | PL-0982 | 1487520 | 915012 | 0,615 |
| PL-0954 | 1517760 | 1186029 | 0,781 | PL-1129 | 1507680 | 1152399 | 0,764 |
| PL-0955 | 1545120 | 1345377 | 0,871 | PL-1131 | 1512000 | 1512000 | 1,000 |
| PL-0956 | 1514880 | 1112282 | 0,734 | PL-1133 | 1512000 | 1512000 | 1,000 |
| PL-0957 | 1529280 | 1118517 | 0,731 | PL-1134 | 1512000 | 1169814 | 0,774 |
| PL-0958 | 1529280 | 1432634 | 0,937 | PL-1135 | 1512000 | 828249 | 0,548 |
| PL-0959 | 1533600 | 991351 | 0,646 | PL-1136 | 1512000 | 868846 | 0,575 |
| PL-0960 | 1533600 | 989436 | 0,645 | PL-1137 | 1512000 | 898557 | 0,594 |
| PL-0961 | 1533600 | 1533600 | 1,000 | PL-1235 | 1473120 | 607354 | 0,412 |
| PL-0962 | 1512000 | 989646 | 0,655 | | | | |

## 5.2 Spatial Querying Functionality and Performance

For the spatial search exercise, three search volumes were defined using spheres at different scales to define the area corresponding to a door, a facade, and an entire building. The size of the spheres was radius 2.46 m, 5.5 m, and 19.42 m respectively. The results were satisfactory, and the system was able to return all the images associated with the search volumes (Fig. 10).

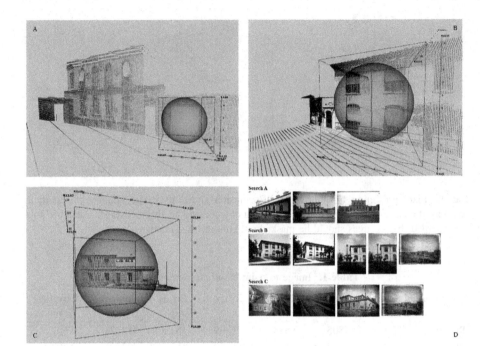

**Fig. 10.** Using spheres of varying size for spatial searching images at different scales (left to right, top to bottom): a) a door and its frame; b) a portion of a facade; c) a complete pavilion; d) retrieved images (Images: a, b, c, d) author).

In a second batch of exercises, spheres of different sizes were distributed throughout the site to carry out searches associated with each of the pavilions. Thus, through a sequence of queries, it was possible to determine the number of photographs related to the different buildings and to gain a better understanding of the photographer's work (Fig. 11).

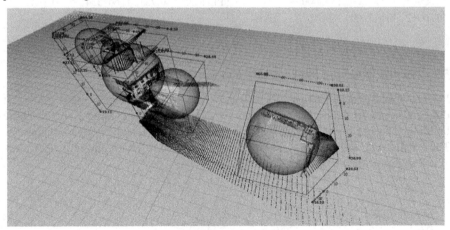

**Fig. 11.** A total of 5 different spheres where used as searching volumes (Image: author).

Finally, the time for each of the search exercises carried out was recorded, the final value being the average of 3 attempts. The same was done for point clouds with lower resolution, processing images at the original size, half, and quarter (Fig. 12).

Average retrieval time (ms) by point cloud resolution

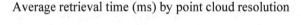

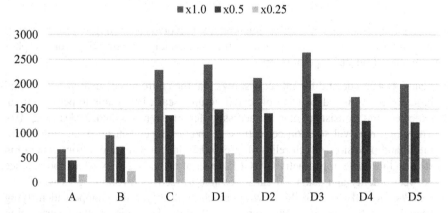

**Fig. 12.** Average retrieval time in milliseconds for each of performed queries at different point cloud resolutions (Image: author).

## 6   Conclusions

The present work has proposed to articulate a novel approach that allows to perform spatial queries to collections of historical images. The results show that the proposed approach is effective and has not been explored until now.

### 6.1   Discussion

Regarding the image to point cloud conversion method, it is found to be certainly possible to recover pixel position in world coordinates, recreating volumetric information from the surfaces that were originally registered by photographic capture means.

- Point cloud generation and storage proved to be an automatable process. The method is scale-independent to the image sensor, being able to project pixels from walls, buildings, and even urban blocks. Generated point cloud resolution and precision is only dependent on i) the accuracy in the calibration of the camera and ii) the fidelity of the volumetry used. It is also noted that both factors can be updated, whenever newer data is available with better resolution or fidelity, without affecting the mechanism or its automation.
- Additionally, the amount of points generated per photograph (See Table 1) is not equivalent to the total number of pixels available in the photographs, since many of

them don't get projected into an actual surface (i.e. pixels corresponding to the sky). From an information preservation standpoint, this limitation could be used on purpose to have better control over the point cloud generation step, projecting the image only on surfaces that have reliable existence. This becomes clear on self-occlusion circumstances, where it is suggested to leave blank areas as-is, avoiding filling them in by hand (Fig. 9a), and in cases where people, trees, and similar objects could be easily masked out manually during point cloud generation step (Fig. 9b).

In regards to the spatial search functionality explored, according to criteria previously established, the new approach results satisfactory at retrieving correct photographs based on this type of query.

- Search tests made at different scale shows that the entire mechanism of point cloud based querying is independent of search volume scale, being able to perform in an expected and consistent manner across different exercises and scales (Fig. 10). Therefore, retrieval solution correctness is mainly dependent on point cloud resolution and precision, which relies on previously mentioned factors from generation step. In this context, geometry CityGML level of detail N°2 showed a good balance between fidelity and actual 3d clues possible to recover (avoiding guesswork).
- Results showed also that this new approach could be used to support identifying spatial distributions in photograph collections. For this matter, performing sequential search tasks helped to spot the number of photos in which individual pavilions and buildings appeared (Fig. 11), providing useful insights for identifying trends in choices made by the photographer on "what to register". Key parameters of search volume turned out to be size and distribution (distance from each other), as well as whether or not some degree of overlap between them is desirable.
- Lastly, search performance and retrieval time at different point cloud resolution shows that the method does not exhibit serious delays for being used in production. Smaller resolution point clouds does help to decrease processing time during search (Fig. 12), but finer elements could not be founded and/or would require bigger search volumes to be able to get accounted for. Nevertheless, some attention should be put in production, tought, since the dataset used in this study is relatively small in total amount of points processed, and could be different from a real case scenario. Finally, storage consumption follows the rule of generated point clouds being 3 times the amount of pixels effectively projected, since they have to keep 3 positional values (latitude, longitude, height).

As stated initially, spatial searching and retrieving of media repositories will certainly become increasingly valuable and relevant in a myriad of heritage studies. As a consequence, this contribution presents implications for a wide span of studies and disciplines. First, for conservation specialists dedicated to historical photographs, the new method is aligned with recovering and preserving the greatest amount of data embedded in them, thus supporting the fight against deterioration due to dissociation - which is the loss of information associated with the object. Secondly, for the administrators of these collections, museums, and cultural institutions, the query mechanism supports the possibility of deploying complex search methods based on spatial attributes, which leads to improving the process of searching and retrieving the photographs but also to discover spatial information associated with images. Finally, for art historians, scholars, and professionals in the cultural heritage field, using search and retrieval systems based on this approach contributes to allowing the use of historical photographs as primary research sources in built heritage studies associated with urban history and disappeared urban and architectural heritage.

## 6.2 Future Work

With the main contribution regarding spatial queries, some interesting topics could be explored in future work. The most manifest one is the need to evaluate a different manner for defining the search volume, as sphere intrinsic geometric constraints do not fit well in scenarios of pseudo-planar surfaces (i.e. walls and floors). Also, a dataset with a large collection of images could be used to test the overall performance; accordingly, it would be necessary to implement any sort of spatial indexing and/or partitioning to be able to search in such a big amount of points. Finally, it would be interesting to implement the aforementioned filtering mechanism to filter and sort the records already retrieved, allowing not only to know the photographs associated with a facade but how those images compare to each other from an information preservation standpoint.

**Acknowledgments.** The present work has been supported by the National Center for Conservation and Restoration from the Ministry of Arts, Culture and Heritage, with the additional help of the Photo Archive Architecture Department from the Ministry of Public Works, and the junior research group Evidencia Visual, Chile.

# References

1. Bruschke, J., Niebling, F., Maiwald, F., Friedrichs, K., Wacker, M., Latoschik, M.E.: Towards browsing repositories of spatially oriented historic photographic images in 3d web environments. In: Proceedings of Web3D 2017, Brisbane, QLD, Australia, 05–07 June 2017
2. Rui, Y., Huang, T.S., Chang, S.-F.: Image retrieval: current techniques, promising directions, and open issues. J. Vis. Commun. Image Represent. **10**, 39–62 (1999)
3. Del Valle, F.: Documentary dimension of photography. In: International Congress on Images and Social Research, México D.F. (México), pp. 28–31 (2002)
4. Hu, Y., Gao, S., Janowicz, K., Yu, B., Li, W., Prasad, S.: Extracting and understanding urban areas of interest using geotagged photos. Comput. Environ. Urban Syst. **54**, 240–254 (2015)
5. Zaragozí, B.: GeoFOV - Incorporating the field of vision into a multimedia geodatabase. Geography Journey 3.0, University of Alicante (2011)
6. Snavely, N., Garg, R., Seitz, S., Szeliski, R.: Finding paths through the world's photos. ACM Trans. Graph. Proc. SIGGRAPH **27**(3), 11–21 (2008)
7. Brivio, P., Benedetti, L., Tarini, M., Ponchio, F., Cignoni, P., Scopigno, R.: PhotoCloud: interactive remote exploration of joint 2d and 3d datasets. IEEE Comput. Graph. Appl. **33** (2), 86–96 (2013). March-April

8. Tyagi, V.: Content-Based Image Retrieval Techniques: A Review. In: Content-Based Image Retrieval, pp. 29–48. Springer, Singapore (2017). https://doi.org/10.1007/978-981-10-6759-4_2

9. González, P.: Skylines III - City point cloud. Blogpost (2014). http://www. patriciogonzalezvivo.com/2014/skylines/skylines.php?v=03. Accessed 15 July 2019

10. Cavallo, M.: 3D city reconstruction from google street view. Comput. Graph. J. (2015)

11. Maiwald, F., et al.: A 4D information system for the exploration of multitemporal images and maps using photogrammetry, web technologies and VR/AR. Virtual Archaeol. Rev. **10** (21), 1–13 (2019)

12. Maiwald, F., Vietze, T., Schneider, D., Münster, S., Niebling, F.: Photogrammetric analysis of historical image repositories for virtual reconstruction in the field of digital humanities. ISPRS – Int. Arch. Photogramm. Remote Sens. Spat. Inf. Sci. **XLII-2/W3**, 447–452 (2017)

13. López-Romero, E.: Out of the box: exploring the 3D modelling potential of ancient image archives. Virtual Archaeol. Rev. (VAR) **5**(10), 107–116 (2014)

14. Aparicio, P., Carmona, J., Fernández, M., Martín, P.: Involuntary photogrammetry: rescuing 3D geometric information from archival photographs. Virtual Archaeol. Rev. (VAR) **5**(10), 11–20 (2014)

15. CityGML Homepage. https://www.opengeospatial.org/standards/citygml. Accessed 15 July 2019

16. Point Cloud Library (PCL) Homepage. http://pointclouds.org. Accessed 15 July 2019

17. Ferrer, P.: Graphic album of the Hygiene Institute of Santiago: presented at the International Congress of Medicine and the Hygiene Exhibition of Buenos Aires, in May 1910. Available on 'Memoria Chilena', National Library of Chile (1910)

18. AFDA (Photographic Archive of Architecture Department, Ministry of Public Works) Homepage. http://www.afda.cl. Accessed 15 July 2019

19. Rosas, J.; Hidalgo, N.; Hidalgo, G.; Strabucchi, W.: Santiago 1910. Construcción planimétrica de la ciudad pre-moderna. Transcripciones entre el fenómeno de la ciudad física dada y la ciudad representada. Investigación Fondecyt Regular, No. 1085253 (2011)

20. Schindler, G., Dellaert, F.: 4D Cities: analyzing, visualizing, and interacting with historical urban photo collections. J. Multimed. **7**(2), 124–131 (2012)

# Visualizing Venice to Visualizing Cities - Advanced Technologies for Historical Cities Visualization

Kristin L. Huffman[1(✉)] and Andrea Giordano[2]

[1] Duke University, Durham, USA
kristin.huffman@duke.edu
[2] University of Padova, 35100 Padova, Italy
andrea.giordano@unipd.it

**Abstract.** Using digital methods, the time has arrived for deepening the scholarly analysis of visual and written documents that validate and/or reveal previously unknown urban circumstances. Traditional methodologies of art, architectural and urban history remain the foundation of rigorous digital approaches; the study of a city necessitates scholarly decryption of information and visual sources that connect them to a broader historical context. As new digital tools and applications have become available, iconographic and textual sources– primary data of exceptional value not only from an historical point of view, but also for interpretative inflections – can now be interwoven as a scientific practice. This is the principal objective of *Visualizing Venice to Visualizing Cities*.

**Keywords:** Cities visualization · HBIM · Virtual museum · Interoperability

## 1 Visualizing Venice to Visualizing Cities

### 1.1 Advanced Technologies for Historical Cities Visualization

There is a demand for deepening the scholarly analysis of documents that validate and/or reveal urban circumstances. Traditional methodologies of architectural and urban history must remain the foundational core of digital approaches; the study of a city will always necessitate scholarly decryption of information and visual sources that connect them to their broader context. We have worked toward complementing the expertise of art and architectural historians with that of architects and visual and media studies experts.

With all of our research projects, art and architectural historians have conducted archival research fundamental to our understanding. And with each of our projects, the process of building a virtual model led to new discoveries in the field. In sum, digital technologies have enabled us to advance our understandings about how to use new tools both as a more integrated part of the research process as well as to new display outcomes.

© Springer Nature Switzerland AG 2021
F. Niebling et al. (Eds.): UHDL 2019, CCIS 1501, pp. 171–187, 2021.
https://doi.org/10.1007/978-3-030-93186-5_8

This paper will trace the development of *Visualizing Venice to Visualizing Cities*, an international research initiative involving Duke University, the University of Padua, and IUAV – Venice, that evolved from the foundational strategies developed by *Visualizing Venice*.

This initiative includes examination of urban systems and sites not only within Venice, but also Padua, Carpi, Athens, and Krakow to demonstrate how the documentation and understanding of cultural sites and their complexities can be understood as part of a multimedia process that includes the interpretation of digital visualizations of historic monuments [1]. Using various examples, this contribution shows three distinct phases for this kind of inquiry:

– Data acquisition: archival research, laser scans and photogrammetric surveys processed and organized through 3D modeling and implemented between interoperable platforms;
– Data communication: the information gathered with the methods listed above conveyed through the design of apps and interactive systems for multimedia devices and web platforms. This process entails designing and testing augmented reality and 3D models for multimedia devices and the implementation of immersive reality;
– Integrating models as a means of analysis into the process of conservation of the architectural assets with the virtual reconstruction of architectural features.

It is possible to apply advanced technologies for the visualization of historical cities and specific sites to demonstrate the ways in which digital methods are potentially useful and applicable to a range of cultural places [2]. This relatively novel methodological approach to the fields of architectural and urban history has resulted in new forms of documentation and understandings as well as innovative public facing, scholarly outcomes with multimedia visualizations. *Visualizing Venice to Visualizing Cities* has developed this methodology over the past ten years, especially with regard to the application of emerging technologies; the resultant expansion of skill sets, expertise, and collaboration; and finally, the volume and types of public facing initiatives represented by publications, international workshops and exhibitions (see Figs. 1a, b, c).

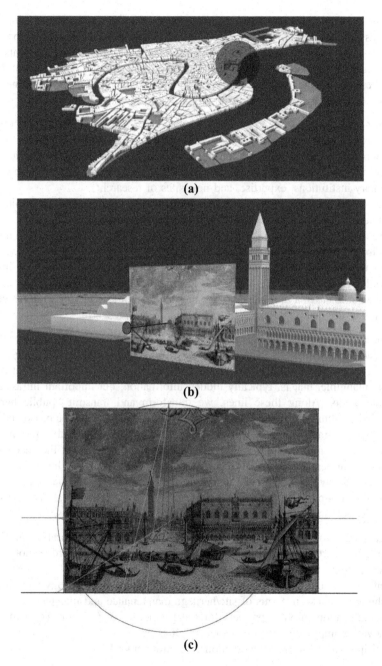

**(a)**

**(b)**

**(c)**

**Fig. 1. a.** The *Senses of Venice* exhibition at Duke University, Durham, USA: the "reinterpretation" of the Map of Venice of Ludovico Ughi (curated by Kristin L. Huffman, model elaboration by Cristina Zago and Martino della Valle). **b.** The *Senses of Venice* exhibition at Duke University, Durham, USA: the position of the observer for an app (curated by Kristin L. Huffman, model elaboration by Cristina Zago and Martino della Valle). **c.** The *Senses of Venice* exhibition at Duke University, Durham, USA: the perspective restitution of the views of the Ughi's Map (curated by Kristin L. Huffman, elaboration Cristina Zago and Martino della Valle).

Most important, this paper serves to emphasize that the application of select digital tools has advanced scholarly knowledge and historical understandings about built environments—how buildings reveal lived experiences—from past moments to the present day. Future progress involves expansion beyond the many lessons learned about these innovative historical studies and their visualizations of urban phenomenon. Looking forward, we would like to highlight the following salient points:

- how to expand our scope to include urban studies programs with engaging on-going research related to a wide variety of cities and their distinctive phenomena;
- how partnership and collaboration might organically become more capacious (with presently unanticipated tasks in the future), as we work in concert with complementary institutions, expertise, and new sites of research;
- how to visualize the progressive transformation of cities over time in pioneering virtual environments, namely with emerging technologies;
- how to highlight each city's distinctive features, built and natural, that mutually reinforce urban evolution as a phenomenon;
- how to articulate clearly and transparently the complex intersection of involved social, political, and economic forces in virtual documented form;
- how to animate in a multi-sensory manner the phenomenology of an urban center's everyday life and experiences from the past to the present.

The challenge, consequently, is to generate a "value chain" of attraction, allowing investigated cities to make visible and accessible their heritage assets: tangible ones (scenery, urban space, culture, art, products and brands, facilities, needs of citizens) as well as intangible, that is, typically hidden information, but important infrastructures and data assets. Along these lines, we transform and transmit "public heritage", including its cultural properties into a "common good" accessible to a broad and varied public. Such a transformation will delineate a remarkable and usable resource, promoting at the same time the dynamics of active participation in the management, protection, and enhancement of urban heritage – e.g., through the activation and promotion of ways to locate resources and funds for cultural and tourism projects.

For this reason, it is essential to reorganize and update what has constituted communication and promotional intervention, in the following areas:

- organization of academic and training strategies of architectural/urban Cultural Heritage (starting from local areas and then moving outward nationally and internationally);
- configuration of an "augmented" multimedia delivery methodology including new technologies, also in terms of site/heritage maintenance and management;
- communication of vital projects for the promotion of Cultural Tourism for the innovative improvement of investigated cities;
- participation in European/international cultural networks.

The realization of this vision must arise from the inherent promise of Information Communication Technologies (ICT), such as ML - machine learning, AI-artificial intelligence, remote monitoring, non-invasive control, data documentation, in an effort to capitalize on, and make connections across, the untapped potential of extensive cultural networks (see Fig. 2).

**Fig. 2.** Potential of BIM and ICT relation: the deviance analysis as a non-invasive operation, the Eremitani Church, Padova (elaboration Paolo Borin, Federico Panarotto, Maria Rosaria Cundari).

### 1.2 Key Challenges, Outcomes and Methodologies

The goals of *Visualizing Venice to Visualizing Cities* are two-fold: to encourage the enlightenment and development of cultural studies and all its branches, including cultural tourism; and to develop and advance a repeatable method. Leveraging ICT generally, this initiative enhances the management, accessibility, and dissemination of data and documentation, optimizing resources and ensuring the inclusive and sustainable use and management of information sources and cultural sites. Recently, the project involves AI-Artificial Intelligence to support select activities, from computer vision techniques to the organization of documents and models along specific paths based on collected data.

The *VV to VC* project systemizes incremental activity in an effort to generate reference procedures that emerge from select case-studies and that could be applicable to others. Its impact on the scholarly community and beyond will open up possible, dynamic social transformations, improving the field of Cultural Heritage, while concomitantly increasing awareness of its substance, global relevance and importance and in advancement of topics such as conservation, salvage, and restoration. The expected outcomes of *VV to VC* consist of strengthening the interplay between theory and practice - learning by doing - with the collaboration between universities, research groups and local partners and a range of expertise, generating progressive effects on:

- quality of culture and consciousness;
- knowledge of places and spaces;

- scientific research and durable/inclusive funding;
- academic and business, market exchange, in particular with academic institutions and Cultural Tourism.

From an operational point of view, the project, therefore, implements innovative methodologies for the acquisition, processing, and communication of data connected to Cultural Heritage. It leverages ICT capabilities, such as AI-supported personalized delivery of multimedia content on mobile devices, along with sensor-supported monitoring of current building conditions. This methodology organizes a platform/infrastructure that manages and monitors architectural heritage, regulating consistency and the dissemination of findings and new discoveries. The ongoing development of apps and websites generates steady and progressive feedback that has an impact on future innovative possibilities for the communication of cultural content; ultimately this approach facilitates the sharing and opening of new information about the history of a city from artistic, architectural and urbanistic points of view.

### 1.3 A Forward-Thinking Methodology and Innovative Visualizations: Our Goals

An ambitious enterprise within digital humanities, the advancement of architectural and urban histories using digital methods necessitates an expanded network of contributors with varying expertise and multi-disciplinary backgrounds. Simple models or digital maps of the city are no longer the goal. Rather, the creation of dynamic interactive and interoperable displays that can reveal and subsequently identify complex urban systems via new modes of communication are needed. In this, visual presentation strategies parallel the complex, ever-changing vitality of the cities themselves.

Dialogues across fields, not to mention, from academic institutions to the professional industry, mark an exciting moment for the field of art, architectural and urban histories. New processes and codes for communicating knowledge-based visualizations have assumed a decidedly important role. The latest technologies have emerged within the professional industry to benefit directly academic research initiatives. It is to these digital tools that we now turn [3].

The *Visualizing Venice to Visualizing Cities* initiative has the following goals:

- technological innovation in the fields of database implementation for the collection and management of information concerning Cultural Heritage;
- implementation of technologies and skills related to the survey of architectural heritage;
- use of technologies and skills that relate to the instrumental survey of surfaces within architectural structures, namely digital interoperable elaboration (SCAN-to-BIM);
- realization of a semantic/interoperable 3D model with Building Information Modeling Systems - BIM;
- realization of the BIM model as a repository for data asset management.

At this stage we intend to work on preliminary findings and the organization of data related to particular scholarly materials: primary sources (scientific as well as archival and documentary research) and secondary sources (published materials, analysis of the actual state of monuments, and study of the geometric-constructive survey) regarding the case study under examination. This foundation will function as a general code that extends understandings of artistic and architectural heritage due to the critical processing of the above-mentioned acquired data. The critical re-elaboration of this material will be structured and made available for further, future investigations through interoperable-digital elaboration protocols and formats.

From a methodological point of view it is possible to begin with a topographic survey of the heritage under examination: a point cloud generated from a laser scanner – provided with geographic coordinates for topographic mapping – guarantees access to geometric/shape information. At the same time, its organization into a proper database enables the following: a) bibliographic references, including digitized documents and major publications; b) a photographic archive that enhances knowledge of the historical evolution of analyzed monuments, opening lines of critical inquiry for subsequent investigation. Managing archive data, metric-shape data (point clouds), and georeferenced data, will generate dialogue among the various types of information and facilitate more profound analysis of artifacts; at this stage, data interoperability connects to several digital tools, providing flexibility for analysis and processing (for example, through the use of even simple formats, such as tables or spreadsheets), making available visualization tools via an open access platform.

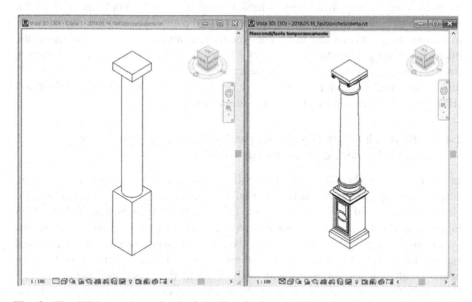

**Fig. 3.** The BIM repository: level of detail – Scoletta del Carmine, Padova (elaboration in REVIT – Autodesk – by Rachele Bernardello, Mirka Dalla Longa, Emanuela Faresin, Giulia Piccinin).

Finally, the definitive goal is to generate detailed interoperable digital models to serve as a repository on which to "load" all the information pertaining to the surveyed artifact (see Fig. 3), including but not limited to archival materials, asset management activities, mapping materials, geometry, measurements, shapes, and material and structural information, such as textures, decay, etc. Integrating and optimizing data into a unified information environment, georeferenced to a web-based system, will ensure ongoing, scholarly access and interpretation. The interoperable digital model will thus become a cornerstone of this research initiative, as it will allow comparative replicability for other cultural sites. This digital "organism" will be capable of verifying consistency and highlighting constituent problems, such as decay, techniques, and substrate background characteristics (in terms of structural and technological issues as well as in relation to the historical-monumental buildings on which these surfaces may exist). Therefore, the process of integration and continuous verification between the current building's situation and the analytical model provides a variety of information in a single digital environment: the structural verification of concerned walls and the analysis and mapping of decay facilitates the discovery of correct strategies for optimizing a structure's maintenance.

In conclusion, *VV to VC* will produce workflows for testing and experimenting models, derived from SCAN-to-BIM operations that include "virtual-augmented-mixed" platforms. The methodology will, therefore, utilize a database inextricably linked to the production of the BIM model to connect all information about the analyzed building directly to the virtual model. This will enable coordination of all the informational assets, not only geometric, visual and metric, but also the current needs of management and maintenance. This model will also be used to investigate the interaction among geometries, shapes, and information with unquestionable feedback for pedagogical initiatives and advanced training, dissemination, cultural tourism and display environments using virtual reality devices, such as Head-Mounted Displays (HMD) and Cave Automatic Virtual Environments (Cave).

### 1.4    LIDAR (Light Detecting Radar) and GPR (Ground Penetrating Radar): Measuring the Seemingly Invisible

In the case of the Eremitani, we used LIDAR, a type of laser scanner, to acquire accurate and specific spatial data (see Fig. 4). This data was converted into a point cloud model, colored points in virtual form that correspond to its existing reality, which in turn helped inform the production of a physical 3D model. For extant structures, this system of measuring data, most especially the inaccessible heights of architectural spaces, has proven the most accurate and reliable tool. Looking from above to down below (vaulted spaces to crypts and tombs beneath the floor), the case of Carpi's Cathedral offered us the chance to use GPR. Practical in the building industry, this tool, a machine that moves systematically across the floor, provided information about modifications to the structure at a foundational level [4].

**Fig. 4.** Spatial data of the Eremitani church, Padova (LIDAR survey and point cloud elaboration by Maria Rosaria Cundari and Christina Boscaro).

Even though strongly suspected or understood in documents related to the history of the building, both of these tools verified understandings hidden from or difficult to calibrate with the human eye, making the invisible visible and the abstract more concrete. Using these methods, we advance the following: architectural heritage based on a deep analysis of the case studies of historical and cultural valuable cities; a semantic 3D database of digital models with varying levels of "certainty", useful in the management of research assets as well as future planning for preservation and heritage management; a GIS updated database of architectural monuments that could map their placement in the city, their accessibility and potential interconnectivity, and their main characteristics; virtual models with different peculiarities adopted according to narrative potentiality, useful for the enhancement of individual architectural monuments through interactive knowledge pathways.

## 1.5    HBIM (Historic Building Information Modeling): Interoperable 3D Modeling

Recording information about historic structures using available technologies offers an anticipatory way to preserve Cultural Heritage sites and ensure that any necessary future interventions follow, as closely as possible, historical precedents. Building Information Modeling (BIM) is one such way. It is referred to as "semantic" modeling given that precise meanings are associated with specific architectural components. The approach to, and management of, historic buildings require the cooperation of many different experts (architects, historians, engineers, superintendents, business corporations) who together are capable of generating a large volume of disparate information such as drawings, documents, on-site analysis, pictures, videos and notes.

Maintaining and finding this information is often very costly and time-consuming. BIM provides static 3D representations of original information used to inspect the building in an effort to progress monitoring and ensure quality. An historic building is however a continuously evolving entity, and never static. An interoperable/semantic HBIM model includes and simulates all information, from historical to structural points of view, involving the building's lifecycle and anticipating what lies in the future. HBIM enables not only the placement within a model of multiple types of information regarding its construction materials and measurements, but also archival content related to transformations at different moments of the building's history (time and geographic coordinates, documentary, and iconographic resources).The model becomes a repository of information related to the monument (see Fig. 5); historical information is literally embedded within the separate building features from larger units, such as outer walls and vaults, to the specific blocks used to build them. These historical sources are overlaid enabling their philological interpretation and contextual relationship over time [5, 6]. At the same time, such a model operates as a dynamic, expressive real-time information system [7]. To serve this purpose it needs to be fed with all types of relevant data (primary and secondary sources: archival materials, 2D and 3D images, videos, progress reports, quality and safety assessments, etc.), which must be astutely selected, fused, compared, and analyzed as planned and coordinated BIM data. Machine Learning and Artificial Intelligence techniques have the potential to play a decisive role in the fulfillment of the above aims with a combination of data and model [8, 9]. Finally, the visualization in the form of a 3D model becomes another type of secondary source; it becomes a structural receptacle for "housing" collected data. For art and architectural historians who must define their scholarly contributions, HBIM offers a solution for the publication of findings within the building itself, both independent documents as well as larger narratives (see Fig. 6). HBIM, therefore, presents the potential for a scholarly publication forum and additional opportunities to share research findings [10–12].

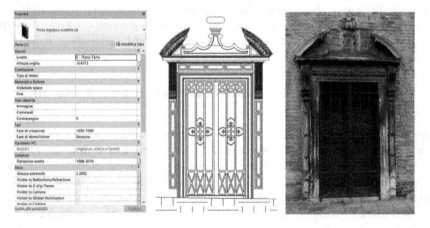

**Fig. 5.** The BIM model as a repository of information related to the monument – Scoletta del Carmine, Padova (elaboration by Rachele Bernardello, Mirka Dalla Longa, Emanuela Faresin, Giulia Piccinin).

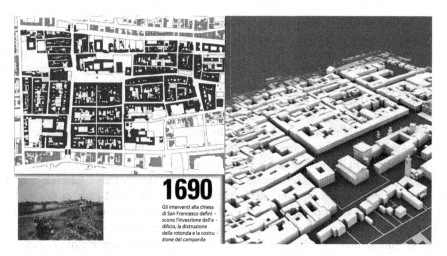

**Fig. 6.** Visualization of Carpi's transformation over time (Elena Svalduz, Cosimo Monteleone, Isabella Friso, Federico Panarotto, Paolo Borin).

Our challenge is to generate an innovative and critical approach to the use and treatment of Cultural Heritage, investigating the integration between BIM and AI/AR, with wide-ranging effects on the enhancement, recuperation, management, and use of Cultural Architectural Heritage. The idea was born from the awareness that both the development of tourism and ongoing management of Cultural Architectural Heritage - economic, protection and safeguarding, etc. – benefit from unprecedented synergies with advanced digital technologies. A side effect with such approaches has been that within a specific digital environment, a multiplicity of information can be adopted to ensure correct (intervention) strategies in relation to the effects a Cultural Heritage site may have – e.g. in terms of flow of visitors, maintenance, restoration, optimization of energy consumption, etc. – within a typical IoT– Internet of Things process [13]. The visitors' immersion in virtual 3D space takes place with portable devices, such as smartphones and tablets, that any operator can easily use: thanks to AR, operators may "enter" the BIM model generated by laser scanner/photogrammetric measurements; the use of the point cloud can be further improved in the investigation of Scan-to-BIM, allowing the virtual inspection of the architecture and the close analysis of all its characteristics by experts in the field. BIM model visualization with AR will revolutionize a user's approach given its apt interface with what the scientific operator has produced, e.g., in situations where it is necessary to view enlarged details or when access to normally inaccessible (fragile and vulnerable) spaces is required for further study.

Essentially, the digital duplicate thus created will allow the automatic analysis and interpretation of documentation connected to a specific structural or decorative apparatus, along with access to a rigorous documentary apparatus. Interestingly, what has been implemented in BIM, may provide further feedback to areas such as the evaluation of design and structural interventions also involving safe use and management topics [14, 15].

Therefore the BIM/AR combination holds great potential for tourism given the historical information in the "semantic" 3D model can be viewed and browsed by tourists and scholars alike through an immersive virtual space, faithful to reality but enhanced with the possible combination of movement and information. Moreover, the reconstruction of digital models, obtained from BIM with material mappings, facilitates study of these artefacts without necessarily being on site or having to intervene with testing, experimentation, and analysis. Finally, the reproduction of tangible, physical models from the digital serves to facilitate the interaction of the visually impaired with such Cultural Heritage, augmenting the inclusivity of the proposal.

In sum, the individual research components allow the systematic creation, and organization, of a building's information [16]. While the interoperable database collects documentation, information, and interpretations, the Scan-to-BIM know-hows lead to the creation of an interoperable virtual model that contains the surveyed architecture, infographics, and information from the database. The result is a semantic model (geometry, information, documents, historical images, thermo-hygrometric values and measurements, etc.) that can be utilized in interactive repositories and visualization platforms (see Fig. 7).

The advantage of using ICT tools becomes essential in the identification of clear, cognitive, navigable paths in digital environments as well as to define networks of relationships between documents and redefine them according to updated needs, newly discovered content, and favorable access points.

**Fig. 7.** From the document to BIM: Baldassarre Peruzzi, San Petronio, Bologna (elaboration by Cosimo Monteleone, Elena Svalduz, Manuela Rossi, for the exhibition Costruire il Tempio, Carpi, 2016).

**Fig. 8.** The App for the Cathedral of Carpi (3D model by Isabella Friso; elaboration: QBGroup).

### 1.6   Augmented Reality: The Transmogrification of the Digital into a Real Experience

The data driven model leads to the visual and narrative content displayed in exhibitions. For example, through the use of intermediary tools, the virtual model of the Cathedral of Carpi, recently restored following destruction caused by an earthquake in 2012, has been experienced in the real world (see Fig. 8). One installation in the exhibition featured an augmented reality; portable devices could lock onto an image of the structure's architectural plan (presented in a 2D vector format), converting that 2D image into a free-standing 3D version that hovers in a way for viewers to experience fully in the round. The 3D HBIM model inter-operated with the digital platform for public display. We have experimented further with this technology projecting digital models of demolished spaces onto the real site in which they originally stood, most notably the Ovetari Chapel in the Eremitani (see Fig. 9a, b).

There, the virtual visualization merged 3D point clouds, geometric primitives and 3D models. The reconstructive virtual models, integrating low-res and high-res 3D point clouds, proved advantageous, not only for scholarly interpretation, but also for Cultural Heritage communication and promotion [16].

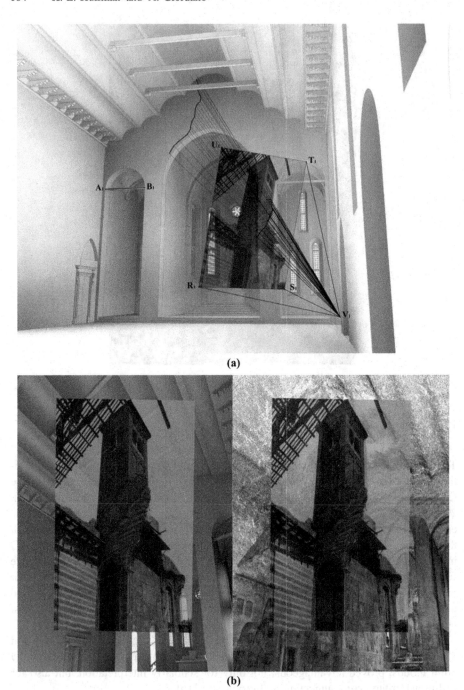

(a)

(b)

**Fig. 9. a.** Projecting demolished spaces on the digital model, Eremitani Church, Padova (elaboration by Paolo Borin, Federico Panarotto). **b.** Projecting demolished spaces on the digital model, Eremitani Church, Padova (elaboration by Paolo Borin, Federico Panarotto).

The implementation of 3D point clouds and BIM models in a database devoted to visualize the architecture can be used as a basis for an Augmented Reality experience. Starting with camera recognition of select spaces or individual architectural elements, AR can be harnessed as a vehicle to add supplemental textual or visual information to the specific decorative element of the architecture as well to visualize reconstructed surroundings that are not accessible or extant. Off-site, via web-based platforms, it is possible to visualize anywhere or anytime the 3D model. Finally, for some case studies it is possible to superimpose concrete information with detected, more speculative ones, visualizing reconstructed geometrical spaces and hypothetical architectural reconstructions. AI/AR will prove fundamental in an effort to test cultural site navigation and the interrogation of the semantic model using innovative tools, such as the implementation of ad hoc sensors [17]. All the partners and various city initiatives involved in *VV to VC* will provide a foundation for future cultural interventions that include technological advancements, notably for the development and innovative use of interoperable models that embed indispensable scholarly research for future study. This initiative highlights local cultural realities and histories, public and private, and stands to enhance architectural heritage for scientific purposes as well as more widely disseminated tourism [18].

## 2   Conclusion and Future Steps

In conclusion, using a range of technologies, such as computerized platforms and interoperable databases and models, web sites, mobile applications, and augmented and virtual realities, combined with historical documentation, it is possible to generate new considerations about the ways in which architectural structures embody any number of social, economic, religious, and political forces throughout history. Such a method also visually reveals how urban environments are in constant flux, changing to respond to historical circumstances and systemic urban phenomena.

The construction of a virtual archive of selected cities can be a test to address several open problems related to ICT, not to mention provide an opportunity to experiment with new systems. The collected data/documentation will respond to content management needs: different types and formats of documents (archival and digital) should be included, and these should be organized and connected. Additionally, the system should update itself dynamically in order to deal with the flow of new information. At the same time, it must guarantee long-term accessibility to data, and therefore, it should remain compatible with newly emerging data retrieval tools. Moreover, the collections of data must be accessible to varying specialized levels, accommodating purposes ranging from scholarly research to dissemination to a broad public, as with tourism. In short, we must address the and identify different paths of knowledge within new and complex information typologies and topologies. The need has risen to take into account the characteristic heterogeneity of cultural heritage to support consistently data integration (the homogeneous representation of different types of documents), the interoperability of content (the possibility to access and edit data through different devices and software), and the scalability of the tools in use (hence a flexibility over time with respect to the quantity and type of input).

We are not only witnessing expansion in the ICT field, but also rapidly changing technical resolutions, functionalities, tools, and software compatibility. The pursuance of the project aims to contribute to the creation of a widespread museum that does not isolate buildings and documents from the urban context, but is rather a dynamic source of knowledge, based on the current use of architectural heritage. It can then become the privileged access point for the enhancement of knowledge and heritage. Looking toward the future, we can expect an integrated reading of varying types of information in visually driven narrative formats that might permit comparative analyses, and, therefore, relational understandings of urban networks. Eventually, cities will become not only museums of knowledge, but ones that have the capacity to speak to one another about continuity and change, differences and similarities.

# References

1. Huffman, K., Giordano, A., Bruzelius, C. (eds.): Visualizing Venice - Mapping and Modeling Time and Change in a City. Routledge, London (2018)
2. Paskins, J.: Paris Under Construction: Building Sites and Urban Transformation in the 1960s. Routledge, New York (2015)
3. Giordano, A.: Mapping Venice. From visualizing Venice to visualizing cities. In: Piga, B.E. A., Salerno, R. (eds.) Urban Design and Representation, pp. 143–151. Springer, Cham (2017). https://doi.org/10.1007/978-3-319-51804-6_11
4. Terpstra, N., Rose, C.: Mapping Space, Sense, and Movement in Florence: Historical GIS and the Early Modern City. Routledge, New York (2016)
5. Giordano, A., Friso, I., Borin, P., Monteleone, C., Panarotto, F.: Time and space in the history of cities. In: Münster, S., Friedrichs, K., Niebling, F., Seidel-Grzesińska, A. (eds.) Digital Research and Education in Architectural Heritage. UHDL 2017, DECH 2017. Communications in Computer and Information Science, vol. 817, pp. 47–62. Springer, Cham (2018). https://doi.org/10.1007/978-3-319-76992-9_4
6. Apollonio, F.I., Gaiani, M., Corsi, C.: A semantic and parametric method for 3D models used in 3D cognitive-information system. In: 28th ECAADE Conference Proceedings, pp. 863–872 (2010)
7. Carpo, M.: The Second Digital Turn: Design Beyond Intelligence, 1st edn. The MIT Press, Cambridge, MA (2017)
8. De Luca, L.: Methods, formalisms and tools for the semantic-based surveying and representation of architectural heritage. Appl. Geomat. (2011)
9. Dore, C., Murphy, M.: Current state of the art historic building information modeling. In: The International Archives of the Photogrammetry, Remote Sensing and Spatial Information Sciences, vol. XLII-2/W5, 2017 26th International CIPA Symposium 2017, 28 August–01 September 2017, Ottawa, Canada (2017)
10. Ferragina, P., Luccio, F.: Computational Thinking: First Algorithms, Then Code, 1st edn. Springer, Cham, Switzerland (2018)
11. Frazer, J.: Parametric computation: history and future. Archit. Des. (2016)
12. Liu, X., Wang, X., Wright, G., Cheng, J., Li, X., Liu, R.: A state-of-the-art review on the integration of building information modeling (BIM) and geographic information system (GIS). ISPRS Int. J. Geo-Inf. **6**(53) (2017)

13. Murphy, M., Govern, E.M., Pavia, S.: Historic building information modelling – adding intelligence to laser and image based surveys of European classical architecture. ISPRS J. Photogramm. Remote Sens. (2013)

14. Yang, H., Zhang, H.: Automatic 3D reconstruction of a polyhedral object from a single line drawing under perspective projection. Comput. Graph. (Pergamon) **65**, 45–59 (2017)

15. Yongwook, J.: A study on the BIM evaluation, analytics, and prediction (EAP) framework and platform in linked building ontologies and reasoners with clouds. Adv. Civil Eng. (2), 1–14 (2018)

16. Oreni, D., Brumana, R., Della Torre, S., Banfi, F., Barazzetti, L., Previtali, M.: Survey turned into HBIM: the restoration and the work involved concerning the Basilica di Collemaggio after the earthquake (L'Aquila). ISPRS Ann. Photogramm. Remote Sens. Spat. Inf. Sci. **II-5**, 267–273 (2014)

17. Bozzelli, G., et al.: An integrated VR/AR framework for user-centric interactive experience of cultural heritage: the arkae vision project. Digit. Appl. Archaeol. Cult. Herit. **15**, e00124 (2019)

18. Zhang, K., Chen, Y., Li, C.: Discovering the tourists' behaviors and perceptions in a tourism destination by analyzing photos' visual content with a computer deep learning model: the case of Beijing. Tour. Manag. **75**, 595–608 (2019)

# Machine Learning and Artificial Intelligence

# Semantic Deep Mapping in the Amsterdam Time Machine: Viewing Late 19th- and Early 20th-Century Theatre and Cinema Culture Through the Lens of Language Use and Socio-Economic Status

Julia Noordegraaf[1(✉)], Marieke van Erp[2], Richard Zijdeman[3,4], Mark Raat[5], Thunnis van Oort[12], Ivo Zandhuis[3,6], Thomas Vermaut[2], Hans Mol[5], Nicoline van der Sijs[7], Kristel Doreleijers[8,13], Vincent Baptist[9], Charlotte Vrielink[1], Brenda Assendelft[10], Claartje Rasterhoff[11], and Ivan Kisjes[1]

[1] University of Amsterdam, Amsterdam, The Netherlands
j.j.noordegraaf@uva.nl
[2] KNAW Humanities Cluster, Amsterdam, The Netherlands
[3] International Institute of Social History, Amsterdam, The Netherlands
[4] University of Stirling, Stirling, UK
[5] Fryske Akademy/HisGIS, Leeuwarden, The Netherlands
[6] Ivo Zandhuis Onderzoek & Advies, Haarlem, The Netherlands
[7] Instituut voor de Nederlandse Taal, Leiden, The Netherlands
[8] Tilburg University, Tilburg, The Netherlands
[9] Erasmus University Rotterdam, Rotterdam, The Netherlands
[10] Leiden University, Leiden, The Netherlands
[11] Maastricht University, Maastricht, The Netherlands
[12] Radboud University, Nijmegen, The Netherlands
[13] Meertens Institute, Amsterdam, The Netherlands

**Abstract.** In this paper, we present our work on semantic deep mapping at scale by combining information from various sources and disciplines to study historical Amsterdam. We model our data according to semantic web standards and ground them in space and time such that we can investigate what happened at a particular time and place from a linguistics, socio-economic and urban historical perspective. In a small use case we test the spatio-temporal infrastructure for research on entertainment culture in Amsterdam around the turn of the 20th century. We explain the bottlenecks we encountered for integrating information from different disciplines and sources and how we resolved or worked around them. Finally, we present a set of recommendations and best practices for adapting semantic deep mapping to other settings.

**Keywords:** Semantic web · Digital humanities · Deep mapping · Linguistics · Social and economic history · Urban history · Media studies

© Springer Nature Switzerland AG 2021
F. Niebling et al. (Eds.): UHDL 2019, CCIS 1501, pp. 191–212, 2021.
https://doi.org/10.1007/978-3-030-93186-5_9

# 1   Introduction

The Amsterdam Time Machine (ATM) aims to provide an integrated platform for presenting historical information about people, places, relations, events, and objects in a spatial and temporal context, with a focus on the city of Amsterdam. The web of data on the history of Amsterdam is created by systematically linking existing datasets from social science and humanities research with municipal and cultural heritage data, where possible in the form of Linked Open Data. The linked data can then be organised and presented in spatial representations, such as geographical and 3D visualisations. The result is a virtual replica of the city, which allows users to explore the city through space and time, at the level of neighbourhoods, streets, or individual houses.

Recently, the authors collaborated in developing a first proof of concept that connects linked data from the Amsterdam cultural heritage institutions and various scholarly research projects to a GIS infrastructure that provides the historical geographical and topological context for these linked datasets, focusing on the period 1832–1921.[1] Such an infrastructure has to be based on precisely identified and localised historical addresses, since these function as the key to a large amount of civil and fiscal data. The Fryske Akademy HisGIS (Historical GIS) team that developed the GIS infrastructure introduced the principle of geographical coordinates as anchor points for all historical data with a spatial component that cannot be tied to specific geometries of buildings or plots. The location points prevent the most common pitfalls of linking historical addresses with specific geometries of parcels or buildings as starting points, which because of changes through time eventually may lead to fuzzy and inaccurate connections caused by historical mutations such as the merging, demolition, split or aggregation of houses and their addresses.

In addition to building the GIS infrastructure, the aim was to test the use of such a geo-spatial platform as an instrument for digital humanities research. Building on the concept of 'deep maps' [3] - geographical representations of data on both the material and experiential dimensions of a place - the Amsterdam Time Machine geo-spatial platform aims to facilitate 'scalable digital humanities research': smoothly navigating historical data from the micro level of one location, anecdote or document to the macro level of patterns in large, linked datasets that expose broader social and cultural processes. The Amsterdam Time Machine operationalises this by investigating the urban history of Amsterdam on a scale that varies between the micro level of a plot, person or place and the macro level of broader societal processes in the city as a whole - a microscope and telescope in one [12,44]. Such research environments offer an unprecedented opportunity to explore the relationship between physical and social space and how this connection was experienced and transformed over time.

---

[1] The temporal focus was based on the availability of already vectorised Napoleonic cadastre from the years 1811–1832 and available data on the introduction of the modern house numbering system in the 1870s and the new neighbourhood system in 1909. We decided to extend this into 1921 to accommodate one of the datasets in the use case.

To test the potential of the ATM platform as a research instrument, the authors conducted a small, pilot use case on Amsterdam entertainment culture in the late 19th and early 20th century. The use case brought together data and insights from three different humanities disciplines - linguistics, socio-economic history, and media studies - to study the emergence of cinema as a new form of entertainment at the turn of the twentieth century against the background of the existing forms of entertainment and the socio-economic composition of the neighbourhoods in which this entertainment was located. Combining data on Amsterdam dialects, occupational status and leisure venues and visualising them in the GIS infrastructure allowed us to test the platform's capacity for interdisciplinary research, by making a connection between social, economic and cultural dimensions of turn of the 20th century urban life in the capital.

## 2   Related Work

The core idea of the Amsterdam Time Machine revolves around anchoring information to time and place. This concept is not novel, but its scale as envisioned by the European Time Machine [48] is. The first project in this consortium to present this grand vision was the Venice Time Machine [23], which showcased a walk through the Venice of 1,000 years ago via digitised and transcribed maps, registries and images. The current constellation of Time Machine projects has been made possible by the groundwork laid by sub-disciplines such as spatial humanities [2,3] and projects such as the Reassembling the Republic of Letters COST Action (2015–2018).[2]

A relatively new development is the cross-over between humanities and semantic web research. Projects such as FDR/Pearl Harbor [22], Agora [50], Dutch Ships and Sailors [8], and the Semantic Sampo portals [21] are exploring the possibilities of representing and connecting concepts from historical documents for advanced search and analysis. The advantage of modelling concepts according to semantic web standards, is that they use a uniform format and when modelled using shared ontologies, can be connected to other sources in the Linked Open Data cloud [33].

The Amsterdam Time Machine project currently focuses on three use cases: linguistics, media studies, and socio-economic history, which are connected through a geotemporal link. Due to its historical focus on the city of Amsterdam, the project is also positioned in the realm of urban history. As this is not a survey paper, we briefly highlight work on the intersection of semantic web and each of these domains. For a broader overview of semantic web technologies in the humanities, the reader is referred to [35].

The linguistics community has been computationally modelling language for over 4 decades, with WordNet as its most famous lexical database [39]. Semantic web-ready models such as the OntoLex-Lemon [34] have evolved into W3C backed standards. Since 2011, the community is working towards keeping track

---

[2] http://www.republicofletters.net/.

of semantic web datasets describing linguistic phenomena in the linguistic linked open data cloud [5].

Many historians in the field of social and economic history work with structured or tabular data such as census data. This type of data lends itself well to integration with the semantic web. In the Netherlands, the CEDAR project [36] and follow-up use cases within CLARIAH-CORE and CLARIAH-PLUS[3] have shown that converting and integrating social and economic data can ease scholarly workflows and lead to new insights [19,37].

Digitised media have been the topic of interest in many semantic web research projects (cf, [46], Multimedian) but often with a focus on improving data annotation and object retrieval. Some work has attempted to create links between media, location and the past (cf. [17]) but to the best of our knowledge, the Amsterdam Time Machine project is the first project that aims to leverage semantic web standards to answer humanities scholars' urban history and media studies research questions.

## 3   Semantic Deep Mapping

### 3.1   Deep Mapping as Concept and Method for Researching Urban History

The focus on space as an angle from which to explore people, places and events in the history of a city is not new. As historian Jo Guldi has explained, the interest of humanities researchers in space as an angle for analysis dates back to the 1880s, "when scholars in history, religion, and psychology reflected on our nature as beings situated in space." [15] From the 1970s, under the influence of French philosophers such as Michel Foucault, Henri Lefebvre, Michel de Certeau and Paul Virilio, the analysis of space has been connected to questions of power, causing a true 'spatial turn' in various humanities disciplines. For urban historians, this meant that they considered the city with a "renewed interest" in the ways in which the "microcosms of everyday life" are related to the "macrocosms of global flows". [15] Or, in the words of historian Charles Tilly, how they rediscovered the city as a "privileged site for study of the interaction between large social processes and routines of local life" [49, p. 704].

This revived interest in space as a core angle for the analysis of everyday local life was greatly aided by the emergence of new, digital technology, in particular the Geographical Information System (GIS) developed in the 1960s by the Canada Land Inventory. GIS allowed scholars in the humanities and social sciences to create digital maps on which data on various phenomena could be visualised and analysed at different levels of aggregation. Within the humanities, GIS has been most routinely employed by archaeologists for organizing and analyzing their excavation data. After that, GIS has also been discovered in other areas, such as Literary Studies [26], Film Studies [20] and History [14,32]. As

---

[3] https://clariah.nl/en/.

David Bodenhamer, John Corrigan and Trevor M. Harris point out, a carto-graphical representation of historical data "provides fresh perspective and new insights into the study of culture and society." [3, p. 2]

In an attempt to do justice to the complexity of human culture that is the topic of humanities research, Bodenhamer, Corrigan and Harris have proposed the concept of 'deep maps' as the next step in humanities research [3]. A deep map extends the focus of geographical information systems on tangible or mate-rial aspects of space with attention for the way people attribute meaning to specific places. [3, p. 3] This takes the form of adding sources that document the use and experience of public space at a given moment and as it evolved over time. Such a 'thickening' of the information layers included in GISs eventually allows for the realisation of 'mirror worlds': virtual places that correspond to actual places [11,24]. It is the ambition of the European Time Machine project to leverage Europe's digital cultural heritage for extending such mirror worlds with the dimension of time, so that we can explore the rich complexity of human culture from both a spatial and temporal perspective.[4]

Various scholars in literature, history, archeology and media studies have experimented with the concept of deep mapping, enriching cartographic repre-sentations of specific places with sources that document the use and experience of the place, for example, as imagined by artists (e.g., [30]) or figuring in pop-ular movies and television series (e.g., [4]). Our approach aims to expand upon such existing work by creating an infrastructure with stable location points and a Linked Open Data approach that allows for deep mapping at scale. Such an app-roach, which harmonises various types of data sources on specific places across different times in one GIS infrastructure, provides the foundation of the mirror world foreseen in the Time Machine project.

## 3.2  GIS Infrastructure

Providing a solid GIS infrastructure for the Amsterdam Time Machine presented us with various challenges. Modelling the data of the use cases into a uniform and spatial accurate system starts with a semantic discussion. This requires an unambiguous explanation and use of seemingly obvious concepts such as 'houses', 'buildings' and 'addresses'. These elements function as a key to a large amount of civil and fiscal data, given the fact that until late in the twentieth century, citizens were registered with their address instead of a personal identification number. Therefore, censuses, resident registrations and fiscal administrations contain a mass of information on people in the past. Together, they provide a 'collective' identification of the people of Amsterdam.

However, in many (or most) cases the present-day address is not the same as a historical address. It often happens that even the physical building is no longer the same. It should also be kept in mind that addresses were originally introduced for fiscal, military or administrative purposes, not as a convenient system for the general public to find the right houses [41,47]. Over the course of

---

[4] https://www.timemachine.eu/.

the 18th and 19th centuries, the system of house registration was changed several times. The first visually shown numbers on Amsterdam facades originate from 1795; the system then was organised by district, which meant that the houses of each district were numbered with consecutive digits. This same principle was used in setting up the numbering of the 1808 and 1853 systems [18].

The modern-day system in which house numbers are linked to streets via an odd and even principle was set up in 1876. In many cases, the order and numbering may have been subject to change. The contemporary building with the address 'Prins Hendrikkade 73', for instance, was known as 'Oude Teertuinen 15' in the year 1876. In 1853, within the footprint of the current building, four smaller houses were situated, each of which had its own house and district number (149, 150, 151 and 152) within the section M of Amsterdam.[5] We find their parcels neatly drawn in the 1832 cadastre, again each with its own specific cadastral address.

These historical addresses can be linked together by stating that the 1853 house number M 150 has the same location as the current Prins Hendrikkade 73 and vice versa, just as M 149, 151 and 152. We chose not to do this as this is conceptually not very accurate and lacks semantic refinement. As Tables 1 and 2 illustrate, the more historical mutations in parcels and house plots have occurred, the more fuzzy and convoluted the data becomes. Therefore, the older geographical infrastructure created by the HisGIS team in 2013 to provide the footprint of the 1832 cadastral parcels and buildings proved unsuitable and did not meet the requirements of the Amsterdam Time Machine project.

For the Amsterdam Time Machine GIS system, the HisGIS team introduced the principle of geographical coordinates as anchor points (represented by a formal identification-number, location-point or locatiepunt in Dutch) for all historical data with a spatial component that cannot be tied to specific geometries of buildings or plots. This system of location points had already been designed and tested as the key geometry in the so-called Time Machine for the Frisian cities, which was officially launched by the Fryske Akademy in May 2017, serving a pilot project concerning the town of Dokkum [42]. It was developed further within the Amsterdam Time Machine project between 2018 and early 2019. The concept of location points prevents common pitfalls of linking historical addresses with specific footprints as geometries of parcels or buildings as starting points. It makes it possible to gain insight into spatial continuity without the system being unyieldingly stuck to all historical mutations caused by joining, merging, demolition, splitting or aggregation of houses and their addresses.

The HisGIS team created a dataset of over 52,000 location points (or coordinate sets) to form the basic GIS infrastructure for the Amsterdam Time Machine. These points are identified by (arbitrarily chosen) identification numbers which the addresses relate to.

The team chose to build this set of linked historical addresses from scratch and leave aside the already existing sets, such as the so-called renumber register

---

[5] As shown in the result of this sparql query: https://druid.datalegend.net/nlgis/-/ queries/address-variations-over-time/1.

**Table 1.** Linking historical addresses via the geometry of buildings or plots causes fuzzy and less accurate geographical relations between historical address identifiers. For example, the 1853 address M 151 relates to four 1832 parcel numbers, but it is unclear which one was the exact same plot.

| Linking addresses via parcel geometry | | | |
|---|---|---|---|
| 2020 address | 1878 address | 1853 address | 1832 parcel numbers |
| Prins Hendrikkade 73 | Oude Teertuinen 15 | District M, no. 149, 150, 151, 152 | Section G, no. 415, 416, 417, 419 |

**Table 2.** Linking historical addresses via a point coordinate provides in more accurate one on one relations. Considering the Table 1 example, the 1853 address M 151 only relates to the correct and specific 1832 parcel plot.

| Linking addresses via point coordinates | | | | |
|---|---|---|---|---|
| Location point | 2020 address | 1878 address | 1853 address | 1832 parcel number |
| 100020 | Prins Hendrikkade 73 | Oude Teertuinen 15 | M, no. 151 | G, no. 416 |
| 100021 | Prins Hendrikkade 73 | Oude Teertuinen 15 | M, no. 152 | G, no. 415 |
| 100022 | Prins Hendrikkade 73 | Oude Teertuinen 15 | M, no. 150 | G, no. 417 |
| 100024 | Prins Hendrikkade 73 | Oude Teertuinen 15 | M, no. 149 | G, no. 419 |

of the Amsterdam city archive in which many historical Amsterdam addresses are linked over time. The reason for doing this is that, despite their comprehensiveness, these and other used systems are flawed by several of the common pitfalls outlined above resulting in an undesirable enlargement of the disarray of accurate spatial locations.

Considering the research focus area and period of the different use cases, the researchers involved decided to bring at least four historical house identifiers of the nineteenth and early twentieth centuries into this system. These are the cadastral parcel numbers of 1832, the so-called district numbers (*wijknummers* in Dutch) of 1853, the house numbers of 1876, and the potential later mutations and additions of the 1876 house numbers recorded in the year 1909. Per address, these four identifiers were linked by visually comparing geographically accurate georeferenced maps: the 1832 cadastral maps, the 1853 district maps, the so-called 'Looman' maps of 1876, and the 1909 *Publieke Werken* maps. In this way, a total of around 120,000 registrations through time are spatially elaborated by the 52,000 location points [40]. Recently, the system has been expanded with an additional set with the house numbers in use in 1943, which resulted in more than 53.000 new locations. We will shortly publish this set as Linked Open Data.[6]

The location points and related house number set does not merely serve academic purposes. Thanks to its Linked Open Data (LOD) structure (see below),

---

[6] The dataset will be published in this repository:
https://druid.datalegend.net/ATM-DEMO/ATM-CLARIAH-DEMO.

every researcher, professional, or hobbyist, may use the GIS infrastructure for his or her own purposes and research goals. Thus, the Amsterdam Time Machine GIS infrastructure can be used as a means of processing every dataset containing historical addresses of Amsterdam, to visualise data and analyse them spatially, in all kinds of fields and disciplines. More generally, this allows researchers to investigate the spatial correlation of certain phenomena, as in the use case discussed below, which focuses on the establishment of theaters and cinemas as cultural entertainment in relation to the socio-economic status of the inhabitants of the various Amsterdam neighbourhoods at the turn of the 20th century.

### 3.3 Linked Open Data Approach

To link the datasets in our project we use a technique called Linked Data [1]. Similarly to how websites can cross-reference each other, databases represented as Linked Data can contain cross-references to each other over the Web. For example, an address may contain many spelling variations, even within one and the same database. By representing an address via a URI (a unique identifier, possibly even approachable via the Web), that particular address can be referenced to without error and across multiple databases. For example, in the Adamlink project[7], the URI https://www.adamlink.nl/geo/street/adriaan-van-swietenhof/64 refers to the street 'Adriaan van Swietenhof'. Rather than having database entries such as 'A. v. Swietenhof' or 'van Swietenhof', we use the URI across various databases so we can link them. This approach is not much different from more traditional GIS databases where multiple entries for the same address are harmonised. The advantage of using URIs is that anyone can reuse them, even without our knowledge, since it is openly available as a public resource.[8] In doing so, datasets using the same URI are automatically linked, hence the term 'Linked Data'.

The transformation of the data into Linked Data in this project facilitates future connections, among others with the images and other historical collections held at the various cultural heritage institutions.[9] As such, the Linked Data approach forms the foundation for the 'deep mapping at scale' that is our ambition.

As it is the central part of our database, we will now describe the data model used to create Linked Data for the HisGIS location points, while we describe the conversion to Linked Data for use case specific datasets in Sect. 4.2. To represent the temporal and geographical variant addresses as Linked Data, we applied the ontology design pattern by [25] for the space-time prism model [16]. Through

---

[7] https://www.adamlink.nl/.

[8] See https://druid.datalegend.net/ATM-DEMO/ATM-CLARIAH-DEMO.

[9] For example, Petra Dreiskämper, not a member of our project, created links between images from the Amsterdam City Archives and the HisGIS location points, as a result of which one can now actually see images of the aforementioned 'Prins Hendrikkade 73' - images that are not included in our own datasets:
https://druid.datalegend.net/ATM-DEMO/-/queries/images-prinsengracht-73/2.

its demonstrated application for $CO_2$ measurements, we recognised similarities with our space and time variant addresses. In the $CO_2$ case, cars drive around a city (space variant) and take multiple (time variant) measurements of the degree of $CO_2$ in the air (value). To model this data, [25] suggest the use of so-called 'control points'. A control point is somewhat like a 'ping' at which the car has a certain location, at a specific time and measures a value. The variant space, time and value measurements are attached to this ping and thus queryable. The latter is important to the space-time-prism model that in this way allows one to derive information on $CO_2$ levels in places and at times where no measurements were taken.

In our study, the HisGIS location points are the control points or 'pings'. The location points are by definition fixed in time, but observed at different points in time, and have different values for 'address'. Figure 1 depicts for a particular location point how time variant addresses can be linked to these location points.

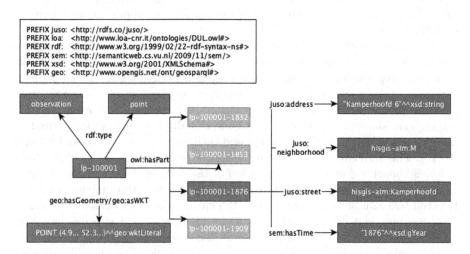

**Fig. 1.** Abridged visualisation of the HisGIS location points model based on the space-time-prism pattern

The figure describes a tree-like pattern, with the location point as the trunk and the addresses as leaves. This means that any historical observation of an address, for example in an advert in a newspaper, can be linked to a location point. In addition, the model also allows us to see whether a change in address is actually related to a move or administrative change, a crucial difference in observation for life course research, for example. While there are but four time points covering the 1832–1909 period, through the space-time-prism model interpolations can be made for other years, as long as the values of the variable of interest are linked to the location points.

## 4    Use Case

### 4.1    Research Question

To test the Amsterdam geo-temporal infrastructure as a platform for urban historical research, we conducted a small pilot study on Amsterdam entertainment culture in the late 19th and early 20th century. The central question is to what extent the location of cinema venues, offering a new form of entertainment around the turn of the 20th century, can be understood in relation to existing forms of entertainment and to the social and economic composition of the neighbourhoods. Are cinemas established in the same neighbourhoods where theatres are located? What is the socio-economic status of those neighbourhoods, defined by income and by the dialects spoken there? What can such a comparison tell us about the status of cultural entertainment in late 19th- and early 20th-century Amsterdam? Such an interdisciplinary study builds on existing socio-economic historical analyses of the city and its inhabitants and enriches these with insights into cultural phenomena, such as language use and the appreciation of cultural entertainment.

Naturally, the location of theatres and cinemas in specific neighbourhoods cannot be seen as a direct indication of cultural appreciation, let alone of cultural consumption: these venues could very well be frequented by people from various parts of the city as well as outside of Amsterdam. At the same time, previous studies of cultural consumption in 19th-century Rotterdam and the Hague have shown that theatres and concert halls were mostly frequented by middle class and elite audiences, who used such visits as markers of social status [10,13]. This indicates a certain correlation between the socio-economic status of a neighbourhood and the appreciation of the cultural venues located there.

Our analysis focuses on the shift in the Amsterdam entertainment landscape between two sample years: 1884, when the city had been expanded with a new, "19th-century belt"[10], and 1915, when the first permanent cinemas had been established in the city. For 1884, we study the correlation between the location of Amsterdam theatres and the socio-economic status of the neighbourhoods, marked by both the 'elite density' in those neighbourhoods and the dialects spoken there. For 1915, we studied, first, how the locations of the Amsterdam theatres have changed compared to 1884, and second, how these correlate with the locations of the cinemas and with the income of the inhabitants of the various neighbourhoods. We conclude with a tentative answer to the question what these patterns tell us about the status of cultural entertainment in late 19th- and early 20th-century Amsterdam.

### 4.2    Datasets

In addition to the geo-data described in Sect. 3.3, we have used various other datasets. The code we have used to clean these data and transpose them to Linked Data is available via Github.[11] For the time being the data can also

---

[10] https://nl.wikipedia.org/wiki/19e-eeuwse-gordel.
[11] https://github.com/CLARIAH/ATM.

directly be queried via the triple store Druid.[12] We will now describe these datasets in more detail.

**Amsterdam Dialects.** According to the 19th-century linguist Johan Winkler and the historian Jan ter Gouw a whopping number of nineteen dialects were spoken in 19th-century Amsterdam, distributed over various neighbourhoods [54], later plotted on a map [7]. Alongside these neighbourhood-specific dialects there were also sociolects spoken throughout the city, especially the slang of thieves and tramps. One of the questions we wanted to answer was whether the dialect variation in 19th-century Amsterdam was as great as Winkler and Ter Gouw claimed. For this, we attempted to reconstruct the dialect variation by collecting all Amsterdam language phenomena mentioned in 45 primary sources, including, for instance, Amsterdam word lists dated between 1800–1940. Subsequently, these language phenomena were manually entered into a database. The resulting database contains 8,020 entries categorised into the following language domains: words, names, idiomatic expressions, speech sounds, word formation, syntax, songs, and speech recordings. For each entry the information given in the original source was added, such as meaning, dating and bibliographical data. Finally, we tried to pinpoint each entry to a specific street or district, based on the information mentioned in the primary sources. In this we succeeded for 70% of the entries. However, it appeared that for fourteen of the nineteen dialects mentioned by Winkler and Ter Gouw, no concrete references to language phenomena could be found. As a next step, the RDF version of the data was modelled using the Lemon lexicon model for ontologies [6].

**Occupational Structure, Tax and 'Elite Density'.** To derive information on people's social and economic position in society, a key variable in sociological and history research, we reused data collected in the early 1980s and preserved thanks to the Dutch scientific data preservation organisation DANS [52,53]. Historian Boudien de Vries took two samples (1854 and 1884) from the electoral roles of the city to obtain data on the Amsterdam elite. In addition to various other variables such as marital status and religion, she entered information on occupation, amount of tax paid and address of residence. We standardised the occupational titles onto the Historical International Classification of Occupations (HISCO) [28] through which we were directly able to attain information on the relative 'position' of these occupations in the occupational structure through HISCAM, an Historical CAMSIS scale [27]. Because it was also available as Linked Data, we could effortlessly add data on population size of every district in Amsterdam through the CEDAR project [36], allowing us to calculate a measure of 'elite density' by relating the number of elites to the population size per district. For the sample year 1915, we based the socio-economic status of the neighbourhoods on the 1915–1916 municipal tax records.[13]

---

[12] https://druid.datalegend.net/ATM-DEMO.

[13] De gemeentelijke inkomstenbelasting 1915-1916, Stat, Med, No, 57.

**Theatre and Cinema.** Data on the location and programming of theatres and cinemas are an important source for studying the broader social, cultural and economic contexts in which these forms of entertainment emerged and operated. Increasingly, such data are being digitised from secondary and primary sources, making them available for computational research [45]. The data for the Amsterdam theatre locations were collected by Charlotte Vrielink from the print publication [31] (Cf. [51]). The dataset is available as a CSV file at DANS.[14] The data on the cinema locations and their programming was collected from Cinema Context[15], a historical data collection for the history of film culture in the Netherlands, which contains information on the cinemas active in Amsterdam and, to a large extent, the films screened there in the early 20th century [9]. For the purpose of this study, the geographic coordinates of the cinema venues contained in Cinema Context were replaced by more precise location points, some newly created by Vincent Baptist. The full dataset is available as a SQL data dump at DANS.[16]

### 4.3   Method

The datasets used in our project, some originating from the early 1980s, were not readily available as Linked Data. We therefore used Python scripts and the CoW tool [38] to transpose our sources to Linked Data. CoW is a CSV-to-RDF converter aimed at researchers that have some computing skills, but are not developers themselves. Because basically anything can be represented via a URI, we were able to create Linked Data for the HisGIS location points, for the dataset on Amsterdam dialects (even including some sound samples of spoken dialect), the data on the locations of Amsterdam theatres and cinemas and the dataset on the occupational structure of the Amsterdam 19th-century elite.

To link the information from the separate databases, we uploaded the Linked Data in one central SPARQL Endpoint, in our case Druid.[17] SPARQL is a query language which allows one to retrieve a selection of data from one or multiple, linked datasets for further analysis. While SPARQL allows for some basic analysis and SPARQL query editors such as YASGUI [43] allow for basic (GIS) visualisations, because of the more complex requirements of our use case we mainly relied on offline tools with more functionality for the visualisation and analysis of our data. Thus, we created SPARQL queries to retrieve relevant subsets of the data that we subsequently analysed and visualised in R and QGIS. For example, we created a query providing information on the elite density, of which the result is downloadable as a CSV file, providing information on the number of elites, the population size and the geographical representation (polygon) per district. This CSV file was then imported into QGIS to visualise

---

[14] https://doi.org/10.17026/dans-z3r-9nyz.

[15] http://cinemacontext.nl/.

[16] https://doi.org/10.17026/dans-z9y-c5g6.

[17] https://druid.datalegend.net/ATM-DEMO/ATM-CLARIAH-DEMO/.

the elite density as a separate layer in our Deep Map. The visualisations of the various data layers in QGIS provided the basis for a qualitative analysis of the patterns observed.

### 4.4   Results

Figure 2 shows the 1884 map of Amsterdam, plotting the location of theatres against the demarcation of the areas of the city in which specific dialects were spoken and the 'elite density' of neighbourhoods.

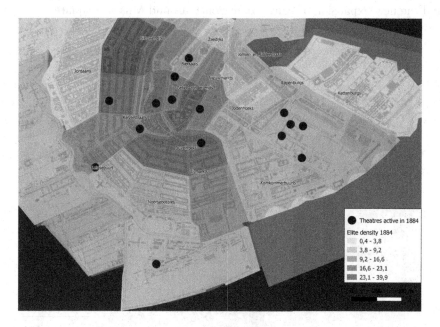

**Fig. 2.** This map combines the three layers from the use case: dialect areas (approximate location indicated by dialect name), elite density (white: low; red: high density, classified using Jenks natural breaks) and the locations of theatres (cyan dots). Base map: Buurtatlas Loman, 1876, https://tiles.amsterdamtimemachine.nl/. (Color figure online)

From this visualisation we observe that all theatres are located in areas with a relatively high elite density. We find no theatres in the relatively poorer areas of the cities, nor in the 'golden bend', the area of the canal ring which is the most affluent. One clear cluster can be observed in the Plantage district in the east of the city, a relatively new urban expansion for the well-to-do [29, p. 195-6], adjacent to the Jodenhoeks dialect on the Winkler dialect map. The area where 'Kalverstraats' was spoken also contains a number of theatres - this dialect can be seen as typically middle-class. One theatre is located at the Keizersgracht, where the upper class lived, speaking an upper class dialect. No theatres can be found in districts where typical working class dialects were spoken, with the exception of one theatre in the 'Zeedijks' or 'Bierkaais' area: De Vereeniging (located at Warmoesstraat 139). Therefore, we can conclude that the majority of theatres were located in the more affluent neighbourhoods and are conspicuously absent in the working-class neighbourhoods, if we regard both the elite density and the dialect information.

To investigate how cinemas found their place in this existing cultural entertainment landscape in the early 20th century, we first observe how the theatre locations have moved in the intervening 30 years. Figure 3 shows the shift of theatre locations between 1884 and 1915 from the inner city to the canal ring and the new expansion of Amsterdam South around Museum Square.

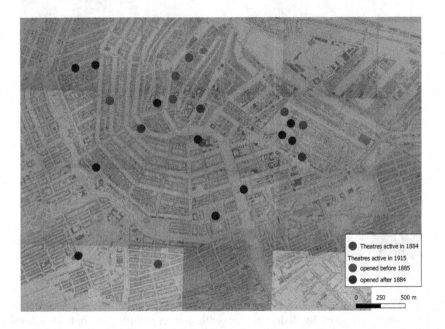

**Fig. 3.** Shift in the location of Amsterdam theatre venues between those active in 1884 (cyan dots) and those active in 1915 (dark blue dots for theatres that were still active since 1884 and green dots for theatres that had opened since 1885). Base map: Dienst der Publieke Werken, 1909, https://tiles.amsterdamtimemachine.nl/. (Color figure online)

Plotting the 1915 theatre locations against the economic status of the neighbourhood (Fig. 4), we observe that some theatres remain in the locations of 1884 (in particular in the area where 'Kalverstraats' is spoken and in the Plantage district), but in general, the theatres have moved in tandem with the city's expansion. Contrary to 1884, we now see two theatres appear in the popular 'Jordaan' district, but otherwise the pattern is the same: most theatres are still located in the more upmarket neighbourhoods - i.e. neighbourhoods in which a relatively high percentage of inhabitants pays the highest tax tariff. As in 1884, the most expensive areas of the city do not contain theatres.

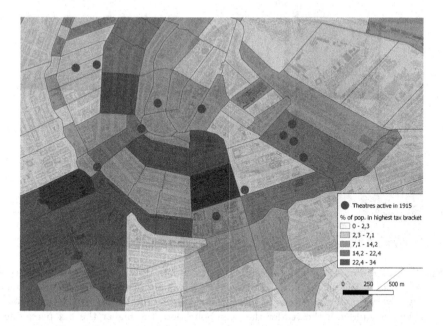

**Fig. 4.** Amsterdam theatre locations in 1915 (dark blue dots) plotted against the economic status of the neighbourhood. The white areas are neighbourhoods where none or only a very small percentage of inhabitants were in the highest tax bracket (over 5,100 Dutch guilders); the redder the neighbourhood, the higher the tax percentage (classified using Jenks natural breaks). Base map: Dienst der Publieke Werken, 1909, https://tiles.amsterdamtimemachine.nl/. (Color figure online)

When looking at the location of cinema theatres in 1915, plotted against the economic status of the neighbourhoods in Fig. 5, compared to theatres we clearly see much more cinemas in the areas with no or few inhabitants in the highest tax bracket areas, here used as a proxy for indicating the areas with poorer inhabitants.

Comparing the 1915 theatre and cinema locations, as plotted against the socio-economic status of the neighbourhoods in Fig. 6, we see striking differences in their location patterns: the cinemas are located in 'older' areas of the city, for example in the North-East corner area of the city where in the 19th century people spoke 'Nieuwendijks', 'Haarlemmerdijks' and 'Jordaans', all of which have been identified as popular dialects. And in the relatively up-market Plantage district, no cinemas can be found, whereas in the Jewish quarter, where in 1884 the 'Jodenhoeks' popular dialect was spoken, we find no fewer than three cinemas (including the 'Tip Top theater' that was known as a Jewish cinema) and no theatres.

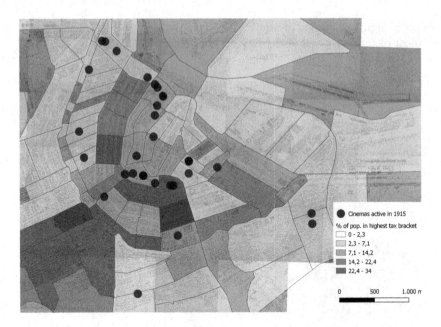

**Fig. 5.** Amsterdam cinema locations in 1915 (magenta dots) plotted against the economic status of the neighbourhood. The white areas are neighbourhoods where none or only a very small percentage of inhabitants were in the highest tax bracket (over 5,100 Dutch guilders); the redder the neighbourhood, the higher the tax percentage (classified using Jenks natural breaks). Base map: Dienst der Publieke Werken, 1909, https://tiles.amsterdamtimemachine.nl/. (Color figure online)

In conclusion, we can note that there is little overlap between the location of theatres and cinemas: the new form of entertainment did not connect to existing venues to create entertainment districts but found a place in other, less affluent areas of the city. This may be explained from the fact that most of the 1915 theatres had already been established in the period 1880–1890, but can also indicate that the new form of entertainment was seen as less respectable and geared towards the lower income groups.

At the same time, the opposition between theatres and cinemas should not be overstated. Within both sectors, there were venues that catered for higher and for lower segments of the markets. For example, there were 'chic' cinema theatres in the 'Kalverstraats' dialect area that catered for a middle class audience by offering the latest premieres (perhaps not accidentally the one area which contains both cinemas and theaters), and cheap theatres that explicitly catered for a working-class audience (such as the Rozentheater in the Jordaan district).

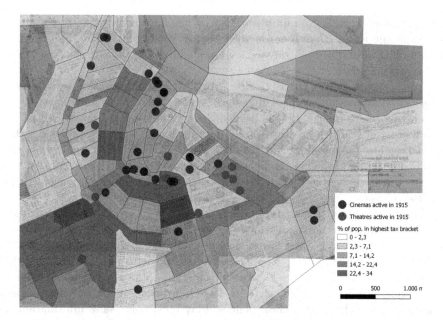

**Fig. 6.** Amsterdam theatre (dark blue dots) and cinema (magenta dots) locations in 1915 plotted against the economic status of the neighbourhood. The white areas are neighbourhoods where none or only a very small percentage of inhabitants were in the highest tax bracket (over 5,100 Dutch guilders); the redder the neighbourhood, the higher the tax percentage (classified using Jenks natural breaks). Base map: Dienst der Publieke Werken, 1909, https://tiles.amsterdamtimemachine.nl/. (Color figure online)

## 5   Discussion

Our effort to create a Semantic Deep Map appears to have been a successful undertaking. We were able to combine multi-typed datasets, from various disciplines and answer a question with the help of these sources.

However, a first point for discussion is that we were unable to follow the Linked Data pipeline up to the point of the analysis because we had to switch from the online dataset collection and dataset querying to the offline data visualisation in QGIS. All the steps needed to get this visualisation, are not stored and therefore not reproducible. In part, this might be improved upon by more advanced SPARQL skills, but for another part it might also be a limitation of the query language, which is not optimised for geographical queries. A solution for this may lay in the use of Jupyter Notebooks, in which one can apply multiple languages (R, Python, SPARQL) to create, query and analyse Linked Data. With a Jupyter Notebook, each language could then be used at its core strength. In addition, all code in the chain could be run for a complete reproduction of the research.

Whilst the Amsterdam Time Machine combined dataset sheds new light on the late 19th- and early 20th-century entertainment industry, it by no means can provide all answers. A core limitation is that the data is incomplete and more a series of 'snapshots' than a continuous record. Thankfully, more digitised data is becoming available every day, which can be linked to the current Amsterdam Time Machine dataset.

Furthermore, whilst the data does provide some information on trends, it does not allow us to switch seamlessly between micro, meso and macro levels. To do this, more information is needed, for example on particular households and their staff living at an address and information on what places besides their residence these people frequented. One limitation of the linguistic data is that rich people living in the most expensive neighbourhoods employed staff that may or may not have lived in their house and spoke another dialect or sociolect than their employers.

When we connect for example the socio-economic data to the dialect data, or the cinema and theatre locations to socio-economic data, we do not know if the people who lived in those areas were actually the ones visiting those venues. While our data does indicate where cinemas and theatres were located, and that in combination with the social status information about the neighbourhood we see correlations between 'higher' and 'lower' cultural venues, our data cannot tell us who actually visited these venues. Play bills, ticket sales information (as cinemas and theatres both used to sell price differentiated tickets to different seating areas), but also mentions of shows in letters and diaries could provide additional insights here. There are several projects ongoing that aim to make this type of data digitally available.[18] Our efforts in this project can serve as a blueprint and anchor for adding such data layers.

## 6    Conclusion

With space as a connecting factor, the Amsterdam Time Machine provides a concrete illustration of the research potential of linking social and economic data with cultural data, allowing researchers to study specific historical and cultural phenomena against the background of broader societal developments. Our approach, based on the identification of location points and the transformation of data into Linked Open Data, allows for the building of a rich tapestry of information about a city and its development over time - both physically and in the way it has been used and experienced. As such, it points towards a 'deep mapping at scale': the creation of a geographical-temporal infrastructure that allows for the querying of multiple types of data in a scalable manner, navigating between the broader patterns of urban life and the micro level of individual people, places and events.

---

[18] Cf.,    for    early    modern    Amsterdam,    the    projects    Golden    Agents-break    (https://www.goldenagents.org/),    The    Freedom    of    the    Streets    (https://www.freedomofthestreets.org/)    and    Virtual    Interiors    (https://virtualinteriorsproject.nl/),    all    funded    by    the    national    research    council NWO.

We conclude that in its present form, the platform provides heuristic support for interdisciplinary digital humanities research, in that the combined visualisation and exploration of different types of data exposes correlations that lead to new hypotheses about historical urban entertainment culture. Our pilot use case showed that in early 20th-century Amsterdam there is little overlap between the locations of theatres and cinemas and that, where theatres were located in relatively affluent areas of the city, cinemas were located in less affluent districts. This generated the hypothesis that cinema as a new form of entertainment was seen as less respectable than theatre and hence 'took place' in less affluent areas of the city. As such, the use case demonstrates the potential of deep mapping as a method that invites experimentation to further test and refine hypotheses.

We are currently in the process of extending the temporal scope of the location points forward in time, to 1943, and back in time to 1647. In the near future, the historical addresses as a dataset and fundamental stepping stone for the Amsterdam Time Machine and its infrastructure will be semantically embedded within the scope of ontologies for historical geographical data on the one hand, and the domain-central HisGIS ontology of the historical cadastral entities on the other. In parallel, we are setting up a sustainable environment for the infrastructure, on the one hand by the creation of sustainable endpoints and a common infrastructure, on the other by establishing an editorial office and editorial board for the Amsterdam Time Machine geodata to ensure that a common strategy and procedure is followed. We encourage future research projects to build upon the Amsterdam Time Machine infrastructure: each new layer of information uncovers another part of the rich history of Amsterdam and its citizens and provides scholars with a new lens through which to study our past.

**Acknowledgments.** The research for this article, conducted in the context of the CLARIAH Amsterdam Time Machine project (2018–2019), was a collaboration between Fryske Akademy (Hans Mol, Mark Raat and Thomas Vermaut), KNAW Humanities Cluster (Gertjan Filarski, Marieke van Erp, Astrid Kulsdom), AdamNet (Henk Wals, Ivo Zandhuis), International Institute of Social History (Richard Zijdeman), Meertens Institute (Nicoline van der Sijs, Kristel Doreleijers, Brenda Assendelft) and University of Amsterdam (Julia Noordegraaf, Claartje Rasterhoff, Thunnis van Oort, Charlotte Vrielink and Vincent Baptist), and was financially supported by the NWO Roadmap for Large-scale Research Infrastructures project CLARIAH. Creating Linked Data for streets and districts and for cultural heritage collections in Amsterdam was done by the AdamNet Foundation in the AdamLink project, financed by the Pica Foundation (Stichting Pica).

# References

1. Berners-Lee, T.: Linked data (2006). https://www.w3.org/DesignIssues/LinkedData.html. Accessed 29 May 2020
2. Bodenhamer, D.J., Corrigan, J., Harris, T.M.: The Spatial Humanities: GIS and the Future of Humanities Scholarship. Indiana University Press, Bloomington (2010)

3. Bodenhamer, D.J., Corrigan, J., Harris, T.M.: Introduction: deep maps and the spatial humanities. In: Bodenhamer, D.J., Corrigan, J., Harris, T.M. (eds.) Deep Maps and Spatial Narratives, pp. 1–6. Indiana University Press, Bloomington (2015)
4. Cateridge, J.: Deep mapping and screen tourism: the Oxford of harry potter and inspector Morse. Humanities 4(3), 320–333 (2015)
5. Chiarcos, C., Hellmann, S., Nordhoff, S.: Towards a linguistic linked open data cloud: The open linguistics working group. TAL 52(3), 245–275 (2011)
6. Cimiano, P., McCrae, J.P., Buitelaar, P.: Lexicon model for ontologies: community report. Technical report, W3C Ontology-Lexicon Community Group (2016)
7. Daan, J.: Hij zeit wat: grepen uit de Amsterdamse volkstaal. Jacob van Campen (1948)
8. de Boer, V., van Rossum, M., Leinenga, J., Hoekstra, R.: Dutch ships and sailors linked data. In: Mika, P., et al. (eds.) ISWC 2014. LNCS, vol. 8796, pp. 229–244. Springer, Cham (2014). https://doi.org/10.1007/978-3-319-11964-9_15
9. Dibbets, K.: Cinema context and the genes of film history. New Rev. Film Telev. Stud. 8(3), 331–342 (2010)
10. Furnée, J.H.: Plaatsen van beschaafd vertier: standsbesef en stedelijke cultuur in Den Haag, 1850–1890. Bert Bakker (2012)
11. Gelernter, D.: Mirror Worlds: or: The Day Software Puts the Universe in a Shoebox... How it Will Happen and What It Will Mean. Oxford University Press, Oxford (1993)
12. Graham, S., Milligan, I., Weingart, S.: Exploring Big Historical Data: The Historian's Macroscope. World Scientific Publishing Company, Singapore (2015)
13. Gras, H., Franses, P.H., van Vliet, H., Pratasik, B.: Theatre as a Prison of Longue Durée. Peter Lang (2011)
14. Gregory, I., Ell, P.: Historical GIS: Technologies, Methodologies, and Scholarship. Cambridge University Press, Cambridge (2007)
15. Guldi, J.: What is the spatial turn? Technical report, University of Virginia Scholar's Lab (2010). spatial humanities: A project of the institute for enabling geospatial scholarship
16. Hagerstrand, T.: What about people inregional science? Papers and Proceedings of the Regional Science Association (1970). https://doi.org/10.1007/BF01936872
17. Hallam, J., Roberts, L.: Locating the Moving Image: New Approaches to Film and Place. The Spatial Humanities, Indiana University Press, Bloomington (2013). https://muse.jhu.edu/book/27089
18. Hameleers, M.: Buurtatlassen tonen oude huisnummeringen. Ons Amsterdam 45, 30–24 (1993)
19. Hoekstra, R.: The datalegend ecosystem for historical statistics. J. Web Semant. 50, 49–61 (2018)
20. Horak, L.: Using digital maps to investigate cinema history. In: Acland, C., Hoyt, E., Horak, L. (eds.) The Arclight Guidebook to Media History and the Digital Humanities, pp. 65–102. Reframe books (2016)
21. Hyvönen, E.: "Sampo" model and semantic portals for digital humanities on the semantic web. In: Proceedings of the Digital Humanities in the Nordic Countries (DHN 2020). CEUR WS Proceedings (2020)
22. Ide, N., Woolner, D.: Exploiting semantic web technologies for intelligent access to historical documents. In: Proceedings of the Fourth International Conference on Language Resources and Evaluation (LREC'04). European Language Resources Association (ELRA), Lisbon (2004). http://www.lrec-conf.org/proceedings/lrec2004/pdf/248.pdf

23. Kaplan, F.: The Venice time machine. In: Proceedings of the 2015 ACM Symposium on Document Engineering, DocEng '15, p. 73. Association for Computing Machinery, New York (2015). https://doi.org/10.1145/2682571.2797071
24. Kelly, K.: AR will spark the next big tech platform - call it mirrorworld. Wired 27 (2019). https://www.wired.com/story/mirrorworld-ar-next-big-tech-platform/
25. Keßler, C., Farmer, C.J.: Querying and integrating spatial-temporal information on the web of data via time geography. J. Web Semant. **35**, 25–34 (2015)
26. Kretzschmar Jr., W.A.: GIS for language and literary study. Literary Studies in the Digital Age: An Evolving Anthology (2013). https://dlsanthology.mla.hcommons.org/gis-for-language-and-literary-study/
27. Lambert, P.S., Zijdeman, R.L., Leeuwen, M.H.D.V., Maas, I., Prandy, K.: The construction of hiscam: a stratification scale based on social interactions for historical comparative research. Hist. Methods: J. Quant. Interdiscip. Hist. **46**(2), 77–89 (2013). https://doi.org/10.1080/01615440.2012.715569
28. Leeuwen, M.H.D.V., Maas, I., Miles, A.: Creating a historical international standard classification of occupations an exercise in multinational interdisciplinary cooperation. Hist. Methods: J. Quant. Interdiscip. Hist. **37**(4), 186–197 (2004). https://doi.org/10.3200/HMTS.37.4.186-197
29. Lesger, C.: Het winkellandschap van Amsterdam: Stedelijke structuur en winkelbedrijf in de vroegmoderne en moderne tijd, 1550–2000. Uitgeverij Verloren (2013)
30. Loeffler, S.: Glas journal: Deep mappings of a harbour or the charting of fragments, traces and possibilities. Humanities **4**(3), 457–475 (2015)
31. Logger, B., Nederland, O., Alexander, E., Alting, M.C.: Theaters in Nederland sinds de zeventiende eeuw. Theater Instituut Nederland (2007)
32. Lünen, A., Travis, C. (eds.): History and GIS: Epistemologies, Considerations and Reflections. Springer, Heidelberg (2013). https://doi.org/10.1007/978-94-007-5009-8
33. McCrae, J., et al.: The linked open data cloud (2020). https://lod-cloud.net/
34. McCrae, J.P., Bosque-Gil, J., Gracia, J., Buitelaar, P., Cimiano, P.: The ontolex-lemon model: development and applications. In: Proceedings of eLex 2017 Conference, pp. 587–597 (2017)
35. Meroño-Peñuela, A., et al.: Semantic technologies for historical research: a survey. Semant. Web **6**, 539–564 (2014). https://doi.org/10.3233/SW-140158
36. Meroño-Peñuela, A., Ashkpour, A., Guéret, C., Schlobach, S.: CEDAR: the Dutch historical censuses as linked open data. Semant. Web **8**(2), 297–310 (2017)
37. Meroño-Peñuela, A., et al.: Ontologies in CLARIAH: towards interoperability in history, language and media. In: Studies on Semantic Web. arXiv preprint https://arxiv.org/abs/2004.02845 (2020)
38. Meroño-Peñuela, A., van der Weerdt, R., Hoekstra, R., Dentler, K., Rijpma, A., Zijdeman, R.L.: sv on the web (cow) converter (2015). https://github.com/CLARIAH/COW
39. Miller, G.A.: Wordnet: a lexical database for English. Commun. ACM **38**(11), 39–41 (1995)
40. Mol, H., Raat, M.: Inventarisatie van de pre-kadastrale uitbreidingsmogelijkheden voor de Amsterdam Time Machine-infrastructuur. Technical report, Fryske Akademy (2019)
41. Raat, M.: Friesland en de landelijke invoering van huisnummers in 1806. sleutels tot het verkrijgen, lokaliseren en integreren van historische bewonersinformatie. De Vrije Fries **96**, 39–60 (2016)

42. Raat, M.: Speuren naar vroege bewoners. Historisch Tijdschrif Fryslân **23**(4) (2017)
43. Rietveld, L., Hoekstra, R.: YASGUI: not just another SPARQL client. In: Cimiano, P., Fernández, M., Lopez, V., Schlobach, S., Völker, J. (eds.) ESWC 2013. LNCS, vol. 7955, pp. 78–86. Springer, Heidelberg (2013). https://doi.org/10.1007/978-3-642-41242-4_7
44. de Rosnay, J.: Le Macroscope: Vers une vision globale. Editions du Seuil (1975)
45. Ross, M., Grauer, M., Freisleben, B.: Digital tools in media studies: analysis and research. An Overview (Bielefeld, Germany: Transcript Verlag, 2009) (2009)
46. Stamou, G., Van Ossenbruggen, J., Pan, J., Schreiber, G., Smith, J.: Multimedia annotations on the semantic web. IEEE Multimedia **13**, 86–90 (2006). https://doi.org/10.1109/MMUL.2006.15
47. Tantner, A.: House Numbers. Pictures of a Forgotten History. Routledge (2015)
48. The Time Machine Organisation: Time Machine Manifesto: Big Data of the past for the future of Europe (2019). https://timemachine.eu
49. Tilly, C.: Explaining Social Processes. Routledge, London (2015)
50. Van Den Akker, C., et al.: Digital hermeneutics: agora and the online understanding of cultural heritage. In: Proceedings of the 3rd International Web Science Conference, pp. 1–7 (2011)
51. Vrielink, C.: In kaart gebracht. een digitale theatergeschiedenis van amsterdam. gis als brug tussen distant en close reading. Ex Tempore **38**(1), 96–113 (2019)
52. de Vries, B.: Electoraat en elite: Sociale structuur en sociale mobiliteit in Amsterdam, 1850–1895. De Bataafsche Leeuw (1986)
53. de Vries, B.: Electoraat en elite: Sociale structuur en sociale mobiliteit in amsterdam, 1850–1895 [data file] (1994). https://doi.org/10.17026/dans-xez-eqdv
54. Winkler, J.: Algemeen nederduitsch en friesch dialecticon. Nijhoff (1874)

# Deep Learning from History
## Unlocking Historical Visual Sources Through Artificial Intelligence

Seyran Khademi$^{(\boxtimes)}$, Tino Mager, and Ronald Siebes

Delft University of Technology, Delft, The Netherlands
S.khademi@tudelft.nl

**Abstract.** Historical photos of towns and villages contain a great deal of information about the built environment of the past. However, it is difficult to evaluate the information of images that are not labeled or incorrectly labeled or not organized in repositories or collections. In order to make the sheer volume of images that are not tagged with metadata found on the Internet or in institutional archives accessible for research, an automated recognition of the image content, in this case of buildings, is necessary. Computer vision can help to address this problem and enable the identification of historical image content. This article describes how artificial intelligence and crowdsourcing are used to identify buildings in nearly half a million historical images of the city of Amsterdam. It explains how computer science and humanities disciplines are linked together to accomplish this task.

**Keywords:** Crowdsourcing · Computer vision · Architectural history · Mixing methods

## 1 Introduction

Computers are widely used in architectural production and help in many ways to calculate and design buildings and structures. Today it is common practice for architects to use CAD processes and to communicate realistic renderings of the products to be created. When it comes to the analysis of the existing built environment, there are also a wealth of digital tools that help to examine selected aspects such as structural aspects, energy efficiency or circulation routes within a building. Architectural history, in turn, is a discipline dedicated to the analysis of the architecture of the past. By dealing with historical buildings, the interest of architectural history lies, among other things, in uncovering the conditions

---

S. Khademi—Author names are simply listed alphabetically and the contribution is equal for all authors.

© Springer Nature Switzerland AG 2021
F. Niebling et al. (Eds.): UHDL 2019, CCIS 1501, pp. 213–233, 2021.
https://doi.org/10.1007/978-3-030-93186-5_10

and characteristics of the built environment of past times. In many cases, the buildings to be analysed no longer exist and are only recorded in textual or visual sources. A wide range of methods is used to examine these sources, including discourse analysis and hermeneutics, areas in which computers play no significant role. Visual sources (historic photographs, drawings, paintings) are the most important source when it comes to analysing the built environment of the past. This concerns buildings that don't exist any more as well as still existing buildings as they most likely have been changed in the course of time. Millions of images have not been used for research yet, as their contents are unknown. Therefore they cannot be considered when it comes to the investigation of a specific object/site. The buildings and the visual sources that document them are a primary source, and in terms of their nature, computer vision can offer a certain potential to expand the range of classical approaches to extracting knowledge from these images [37].

The architectural production, but also the documentation of the built environment has left a wealth of visual material, since the mid-19th century mainly photographs. Digitisation is an essential measure to facilitate access to this enormous stock of visual material, which is particularly revealing for research. Furthermore, digital cataloguing is essential to provide comprehensive and efficient information about the existence and (virtual) location of the material. Digital catalogues (such as Europeana, the German Digital Library or the Digital Public Library of America) provide access to millions of digitised documents, including historical images of architecture and urban planning, and architectural history repositories such as the Colonial architecture and city planning repository (http://colonialarchitecture.eu) contain further collections of visual resources. Their digital availability is important for in-depth research, as they can be visualized and analysed without much effort.

In addition to the digital availability of the images, annotation with meta-information is required to locate the repositories' contents. The names of objects, places and persons as well as keywords stored in them are ultimately meta tags that have been assigned to the images at a certain point in time - in the best case systematically and correctly. Defective, wrong or missing meta tags mean that the image material may not be found at all. This is particularly relevant for the many images whose content is largely unknown or undiscovered. As a result, millions of images end up in repositories without any real possibility of finding them or their content. Researchers and experts cannot take on this task, as they could only handle a tiny part of the media concerned. Given the abundance of material, even larger teams would not be able to maintain a significant amount of material. This is precisely why the use of computer vision seems to be a significant contribution here. How can state-of-the-art computer technology help humanities scholars to manoeuvre through the wealth of digitally available visual material by recognising its content? This would be helpful in accessing image material related to under-researched areas of architectural history like informal housing or pre-colonial architecture, anything that is not part of the canon of western architecture. Moreover, the abundance of image material could also be helpful in analysing short- or medium-term developments in cities and neighbourhoods. This refers to the potential of analysing visible changes in the built environment and their relation to e.g. processes of gentrification or the development of property values. The article deals with achieving the first steps in this direction. It outlines the research work of the European research project ArchiMediaL that deals with automatic image content recognition for historical images of the built environment. ArchiMedial is applying mixed methods to combine qualitative research in the built environment with quantitative research regarding the analysis of the visual representations of the built environment. It explains the profound learning processes, linked data and crowdsourcing approaches that led to a successful algorithm for the recognition of buildings in historical photographs from different domains.

## 2 ArchiMediaL

As a research project involving four European universities, ArchiMediaL is investigating the possibilities of using current information technologies to open up previously unexplored architectural and urban images for research [29]. To this end, strategies for automatic recognition of image content are being developed. Starting point of the research project was the investigation of automatic building recognition in historical images by AI. Despite the progress made in recent years in the recognition of forms, this is an unprecedented task, which initially requires basic research and the meeting and communication of different disciplines and deep expertise in the humanities. Such a task has not been pursued so far. Parallels exist only with the Urban Panorama research project, which also investigates historical visual material from urban contexts [2]. Despite the goal of facilitating the opening of large image sets to less known or little researched topics, research must start in a fairly well documented area of architectural and urban history, since the performance and reliability of the automatic recognition model can only be tested with respect to a *ground truth* which is human annotation in this case. In order to develop good visual recognition models, the images must provide sufficient meta-information to enable the results to be verified. To meet this requirement, a database of images with a sufficient amount of meta information was sought. The solution was found in the Beeldbank depot of the city of Amsterdam in the form of several hundred thousand pictures taken in the streets of Amsterdam since the end of the 19th century [1].

The city of Amsterdam is well covered by Geo-located online images with street views. This is important because buildings can be clearly identified by their address or geolocation. This information can be determined using a visual reference system that contains images of building facades and their Geo-locations. It can be obtained, for example, from online mapping services that provide images of facades such as Mapillary [3]. In Mapillary, a large part of Amsterdam's buildings are photographed and provided with address data. If a building in a historical photo can be identified in a Mapillary photo, the location of the building in the historical photo and thus the building itself is identified. However, a location may contain different buildings at different times, which in turn may be subject to changes such as partial demolition, extensions, additions or renovations. The core of the project is therefore to use computer vision to automatically identify buildings in historical photographs that are Geo-located in the Mapillary repository. If the visually intelligent machine can handle the challenging task of building recognition despite the significant appearance change, in the object and the context, the precise identification of old buildings becomes possible.

In another level, ArchiMediaL is a unique interdisciplinary project that serves both humanities and computer science, which is rare in the context of collaborative research between the two fields. The training of state-of-the-art AI models on available historical image data repositories can effectively help computers to become more intelligent and expert in the domain of historical data, in return, the librarians can make use of these models to better interact with the visual archives and to open up their contents. This mutual interaction between computer scientists and humanity researchers can break the classical pattern of computer science serving the humanities without a real reciprocal conversation between the two parties. The authors believe that this is a step towards an interpretable AI that can act as an artificial research assistant for the analysis of visual data in the digital humanities.

## 3    Computer Vision

### 3.1    Context

In the case of historical visual material, metadata is created by human annotation, the acquisition of which is very expensive, relatively slow and requires specialist knowledge. Moreover, images collections without trusted and rich commentary tags are very inefficient to explore for both librarians and researchers. In this work, we describe the challenges of automatic annotation of visual archival data related to the built environment. Specifically, we focus on style-agnostic content-based image retrieval (CBIR) that can effectively retrieve semantic objects from a set of images (see Fig. 1).

Query (Westerkerk Amsterdam)

Gallery (Churches)

**Fig. 1.** Content-based image retrieval example: given a query image, we want to retrieve a similar image from a gallery. In this example we have Westerkerk from Amsterdam and we have a gallery of churches around the work including pictures from Westerkerk.

In this context, classical non-learning local feature methods such as SIFT [36] and its variants [19,34] are used to transform image patches to vector descriptors. In turn, aggregation methods including [38] used these local features to describe the image as a whole. Currently, pre-trained (learned) neural network models [20, 43] are predominantly used that are proved to perform significantly superior to their feature-engineered predecessors. Moreover, in image representation learning models [20], the input image is transformed to a vector representation in an end-to-end manner and no aggregation step is required to be followed. This is unlike local descriptor models such as [43], where many descriptors for an image are generated that are combined to output the vector representation. Accordingly, in this work, we focus on data-driven representation learning methods to solve the CBIR task. Nevertheless, the significant performance of modern computer vision is based on a large number of images that are annotated by humans. It takes millions of images that are labeled with hundred thousand of object classes to teach a computer to 'see' the world. Notably, the collected image sets for visual learning are all from the contemporary era, thus our 'intelligent' companions have not seen our past yet. To teach computers human history, we need to show them how the world looked like before the advent of digital cameras or else our computer assistants are unable to recognize and detect objects and semantics of the past.

## 3.2    Convolutional Neural Network (CNN)

The brain-like computer architectures, referred to as convolutional neural networks (CNNs) [33], extract effective features, in form of vector representation [21], by seeing a large number of images in their training process for the desired visual task, e.g. object recognition. These trained models are later used for inference on visual data. In general the test data are not seen by the CNN model during the training, thus the CNN models must learn syntax in the training process and generalize it to the unseen data when they are deployed to use (inductive learning). This is consistent with the human intelligence where the learned skills are used in real-world scenarios which might not have been fully covered in the training period. The more correlated the training and the test scenarios are, the more effective the learning is, for both the human and the machine intelligence. Accordingly, once a CNN model is trained on high-quality natural contemporary images for visual recognition, it cannot effectively perform the task on illustrations, low-quality and blurred images, drawings and paintings, that are often found in archival records. In short, to develop intelligent tools that can handle the latter, we need to adapt the CNN models to archival image collections or else we create incompetent tools [41].

Currently trained computer models that are used in the context of visual history often take the image style (e.g. black and white or blurred) as a discriminative attribute rather than the image content. This is inevitable since colour and texture are among the most discriminative attributes when it comes to image understanding [25]. We need to re-think these associations for archival images when colour and texture are not only related to the depicted object in the image but are also affected by the quality and the depiction style and format of the image being illustration, photo or a sketch.

## 3.3    Semantic Similarity Learning

The most popular approach to representation learning is to use a pre-trained CNN model on a classification task and a large dataset such as ImageNet [23]. This is due to the availability of CNN models trained on these benchmarks and the popularity of the image classification task. Recent research literature shows that similarity learning maybe more powerful for gaining insight to the data which does not express explicit class formation [22,31]. Moreover, similarity learning is often less laborious as only positive and negative labels are required for similar and dissimilar pairs, respectively. The deep similarity learning method is particularly effective for classification tasks where severe class imbalance exists, e.g. few samples available for certain classes or in an extreme case a novel class appears in the test that was not included in the training process. If a classification setting is considered for the latter problem then the novel sample will be wrongly classified as a member of the already existing classes. In contrast, in similarity mapping, a novel sample can be placed in a high-dimensional latent space without making a specific claim to membership.

Considering the large variety of objects and therefore classes in most archival data and our case study, a cross-time dataset of historical and current street views of Amsterdam [1], we use deep similarity learning for representation learning. Thereby, we address the cross-domain image retrieval task, formulated as CBIR, where the semantic similarity needs to be learned to find the most similar images in the gallery w.r.t. the query image. We chose a Siamese network (See Fig. 2 for similarity learning. Siamese networks use two sister networks with shared learning parameters for the training process. The training tuples are images and their labels, in contrast to the classification where the training pair is the image and the label. The CNN network learns to project an image to a vector (latent) space such that the similar images are placed closer, in terms of Euclidean distance, compared to dissimilar images.

In other words, deep CNN is a mapping function $f$ from an image of size $w \times h$ with $r$ color channels to a $k$-dimensional representation space, $f : \mathbb{N}^{w \times h \times r} \rightarrow \mathbb{R}^k$ where distances in $\mathbb{R}^k$ between similar image pairs, $d_{\text{Positive}}$, are smaller than distances to dissimilar image pairs, $d_{\text{Negative}}$, by a predefined margin $m$ in the desired metric space, i.e., $d_{\text{Positive}} + m \leq d_{\text{Negative}}$, where

$$d_{\text{Positive}} = d(f(I), f(I')|y = 1), \tag{1}$$

$$d_{\text{Negative}} = d(f(I), f(I')|y = 0). \tag{2}$$

Similar image pairs have the label $y = 1$ and dissimilar image pairs the label $y = 0$. We consider a Euclidean metric space where $d(f(I), f(I'))$ outputs the Euclidean distance between two vectors of representations for an image pair $\{I, I'\}$.

Once the network trained for similarity learning, it is used to map all the images in the dataset to a vector space. The distances between the vector representations in Euclidean sense are considered as similarity score. In a retrieval task, the distance between the vector representation of the query image is computed w.r.t. all vector representations of the images in the gallery. The images are then ranked in ascending order w.r.t. their distances to the query. The top ranked images are taken as the result for this search query.

### 3.4   Cross-Domain Retrieval

In the context of cross-domain CBIR, the representation of the object(s) in the gallery database can be potentially different from the query image. For example the images in the gallery may contain sketches, paintings or old photos as shown in Fig. 3. A common failure mode when it comes to deploying the CNN models that are trained only on single-domain images for a cross-domain CBIR task is that the network places the similar-style images in a neighbourhood even though different objects are depicted as it has never seen an object from the second domain (being historical images here). To resolve this domain-disparity issue, we propose to learn domain invariant image representations that focuses on semantics rather than on image style or colour. This leads to a specialized CNN model, which learns indifferent image representations for archival and contemporary image domains whereas it is discriminative on content level. As of any data-driven AI model we need annotated data with cross-domain similarity labels for training purposes. We spot the invaluable amount of visual archival data available in Amsterdam's city archive [1] for training style-agnostic computer models that can detect semantic objects mostly being built-form structures regardless of the image representation. For supervised training and evaluation set we need an image pair including identical objects in different domains being historical images and current images of the same site. This is exactly the task that we want to automate using a computer vision model and thus we are collecting human annotation accordingly. The process of data collection and labeling are described in Sect. 4. The following is a literature review of the cross-domain image search task.

### 3.5   Related Work

There is relatively little literature dealing with variations of cross-domain image search tasks [24,30,32,40]. Nevertheless, we are the first to consider the time-lag between sensing the same object as the cause of domain disparity.

There is a variety of methods that can impose the style-invariance constraint to the features learned by CNN models. A transductive approach is to let the CNN model see the historical images during the training process so it can come up with representations that are indifferent between contemporary and historical objects/images but yet discriminative on a semantic level. This is an unsupervised domain adaptation technique which does not require image labels from the historical image domain. Please refer to [41] for a survey on unsupervised domain adaptation techniques. In an earlier work we tried to develop a deep domain adaptation model for similarity learning [35] which is an essential building block for unsupervised domain adaption. in [35], a generative model is used to generate a synthetic pseudo-dataset for cross-domain training where original street-view data was transformed to another style to construct the similar pairs (automatic labeling).

Another line of research tries to insert attention modules to the network to guide it towards learning more powerful features rather than unwanted biases in the dataset such as photo style [28]. In our recent work, a combination of both attention and domain adaption is used to train robust CNN networks for an age-agnostic image retrieval task where historic views of Amsterdam are matched with the current street-view of the city [42]. In [42] similarity is learned by training a Siamese network on images with the same Geo-tags in the contemporary image domain, i.e. street-views of Amsterdam from Mapillary. This is commonly referred to as weakly supervised learning as the labels for training are not the same as the ones for testing. In our case the test (evaluation) set contains a query from historical Amsterdam and the gallery is current street-views of Amsterdam. The results of [42] reveal the performance gap while the intra-domain trained model on street-view images are tested in cross-domain data indicating a drop from 99% top 20 accuracy to 28% respectively. The main conclusion is that full supervision is required to achieve reasonable performance for the cross-domain image retrieval task.

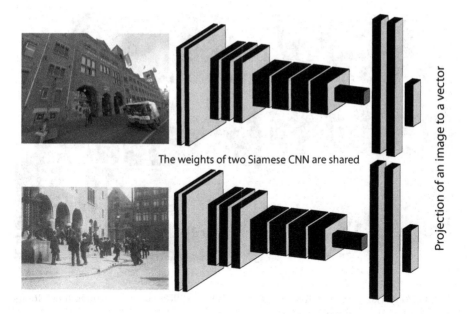

The weights of two Siamese CNN are shared

Projection of an image to a vector

**Fig. 2.** Siamese networks are one of the most popular CNN network for similarity learning in computer vision, where they are consist of two sister networks that share weights. The networks trains on similar and dissimilar image pairs where the projected images of similar content are place closer in representation space compared to the dissimilar images.

## 3.6   Computer Vision Research Question

The main research challenge that we try to solve is the task of cross-time image matching. The meta research question for the computer vision science perspective is how to extract representation-agnostic features that can detect semantic objects regardless of their different manifestations? The answer so far is that there is no one-size-fits-all solution when it comes to learning representative features for various visual domains [44]. Let alone that the famous CNN model pre-trained on standard benchmarks will not work on your non-standard image dataset with different-style images and sizes [26]. To approach this fundamental research question we study a well-served case, distant enough from the standard benchmarks to evaluate the learned representations: Art and visual history.

In our experimental setup in [42] we showed that unsupervised or weakly supervised methods perform poorly in our case of archival visual data, therefore some form of supervised learning is inevitable for feature learning. The contribution of supervised learning to cross-domain image retrieval is only revealed once we have enough data for training deep neural networks for such a challenging task. The *cross-time* dataset aims at bridging the data gap to answer this research question and at the same time establishes a foundation for development of tailor-made AI models for digital humanity.

**Fig. 3.** Westerkerk in Amsterdam is depicted in different images including Google street-view and historical pictures.

# 4    Crowdsourcing Image Pairs

The principle of crowdsourcing is a valuable approach to reduce the cost and time of the data collection process for training and evaluation of machine learning models. Motivating volunteers to participate in the data curation procedure can be done in different ways. One has to take into account the required expertise and familiarity of the crowd with the domain. Some tasks are generic enough to be done via Captchas [17], but annotating historical street-view images requires some familiarity with the geographic area depicted. The latter applies to our crowdsourcing task since deciding where a historical image was taken often requires familiarity with the location. Geo-tagging is the process of attributing Geo-coordinates to objects, which are historical images in our case so the more familiar the annotator is with the location, the higher the likelihood the annotator will recognize the location depicted in the historical image.

## 4.1    Dataset and Crowdsourcing Platform

The selection procedure for the best historical image dataset was relatively time consuming. Since deep learning models require a large set of high-quality training data we had to focus on a significant amount of our resources to find a dataset where it is likely that we can get many people that are willing to help annotating. Moreover, the data has to be free from copyright, since it shall be published as benchmark dataset for deep learning. The Amsterdam Beeldbank [1] proved to be ideal. It is a historical image collection owned by the city archive of the Amsterdam municipality. The dataset currently contains more than 441K high resolution images of photos, drawings and paintings depicting street-views, portraits, aerial views, interiors etc. Every image is accompanied with a (partially) completed meta-data template.

In crowdsourcing platforms, the significant extrinsic motivational factors are reputation, status, peer pressure, fame, community identification and fun. Enjoyment is considered as the leading intrinsic motivational factor prevalent in online platforms [27]. We try to appeal to both the enjoyment factor and the sense of community identification by offering an online tool to share historical knowledge with friends and the research community. The task should be easy combined with a gaming experience where the annotator is shown a historical image and a 3D street-view navigator mostly positioned close to the expected location where the historical image is being taken. The user can virtually move through the streets until the exact location is found and pan/zoom the camera to match the respective historical image.

We use any available metadata (for example a street name or the name of a neighborhood) to help the annotator with a first approximation of the location by using the address lookup functionality of Google Maps. The advantage of this is that the annotator can select images of a neighborhood (s)he is most familiar with. The task then is to navigate the camera to a position that is roughly comparable with the camera's position in the historical photograph. Different focus lengths, restrictions in movement and obstructing objects like trees or cars limit comparability of the chosen section with the historic photograph. Here there is the possibility to tick check boxes that explain the main differences, e.g.: partly obstructed, building added, unreachable, large distance. To be able to set a meaningful starting location for the user, at least some metadata that contains geographical information is required. This could be the name of a neighbourhood or a street/range of streets. Otherwise it would be quite laborious to find the corresponding scene. Thus, metadata is still required for compiling the training set. Once the CNN model is trained, it does not need images with meta tags to identify the content.

In order for the crowdsourcing task to be interesting enough to be carried out without financial reward, we have been inspired by research on 'serious games' [16] where the entertaining aspect of games is deployed for educational and scientific purposes like gathering research data to build the ArchiMediaL annotation tool. The idea behind the game is for the participant to find the exact location where a historical image is being taken by virtually navigating through a 360° panoramic street-view screen built by Mapillary [3]. Once the participant navigated to the approximate location, (s)he can use the rotating, panning and zooming features to approximate the historical image. The participant can choose which area (s)he would likes to play by navigating on a map and then click on the blue markers in the desired neighborhood. An orange marker indicates that this historical image is annotated and currently under review. A green marker indicates that at least one successful annotation is already added (see Fig. 6). In case the historical image is not a street-view image (e.g. interior, an aerial photo or other), the user can skip this task by selecting the appropriate checkbox and submit the result. Otherwise, the navigation procedure described above can begin and when it is finished, some check boxes can be selected to describe the current street view situation compared to the situation from the historical street view. For example, buildings can be added or removed, or the street view panoramic tool cannot reach the point where the photographer of the historical image took the picture. Every submission is manually verified by one of the ArchiMediaL administrators which takes only a fraction of the time per image in comparison to the annotation task itself.

The goal is to make the software and data open-source and free to share with the public. It took quite some effort to find a mix of technology, software libraries and data that in combination fulfills the requirement for the open source publication. For example, despite the high-quality content, Google Street-view data, professional web front-ends, GIS platforms like ArcGIS etc. have restrictive licenses or are too expensive which rendered them unsuitable for the project. It was possible to gather a blend that allowed us to implement the annotation platform. It contains the elements described below.

## 4.2    Technical Details

### Functionality

*Dynamic loading* should be realized for this project. Since the rendering of the data-points and metadata happens at the client side, and there are 200K+ data-points, loading everything will take too much bandwidth and memory consumption. Therefore a clustering approach is required. Once a user zooms into a location, only *that* data is loaded.

*Account management with various user types and groups* are considered for user identification. There are three user types: 1) *Annotators*, the target audience for this crowd-sourcing platform, 2) *Validators*, those who check the quality of the annotations and 3) *Administrators* who can modify accounts and dataset settings.

*Informative marker design* are required to reflect three different types of information using icons and colors: 1) each marker contains an icon that is unique for each dataset, 2) the datatype (e.g. aerial, interior, street-view) has its own icon, and the status of the annotation (i.e., todo, under-review, accepted) is reflected in the color.

*Open-source common libraries* are essential to our design. The implementation should be based on popular open source tools and libraries for handling and visualizing GIS data since it is well documented and makes our tool easier to be understood and extended by external developers.

**Modules.** In the following list we introduce our choices of design elements for the open-source annotation platform:

*Mapillary* is a street-level imagery platform that uses computer vision to automatically annotate maps. Mapillary brings together a global network of contributors who want to make the world accessible to everyone by visualizing the world and building richer maps. In order to make use of their widgets one has to register for a free API key which can be invoked by their well documented JavaScript library [4].

*Open Streetmaps* [39] is an editable map database built and maintained by volunteers and distributed under the Open Data Commons Open Database License. Mapping takes place not only at computers but also out in the world. From car trips to casual jogs, photos, videos, GPS traces, and hand-taken notes provide OSM with Geo-spatial information. The mapping infrastructure, along with many of the associated OSM projects, is maintained and developed by volunteers as well. Computing and network resources are donated by universities and organizations.

*Leaflet* [18] is a widely used open source JavaScript library used to build web mapping applications. First released in 2011 [15], it supports most mobile and desktop platforms, supporting HTML5 and CSS3. Leaflet allows developers without a GIS background to very easily display tiled web maps hosted on a public server, with optional tiled overlays. It can load feature data from GeoJSON files, style it and create interactive layers, such as markers with popups when clicked.

*Google maps Geo-coordinate resolver* is the most popular of navigation systems. One types in some details describing the location like the address or the title (e.g. Eiffel tower) and the location is displayed on a map. Google also provides the latitude and longitude coordinates which we use to map the title and description meta-data from the Amsterdam Beeldbank to these coordinates. It is an important feature of our tool to already guess an approximate location of the historical image content. This is where the markers on the ArchiMediaL annotator are placed. We wrote custom code in JAVA to automate this procedure for the 400K+ historical images from Beeldbank.

*PostGIS* [9] is a spatial database extender for PostgreSQL [10] object-relational database. It adds support for geographic objects allowing location queries to be run in SQL. In order to store the locations internally in PostGIS, the lat-lon coordinates from the previous step, a transformation needs to be applied [11].

**Additional JavaScript Libraries**

*jQuery.* jQuery [6] is a JavaScript library designed to simplify HTML DOM tree traversal and manipulation, as well as event handling, CSS animation, and Ajax. It is free, open-source software using the permissive MIT License.

*Leaflet.MarkerCluster* [7], as the name implies, used for clustering markers in Leaflet. It uses a grid-based clustering method which makes it ideal for a fast solution to the many-markers problem.

*Tabulator* [13] creates interactive tables any HTML Tables, JavaScript Arrays, AJAX data sources or JSON formatted data. Tabulator is used for various components in the ArchiMediaL Annotator, for example to display the table of annotations attached to the markers or for the administrator panel to verify pending reviews.

*FontAwesome* [5] is a popular icon toolkit featuring icon font ligatures, an SVG framework, official NPM packages for popular front-end libraries like React, and access to a new CDN. Most of the ArchiMediaL annotator icons have FontAwesome as the source.

*Node.js* [8] is a platform built on Chrome's JavaScript runtime for easily building fast and scaleable network applications. Node.js uses an event-driven, non-blocking I/O model that makes it lightweight and efficient, perfect for data-intensive real-time applications that run across distributed devices. Node.js serves as the larger part of the ArchiMedial back-end.

*Puppeteer for Node.js* [12] is a Node.js [8] library which provides a high-level API to control Chrome or Chromium over the DevTools Protocol. Puppeteer runs headless by default, but can be configured to run full (non-headless) on Chrome or Chromium.

## 4.3   Users

Despite the relative short period between the test release of the platform and the write-up of this article, we already experimented with various strategies to attract new annotators to our platform. The easiest and most successful one is to tap in the rich source of student enthusiasm during lectures to give them some time to experiment. The largest peak of new subscriptions was actually during one of the lectures at the TU-Delft seen in the week of December 16th, 2019 in Fig. 8. Unfortunately, this stress test lead to an unforeseen unacceptable spike in use of computational resources on the shared servers, and the host decided to temporarily kill all processes. Since that even a significant amount of time was spent to make the processes more efficient. For example, making a screenshot of the Mapillary screen from the user requires spawning a Google Chrome instance on the server, which is already about 100 MB in memory usage. With hundred simultaneous users, it leads easily to GBs of memory usage which is way above our 1 GB max. This was solved by having an instance pool of Chrome engines handled by Puppeteer for Node.js [12] that take the user jobs respectively. When more than 4 in our case need an instance, they have to wait, mostly for a couple of seconds, in a queue until its their time. We hoped that the students would continue to play around with the annotator and help us with more annotations, but that did not happen. This explains that, although most new registrations happened during that event, most of them never submitted an annotation then or afterwards (cf. Fig. 9). Another interesting observation when looking at Fig. 9 is the highly skewed distribution. Only few users are responsible for the a large portion of the annotations. This is similar to what happens to the contributions on WikiPedia [14]. Figure 8 shows the weekly number of new subscriptions to our platform. In retrospect we can verify the effectiveness of the actions we took to attract new subscribers (Tables 1, 2 and Figs. 4, 5).

**Table 1.** Total accepted, pending and rejected annotations per category

|  | Street-view | Interior | Aerial | Other | *Total* |
|---|---|---|---|---|---|
| Accepted | 835 | 243 | 84 | 165 | 1327 |
| Rejected | 278 | 12 | 11 | 25 | 326 |
| Pending review | 3 | 0 | 0 | 0 | 3 |
| *Total* | 1116 | 255 | 95 | 190 | **1656** |

**Table 2.** Statistics on street-view situations for accepted annotations

| Street-view situation | Total (percentage) |
|---|---|
| (Partially) blocked | 103 (12.3%) |
| Large distance | 50 (6.0%) |
| Unreachable | 45 (5.4%) |
| Buildings removed | 60 (7.2%) |
| Buildings added | 79 (9.5%) |
| None | 565 (67.7%) |

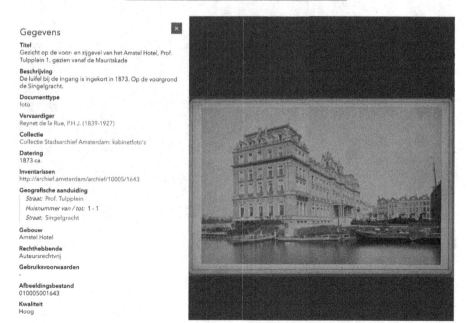

**Fig. 4.** Screenshot of the Amsterdam Beeldbank portal containing a historical image accompanied with its meta data.

**Fig. 5.** Screenshot of the ArchiMediaL annotator where the annotator managed to match the Mapillary street-view with the historical image

**Fig. 6.** Three types of markers indicating 1: todo (blue), 2: under-review (orange) and 3: accepted (green) (Color figure online)

### 4.4 Crowdsourcing Research Question

The research question we have used as a basis for generating the training dataset is: "What is the best practice for obtaining geo-tagged historical images of a

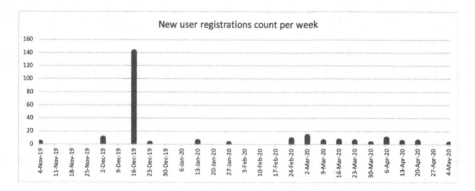

**Fig. 7.** Weekly amount of new registered annotators

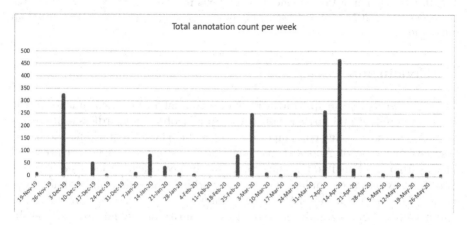

**Fig. 8.** Weekly amount of contributed annotations

city by crowdsourcing? The implementation and data acquisition of ArchiMe-diaL's annotation tool were successfully tested for the collection of image pairs in order to create the first cross-time dataset with historical and contemporary image pairs. Nevertheless, our experience has shown that a great deal of effort is required to motivate people to contribute, unless they have strong research incentives. In continuing the work, we have used financial rewards to collect enough data to automate the task of historical location recognition. The dataset will soon be released, which will be a major step for computer vision experts to solve the cross-domain image matching task (Fig. 7).

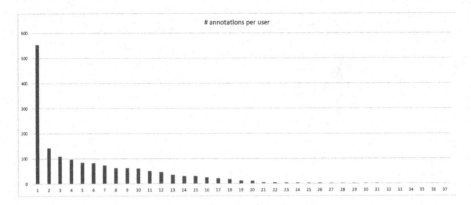

**Fig. 9.** Distribution of the amount of annotations per single user. Note that from the total amount of 207 registered users only 37 have actually successfully submitted an annotation

## 5  Conclusion

Computer vision can help to identify image content in historical images of the built environment and further pair it with similar objects regardless of its representation form including contemporary photos, sketches, illustrations, and paintings. As the case of Amsterdam exemplifies, a stock of +400k architectural images from the Beeldbank archives has not yet been clearly identified in terms of content. Millions of similar images exist worldwide in online and offline repositories. The identification of the image content is not possible for architectural and urban historians simply because of the quantity of the images. As a result, valuable visual source material for research in the humanities is lost. Computer vision seems to be helpful here, e.g., by finding the contemporary footprint of the historical buildings for further research on changes in the built environment, gentrification of neighborhoods, sustainability and resilience of buildings, etc. In this paper, we introduce cross-time image matching for historical and contemporary street-view images. Our initial experiments with off-the-shelf computer vision models including classical feature engineering methods and modern pre-trained models on image benchmarks showed very poor performance. This opens up a new research direction for computer vision experts as the task seems challenging enough to be studied for further improvement. We identified two reasons that are associated with the moderate performance of existing CNN models on this task. First, that contemporary street view images of the buildings vary in terms of the view-point, occlusion, appearance compared to the historical images. Second, the image quality and color representation are relatively different from that of new photos which cause domain disparity from the source query object (historical image) to the gallery object (street-view) images. Moreover, using pre-trained CNN models on contemporary benchmarks seems to add to the domain disparity and these models tend to be more discriminative in the image-style level rather than semantic level.

To study the challenge of cross-domain image matching, we decided to collect human-annotated image pairs to be able to quantitatively evaluate different computer vision models and further to use the human baseline for training the neural network models to automate the task. For this purpose, a crowdsourcing image matching tool has been developed that allows finding the location of a building in a historical image by navigating the current scenery of the image in a 3D street view mode. Through advertising in university courses and social media, volunteers helped to pair 1656 images. A review and correction of these pairs resulted in a set of 902 useful image pairs that can be used for evaluation purposes. We hope to achieve more labeled pairs to train the best performing model end-to-end to quantify the level of human supervision that is required for this task. We challenge the computer vision community to approach the unsolved task of the cross-time image retrieval once the dataset including both historical and contemporary images matches the Amsterdam buildings is released.

On another level, a unique feature of this research is the mixed methodological approach that combines architectural history with machine learning and crowd-sourcing solutions. While research in the field of artificial intelligence (AI) requires high-quality data, e.g., to advance neural networks, it is common to use datasets that are very well suited for bench-marking technical advances. On the other hand, research in the humanities applies qualitative methods and focuses on a limited number of case studies. Our goal is to combine useful approaches in both fields of data science and humanities by identifying research questions that are exciting for both scientific parties. This means that AI research is not seen as a supplier for the solution of a humanities problem, but that the joint research must be interesting for the researchers involved from all disciplines. In our case, the identification of historical buildings in photographs helps researchers to assign these images to specific objects and thus make them usable as important resources. At the same time, it is a new challenge for the computer vision community to realize image recognition with historical photographs from very different domains. The deep combination of humanities and computer science research can help to make progress in both areas and to uncover new insights. In addition, it offers the opportunity to formulate novel research questions and to advance to the more complex interdisciplinary research designs.

**Acknowledgements.** We would like to thank our colleagues in the ArchiMediaL project, especially Dr. Beate Löffler for her generous help with data collection. We would also like to thank the Volkswagen Foundation for its financial support of this project.

# References

1. Beeldbank stadsarchief amsterdam. https://archief.amsterdam/beeldbank/
2. North Carolina state university: Urban panorama. https://www.visualnarrative. ncsu.edu/projects/urban-panorama/
3. Mapillary (2020). http://mapillary.com. Accessed 4 June 2020

4. The Mapillary API (2020). https://www.mapillary.com/developer/api-documentation/. Accessed 4 June 2020
5. Fontawesome (2020). https://github.com/FortAwesome/Font-Awesome. Accessed 5 June 2020
6. jquery (2020). https://jquery.com/. Accessed 5 June 2020
7. Leaflet.markercluster (2020). https://github.com/Leaflet/Leaflet.markercluster. Accessed 5 June 2020
8. Node.js (2020). https://nodejs.org/en/. Accessed 5 June 2020
9. Postgis (2020). https://postgis.net/. Accessed 5 June 2020
10. Postgresql (2020). https://www.postgresql.org/. Accessed 5 June 2020
11. Postgresql-lat-lon (2020). https://postgis.net/docs/ST_MakePoint.html. Accessed 5 June 2020
12. Puppeteer for node.js (2020). https://github.com/puppeteer/puppeteer. Accessed 5 June 2020
13. Tabulator (2020). http://tabulator.info/. Accessed 5 June 2020
14. Wikipedia: list of Wikipedians by number of edits (2020). https://en.wikipedia.org/wiki/Wikipedia:List_of_Wikipedians_by_number_of_edits. Accessed 5 June 2020
15. Leaflet wikipedia (2020). https://en.wikipedia.org/wiki/Leaflet_(software). Accessed 28 May 2020
16. Abt, C.C.: Serious Games. University Press of America (1987)
17. von Ahn, L., Blum, M., Hopper, N.J., Langford, J.: CAPTCHA: using hard AI problems for security. In: Biham, E. (ed.) EUROCRYPT 2003. LNCS, vol. 2656, pp. 294–311. Springer, Heidelberg (2003). https://doi.org/10.1007/3-540-39200-9_18
18. et al., V.A.: Leaflet (2020). https://leafletjs.com/. Accessed 2 June 2020
19. Arandjelovic, R., Zisserman, A.: All about VLAD. In: 2013 IEEE Conference on Computer Vision and Pattern Recognition, pp. 1578–1585 (2013). https://doi.org/10.1109/CVPR.2013.207
20. Arandjelović, R., Gronat, P., Torii, A., Pajdla, T., Sivic, J.: NetVLAD: CNN architecture for weakly supervised place recognition. IEEE Trans. Pattern Anal. Mach. Intell. **40**(6), 1437–1451 (2018). https://doi.org/10.1109/TPAMI.2017.2711011
21. Bengio, Y., Courville, A.C., Vincent, P.: Unsupervised feature learning and deep learning: a review and new perspectives. CoRR abs/1206.5538 (2012)
22. Chopra, S., Hadsell, R., Lecun, Y.: Learning a similarity metric discriminatively, with application to face verification. vol. 1, pp. 539–546, July 2005. https://doi.org/10.1109/CVPR.2005.202
23. Deng, J., Dong, W., Socher, R., Li, L.J., Li, K., Fei-Fei, L.: ImageNet: a large-scale hierarchical image database. In: CVPR 2009 (2009)
24. Fernando, B., Tommasi, T., Tuytelaars, T.: Location recognition over large time lags. Comput. Vis. Image Underst. **139**, 21–28 (2015)
25. Geirhos, R., Rubisch, P., Michaelis, C., Bethge, M., Wichmann, F., Brendel, W.: ImageNet-trained CNNs are biased towards texture; increasing shape bias improves accuracy and robustness. ArXiv abs/1811.12231 (2019)
26. Geirhos, R., Rubisch, P., Michaelis, C., Bethge, M., Wichmann, F.A., Brendel, W.: ImageNet-trained CNNs are biased towards texture; increasing shape bias improves accuracy and robustness. CoRR abs/1811.12231 (2018). http://arxiv.org/abs/1811.12231
27. Hossain, M.: Crowdsourcing: activities, incentives and users' motivations to participate. In: 2012 International Conference on Innovation, Management and Technology Research, ICIMTR 2012, Malacca, 21–22 May 2012, pp. 501–506 (2012)

28. Ji, X., Wang, W., Zhang, M., Yang, Y.: Cross-domain image retrieval with attention modeling. In: 2017 ACM Multimedia Conference (2017)
29. Khademi, S., et al.: Research project archimedial - enriching and linking historical architectural and urban image collections. https://archimedial.eu
30. Kim, T., Cha, M., Kim, H., Lee, J.K., Kim, J.: Learning to discover cross-domain relations with generative adversarial networks. arXiv: 1703.05192 (2017)
31. Koch, G., Zemel, R., Salakhutdinov, R.: Siamese neural networks for one-shot image recognition (2015)
32. Kong, B., III, J.S.S., Ramanan, D., Fowlkes, C.C.: Cross-domain image matching with deep feature maps. arXiv preprint arXiv:1804.02367 (2018)
33. Krizhevsky, A., Sutskever, I., Hinton, G.E.: ImageNet classification with deep convolutional neural networks. In: Pereira, F., Burges, C.J.C., Bottou, L., Weinberger, K.Q. (eds.) Advances in Neural Information Processing Systems, vol. 25, pp. 1097–1105. Curran Associates, Inc. (2012). http://papers.nips.cc/paper/4824-imagenet-classification-with-deep-convolutional-neural-networks.pdf
34. Li, J., Hu, Q., Ai, M.: RIFT: multi-modal image matching based on radiation-invariant feature transform. CoRR abs/1804.09493 (2018). http://arxiv.org/abs/1804.09493
35. Liu, X., Khademi, S., Van Gemert, J.: Cross domain image matching in presence of outliers. In: The IEEE International Conference on Computer Vision (ICCV) Workshops, October 2019
36. Lowe, D.G.: Distinctive image features from scale-invariant keypoints. Int. J. Comput. Vis. **60**, 91–110 (2004)
37. Löffler, B., Hein, C., Mager, T.: Searching for Meiji-Tokyo: heterogeneous visual media and the turn to global urban history, digitalization, and deep learning. Global Urban History, 20 March 2018 (2018)
38. Muñoz, X., Martí, R.: Which is the best way to organize/classify images by content? Image Vis. Comput. **25**, 778–791 (2007). https://doi.org/10.1016/j.imavis.2006.07.015
39. OpenStreetMap contributors: Planet dump (2017). https://planet.osm.org. https://www.openstreetmap.org
40. Tian, Y., Chen, C., Shah, M.: Cross-view image matching for geo-localization in urban environments. In: CVPR (2017)
41. Wang, M., Deng, W.: Deep visual domain adaptation: a survey. CoRR abs/1802.03601 (2018). http://arxiv.org/abs/1802.03601
42. Wang, Z., Li, J., Khademi, S., van Gemert, J.: Attention-aware age-agnostic visual place recognition. In: The IEEE International Conference on Computer Vision (ICCV) Workshops, October 2019
43. Yi, K.M., Trulls, E., Lepetit, V., Fua, P.: LIFT: learned invariant feature transform. In: Leibe, B., Matas, J., Sebe, N., Welling, M. (eds.) ECCV 2016. LNCS, vol. 9910, pp. 467–483. Springer, Cham (2016). https://doi.org/10.1007/978-3-319-46466-4_28
44. Zhai, X., et al.: A large-scale study of representation learning with the visual task adaptation benchmark (2019)

# Policies, Legislation and Standards

# A Framework to Support Digital Humanities and Cultural Heritage Studies Research

Selda Ulutas Aydogan[1]([⊠]), Sander Münster[1], Dino Girardi[2,3],
Monica Palmirani[2], and Fabio Vitali[4]

[1] Digital Humanities, Friedrich Schiller University Jena, Fürstengraben 1,
07743 Jena, Germany
selda.ulutas@uni-jena.de

[2] CIRSFID-Alma-AI, University of Bologna, 40121 Bologna, Italy

[3] Institute for Law and Informatics, University of Lapland, 96101 Rovaniemi,
Finland

[4] DISI, University of Bologna, 40121 Bologna, Italy

**Abstract.** Developments in information and communication technologies and their repercussions for how cultural heritage is preserved, used and produced are the subject of several research and innovation efforts in Europe. Advanced digital technologies create new opportunities for cultural heritage to drive innovation. Digital humanities are an important domain for cultural heritage research in Europe and beyond. Digital tools and methods can be used in innovative ways in cultural heritage research. The research and innovation efforts and framework of digital humanities, and cultural heritage as one of its research fields, are influenced by EU policies and legislation. This article describes the existing policy initiatives, practices and related legal setting as framework conditions for digital humanities and cultural heritage research and innovation in Europe – focusing on urban history applications in the age of digital libraries. This is a multifaceted study of the state of the art in policies, legislation and standards – using a survey with 1000 participants, literature surveys on copyrights and policies.

**Keywords:** Digitisation · Cultural heritage · European policy · Legal framework · Research and innovation

## 1 Introduction

In this article, we present the framework demands and analyse the current state of the art of legal and policy issues related to research and innovation on digitisation and cultural heritage. This is done in three main parts. First of all, we present the results of an online community survey of needs for a supportive policy and legal framework concerning digitisation and cultural heritage. Secondly, we analyse the most recent EU policy and funding schemes, to present the context and trends which impact on research and innovation processes in relation to cultural heritage and digitisation. Third, we

© Springer Nature Switzerland AG 2021
F. Niebling et al. (Eds.): UHDL 2019, CCIS 1501, pp. 237–267, 2021.
https://doi.org/10.1007/978-3-030-93186-5_11

analyse the current legal framework to reach a broader understanding of the conditions which affect and structure these research and innovation processes in digital cultural heritage (DCH).

## 2  Survey

To analyse current demands from a community point of view we conducted an online survey. The specific interests related to investigations are:

- What is the digital heritage community and where are its members from?
- What are demands do they make concerning framework conditions?

### 2.1  Theoretical Framework

From a theoretical perspective several approaches focus on historical, philosophical and sociological aspects [1/ 65,2]. A prominent concept provided by science and technology studies characterises fields of research by specific epistemic cultures in terms of "architectures of empirical approaches, specific constructions of the referent, particular ontologies of instruments, and different social machines" [3, p. 3], techniques to gain insights, different vocabularies, different publication bodies and habits [4]. According to this approach, scholarly fields "(a) have a particular object of research [...], (b) have a body of accumulated specialist knowledge [...], (c) have theories and concepts [...], (d) use specific terminologies [...], (e) have developed specific research methods [...], and (f) must have some institutional manifestation in the form of subjects taught at universities or colleges" [2].

**Quantitative Studies**
**Various surveys** have been conducted to investigate digital use and practices in the humanities. The DARIAH DIMPO survey published in 2016 had 2100 participants and focused on regional coverage and the use of digital methods [5]. Its main finding was that the digital humanities community in Europe is widely driven by German and French researchers. Similarly, the e-Science survey series with 860 participants covered the private and professional use of digital tools: its main finding was that the private use of digital tools does not differ much between researchers from the humanities and other disciplines. In contrast professional use is highly divergent between single humanities disciplines but digital tools are less used than in other disciplines [6]. In the context of digital heritage studies various surveys were carried out on specific topics. The ViMM survey with 700 participants queried digital challenges and protagonists [7]. The surveys by INCEPTION, the VIGIE study and the Europeana 3D task group focused on the use of 3D [8].

Scholarly communities in digital humanities have been examined with regards to conference contributions and related patterns in various investigations[1]. Most relevant for the community of digital humanities is the research of Scott Weingart on the ADHO DH conferences [9]. For a fundamental analysis of topics in the humanities, see Leydesdorff et al. [10]. For digital heritage studies, Spugnoli investigated topics of an Italian conference series [11]. Muenster et al. analysed 4500 international publications stemming from six major conferences in digital heritage studies and dating from 1973 to 2015 [12, 13] as well as three panel surveys since 2017 [14, 15].

## 2.2 Methodology

The methodology of the survey was as follows:

- **Open-ended questions:** The survey used open questions only, to allow for diverse answers and to retrieve additional items [16].
- **Sampling:** During May and June 2019, the survey was sent to ~5000 individuals who were authors of papers in the main conferences in DCH as the ICOMOS CIPA Symposium, DIGITAL HERITAGE, EUROMED, CAA the CIPA 3DArch workshop [cf. 12] and members of international associations as the International Centre of Archival Research (ICARUS), the International Centre for the Study of the Preservation and Restoration of Cultural Property (ICCROM) and the Time Machine Organisation (TMO).
- **Survey participants:** In total 968 individuals responded; of these, 406 completed the survey. Since the questions did not depend on each other, we included only partly filled forms in the evaluation.
- **Data analysis:** Data was clustered via alternating inductive and deductive steps of qualitative content analysis [17].
- **Ethics:** All responses were anonymous. The acquired metadata contained information about location only. This data was used to investigate the geographical coverage of the survey.

## 2.3 Findings

The survey included six questions. The following findings are taken from responses to one Question: The Time Machine will have impact on standardisation, policies and law in Europe and its nations. What actions on these topics would you suggest to include in a roadmap? We received 590 answers to this question (Fig. 1).

---

[1] An overview can be found at: http://scottbot.net/dh-quantified/.

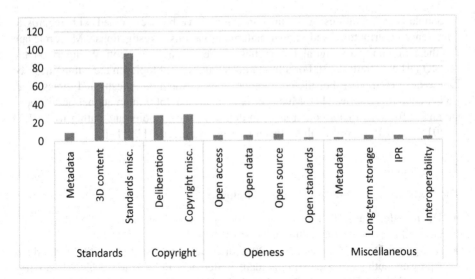

**Fig. 1.** Question: The Time Machine will have impact on standardisation, policies and law in Europe and its nations. What actions on these topics would you suggest to include in a roadmap? **Coding: 265 answers with min. occurrence 3 nominations per group selected out of total 590**

Overall, standards are the most frequently mentioned topic on which respondents see the need to take action. Most answers did not further specify which type of standards they meant, so these have been categorised as miscellaneous (misc.). The most frequently mentioned standards, on which 60+ respondents demanded action, was 3D content. 10 respondents asked for metadata standards. Occasionally standards for other media, such as "musical records" were also requested.

Concerning copyright, around 30 of the answers mentioned copyright without further explanations and the deliberation of copyright. Less frequently, openness in terms of source, data, access and standards are mentioned by less than ten participants each. Occasionally, other aspects not fitting in these categories were mentioned (e.g. intellectual property rights).

## 2.4 Discussion

From the survey there evolved a very clear view that standards, and specifically 3D standards, are of highest relevance for taking action. This finding is in line with various European-scale endeavours – e.g. the Europeana 3D task group [8], European Commission tender on 3D digitisation and the DT-20 Competence Center CSA[2]. In addition, various EU projects developed standards and workflows for 3D digitisation, including 3D-COFORM, 3D-ICONS, CARARE, PARTHENOS and Share3D [cf. 18].

---

[2] https://ec.europa.eu/digital-single-market/en/news/study-quality-3d-digitisation-tangible-cultural-heritage.

Even after 30 years of 3D related activities and various standard setting initiatives there is no established consensus about 3D data standards beyond file metadata.

Surprisingly, openness is only occasionally named as challenge. This may be for the technical reason that open access was not explicitly named in the question text. Since even deliberated copyright was demanded by 30 participants only, it seems questionable whether openness as a main challenge in current EU research policies[3] is that relevant for DCH to date. The concrete demands concerning copyright (e.g. homogenisation of copyright, open access and simplified rules) are also unclear.

# 3 State of the Art in Policy and Funding Practices

Cultural heritage has gradually gained ground as a subject for research and innovation policy in Europe. It is a multidisciplinary domain in relation to the ICT sector, digitisation and innovation for economic and social impact. The EU dedicates resources and efforts to cultural heritage via research and innovation framework programmes, policy initiatives, expert groups and tailored events.

Below, we analyse the most recent EU policy and funding schemes relevant to cultural heritage and digitisation. The focus is on current research and innovation policy and funding programmes, including the impact of the COVID-19 crisis on policy and funding practices on digitisation of cultural heritage.

## 3.1 Theoretical Framework

Scholars have addressed various aspects of the European policy framework supporting digitisation of cultural heritage. The relevant literature focuses on three major and interwoven areas.

One strand of research discusses European cultural heritage policy framework and funding context entailing aspects and focus of innovation and digitisation [19, 20, 21, 22]. Other scholars focus more on digitisation, cultural heritage and European policy framework [23, 24]. Another set of scholars focus on digitisation, digital innovation and implications for European cultural assets for economic and societal benefits, challenges for cultural heritage institutions illustrated through EU projects, stakeholder networks and cases [25, 26, 27, 28, 29]. Scholarly articles present major European policies, strategies and initiatives in relation to digitisation and cultural heritage such as i2010 Digital Libraries Initiative (2005) [30], Digital Agenda for Europe (2010) [31], European Year of Cultural Heritage (2018) [32], European Heritage Strategy for 21st Century [33], European Framework for Action on Cultural Heritage [34], New Strategic Agenda for the EU (2019–2024) [35], Work Plan for Culture 2019–2022 [36] among others [e.g. 20, 22, 24, 28].

The European Commission's "Mapping of Cultural Heritage actions in European Union policies, programmes and activities, August 2017" [37] presents recent EU policies and actions with regards to cultural heritage.

---

[3] See e.g. https://ec.europa.eu/research/openscience/index.cfm?pg=openaccess.

**Methodology**

The study is primarily based on analysis of most recent policy documents with specific emphasis or correlation to digitisation and cultural heritage in Europe.

**Data Retrieval:** For our study, data sources were analysed to derive out policy content, objectives and approaches. The focus is on three sets of data:

1. Scholarly articles on cultural heritage, digitisation and innovation.
2. EU policy documents on cultural heritage, digitisation, research and innovation.
3. Information on EU research and innovation funding schemes relevant to cultural heritage.

Relevant articles were identified via a keyword search in Google Scholar database as well as in the Publications Office of the EU database. Out of a total of 24260 retrieved articles and publications we selected 70 for further analysis based on criteria that they entail European level research, innovation and digitisation policy content on cultural heritage.

**Evaluation and Analysis:** We applied two-stage inductive and deductive qualitative content analysis as per Mayring (2000) [17] for systematic analysis of text to retrieve manifest content and to understand the policy concepts with regards to digitisation and cultural heritage.

**Theoretical Framework:** The EU level reports, strategies, communications and other official documents were confined to those having contemporary effect.

In this sense, a "design science" framework is applied. The method used is based on the work of Romme and Meijer (2020) offering a contribution to discourse by combining "retrospective research" based on "scientific validation" and "prospective research" as "creative design" [38, p. 1, 2]. Beyond traditional approaches based on linear and top-down oriented processes, their work is about developing a design approach for public policy and administration (PPA) that integrates validation and intervention-oriented design. It affirms the role of user engagement, creativity in prospective design and validation of retrospective research. Where design is about generating and elaborating new practices of PPA, validation is about theorising the practices created. This integrated approach enables theoretical understanding of policy, practices and interventions to improve them [38]. The community survey presented in Sect. 2 is used to shed light on policy and practices (Sect. 3) and legal framework analysis (Sect. 4). Based on theorisation of community needs, design science approach is taken to the policy and legal framework for digitisation of cultural heritage and intervention for new practices.

## 3.2    European Policy and Practices on Cultural Heritage and Digitisation

The most recent policies and initiatives with an impact on post-2020 research and innovation agenda in Europe are examined below in terms of their key function and call for action to enhance the digitisation and innovation of cultural heritage. This exercise feeds into the analysis of the current policy and legal framework in this field. This framework provides a basis for bottom-up initiatives aiming to reinforce DCH research and innovation landscape in Europe.

### 3.2.1    The European Heritage Strategy for the 21st Century

The Recommendation of the Committee of Ministers to Member States on the European Cultural Heritage Strategy for the 21st century (Strategy 21) was adopted on 22 February 2017 [33]. Strategy 21 builds on past initiatives and achievements structuring heritage policies and the resulting cooperation across Europe over the preceding 40 years. It aims to enable a common approach to cultural heritage and its effective and integrated management by main actors at national, European and international levels. It aims to build synergy among extant policies and tools, especially among European and international legal instruments. Another objective of Strategy 21 is to increase visibility of European countries' practices and achievements through an information network called the HEREIN system [33].

Strategy 21 rests on three priority components: "social"; "territorial and economic development"; "knowledge and education" [33, p. 6]. Under each component, recommendations are made to member states and these are for members states to apply in line with their resources, priorities and instruments to meet the challenges identified. Each component give reference to digital tools, techniques and innovative approaches for cultural heritage. In the strategy, cultural heritage is presented as a strong component of social and economic development and correlated with other sectors. It is also perceived as a vital asset for "education, employment, tourism and sustainable development" [33 p. 4].

Under the "social" component of the Strategy 21 [33] member states are called to make visible and employ digital tools to promote citizen involvement in capturing the value of their heritage. Utilisation of digital instruments, the latest technologies and interdisciplinarity are emphasised for enhanced access to heritage. Digital forms and reuse of heritage are associated with asserting European values and promoting dialogue among different cultures and generations.

The territorial and economic development component includes enhanced use of new technologies such as "augmented reality", "digitisation", and "3D scanners" [33, p. 18] to protect, restore and promote heritage. In the component on knowledge and education, the aim is to make information on digital heritage more accessible, open and practical to support the integration of heritage-related content in school education [33].

From a macro-perspective, Strategy 21 aims to enhance the concerted efforts across member states to exploit the benefits of digital tools and technologies for cultural heritage. The recommendations stress the value of a supportive framework to effectively implement digitisation, standardisation and open access.

### 3.2.2    The European Year of Cultural Heritage 2018

Launched by the European Commission, the European Year of Cultural Heritage (EYCH) 2018 aimed to boost people's engagement with Europe's past and a common sense of belonging to Europe [32]. It entailed a series of events and initiatives accross Europe. The Year gave its label to over 13,000 events organised in Europe. Also, more than 620 events/initiatives of third countries were associated with the Year [39, p. 4].

The Commission and key stakeholders launched ten European Initiatives[4] for the EYCH in connection to its four key principles: "Engagement, Sustainability, Protection and Innovation" [40]. The aim was to make a long-lasting impact beyond 2018. The initiatives were intended to enable joint action and reach various target groups across Europe. The innovation principle entailed three initiatives: "Heritage-related skills: better education and training for traditional and new professions"; "All for heritage: fostering social innovation and people's and communities' participation"; "Science for heritage: research, innovation, science and technology for the benefit of heritage" [40].

EYCH 2018 is an example of a comprehensive and far-reaching initiative for creating and sustaining the value and role of cultural heritage widely across research and innovation communities and citizens of Europe.

### 3.2.3    A New European Agenda for Culture

The New Agenda for Culture was proposed by the European Commission in 2018 in response to European Council's call to enhance the efforts and momentum caught by previous EU level policies, initiatives and member state level activities. The underlying rationale of this agenda is European Council's call "*to examine further possible measures addressing,* among others, *the legal and financial framework conditions for the development of cultural and creative industries and the mobility of professionals of the cultural sector.*" based on the European Council Conclusions of 2017 [41, p. 2, 42].

The New Agenda is based on three strategic objectives revolving around social, economic and external relations. The role of culture for innovation as a factor in economic growth and employment is mentioned within *Economic dimension - supporting culture-based creativity in education and innovation, and for jobs and growth* [41, p. 4]. Enabling favourable environments, facilitating access to finance and enhancing innovation capacity, promoting digital and entrepreneurial skills, and fair remuneration are among the actions described for cultural and creative industries, authors and creators [41, p. 4]. The potential of cultural and creative sectors to catalyse innovative solutions when combined with other sectors in information and communication technologies, manufacturing, tourism and other sectors is mentioned as "transformative power" [41, p. 4, 10]. In support of this, the Commission aims to generate favourable conditions for culture-driven innovation [41].

The New Agenda is a critical intervention aiming to enable a favourable system framework for cultural heritage-driven creativity, innovations and the resulting benefits for the economy and society. It emphasises enablers such as legal and financial frameworks, entrepreneurial skills and innovation capacity in support of the cultural sector.

---

[4] These are: Shared heritage, Heritage at school, Youth for heritage, Heritage in transition, Tourism and heritage, Cherishing heritage, Heritage at risk, Heritage-related skills, All for heritage, Science for heritage.

### 3.2.4    The Work Plan for Culture 2019–2022

Adopted in November 2018 by the Council of the European Union, the Work Plan 2019–2022 rests on five priorities: "Sustainability in cultural heritage"; "Cohesion and well-being"; "An ecosystem supporting artists, cultural and creative professionals and European content"; "Gender equality"; "International cultural relations". Digitalisation and cultural statistics are considered as crucial horizontal issues in the plan. It is stated that digitalisation generates "new and innovative possibilities for art and culture in terms of access, expression, preservation, dissemination and consumption" [36, p. 13].

The importance of digital technologies is underlined for "audience development and innovative methods of participation" in support of the cohesion and well-being priority. Relations with other sectors such as education, science and technology, territorial development and culture-driven social innovations are seen as contributing to the same priority [36, p. 14].

Under the priority of "An ecosystem supporting artists, cultural and creative professionals and European content", the role of creative and cultural resources is emphasised for Europe's competitive power and boosting innovation. Skills development, mobility, cross-border relations and access to financial resources are among the issues depicted for this priority in relation to European-scale exchange and research [36, p. 14]. One of the action topics of the Work Plan is to identify alternative funding sources in support of cultural heritage to ensure its economic sustainability [36, p. 16]. Novel instruments and guidelines are mentioned as a subject of an expert group led by the Commission to respond to the need for organisations to understand their digital audiences and adapt to digital developments in flux [36, p. 17]. Access to financing and support for the innovation potential and creativity of young people are seen as subject to future expert work and recommendations at European level [36, p. 17, 20].

In a similar vein to the New Agenda for Culture, this Work Plan emphasises the measures that target innovations and creativity in the culture sector. Development of skills, a favourable ecosystem, enhanced mobility, facilitated access to finance and organisational adaptation to digital developments are emphasised as a supportive framework for innovations.

### 3.2.5    The Recovery Plan for Europe

The Recovery Plan for Europe was proposed on 27 May 2020 as a comprehensive European response to "repair damage from the crisis and prepare a better future for the next generation" [43, p. 1]. As a collective action the recovery process is to enable "green and digital transitions" [43, p. 1] for enhancing the competitiveness, resilience and global role of Europe. The recovery process is based on an egalitarian approach and targets cohesion and convergence of across Europe. In the Recovery Plan, €1.85 trillion is proposed to push the European economy forward [43, p. 2, 44].

Despite the high level of uncertainty, the anatomy of the economic crisis is elaborated to reach a rationale for investments and actions. Some estimates were made with respect to the economic damage caused by the crisis. According to these estimations "tourism, the social economy and the creative and cultural ecosystems" could face a more than 70% decline of turnover in the second quarter of 2020 [43, p. 2, 3].

In this respect, we analyse the Recovery Plan for the scope of its support measures for the cultural sector. Within the Plan, REACT-EU is introduced as a new initiative by the European Commission to enable cohesion policy funding for member states to respond to crises. Digital transitions, tourism and culture are among the target sectors of this support. The Commission also proposes to strengthen EU programmes including Horizon Europe, Creative Europe and Digital Europe [43, p. 5, 6, 7, 14]. These programmes entail instruments to support digitisation and cultural heritage-related actions.

Deepening and digitising the single market are among the policy fundamentals of the Plan, as the pandemic showed the vitality of digitisation; these technologies enabled business, services and communication. In this vein, technology fields such as "artificial intelligence", "cloud infrastructure", and "supercomputers" will have priority and receive investments [43, p. 8].

The Recovery Plan added a new layer to the trend of digitisation as a response to the crisis caused by COVID-19. This has implications for the cultural and creative sectors, both for greater crisis-resilience and for more cultural heritage-led innovations driven by digital technologies.

### 3.2.6  Public Consultation on Opportunities Offered by Digital Technologies for the Culture Heritage Sector

On 22 July 2020, the European Commission launched a public consultation to pave the way for a more responsive policy framework of digitisation and cultural heritage. The survey included the option to offer in-depth evaluations of one of the Commission's main policy tools: the Recommendation on digitisation and online accessibility of cultural material and digital preservation [45, 46, 95].

The main motives of the consultation are to gather the views of European cultural heritage actors at large, to better grasp the importance of digitisation of cultural heritage, support processes for this and gain input for the EU policy framework. Through this consultation, the Commission asks for the contributions of member state authorities of relevance, cultural heritage institutions, international organisations, umbrella organisations of relevant stakeholders and the public [46, 96].

The COVID-19 pandemic is meant to highlight the importance of digitisation for the cultural heritage sector. The public consultation seeks to evaluate the impact of the pandemic on cultural heritage sector and help to erect supportive measures to capture the value of digitisation. A set of questions in the survey focus on the cultural heritage sector in the context of the crisis caused by pandemic, the importance and role of using and reusing digitised cultural heritage assets, the perception of digital transformation and specific elaborations on the Recommendation [46, 96].

The public consultation is critical for shaping the policy framework for the digitisation of cultural heritage through a better grasp of the effect of the COVID-19 pandemic and offers a policy window for cultural heritage institutions and professionals at regional, European and international levels.

### 3.2.7  EU Research and Innovation Funding; Horizon Europe Programme

Zabeo and Pellizzon (2017) refer to the EU funding programmes of 2014–2020 and funding initiatives most relevant for cultural heritage-related actions as the EU Structural Funds, Creative Europe, Joint Programming Initiative in Cultural Heritage and Global Change, Horizon 2020, ERASMUS+, Europe For Citizens, COST Actions, Humanities in the European Research Area (HERA) ERA-NET Cofund project [19, p. 71, 72, 73].

Horizon Europe is the new Research and Innovation Framework Programme of EU for 2021–2027. Horizon Europe will have three pillars as "Pillar 1, Excellent Science"; "Pillar 2, Global Challenges and European Industrial Competitiveness"; "Pillar 3, Innovative Europe", underpinned by the measures for "Widening Participation and Strengthening the European Research Area" [47, p. 2].

The document "Orientations towards the first Strategic Plan for Horizon Europe, Revised following the co-design process, Version of 31 October 2019" presents the results of the extensive co-design process in preparation for the Strategic Plan during 2019 [47, p. 1]. This Plan sets forth the strategic orientations for the Programme's investments of initial 4 years [48].

Cultural heritage is mostly included in Pillar 2 under "Cluster 2: Culture, Creativity and Inclusive Society". The challenges for this Cluster are related to "democratic governance, cultural heritage and the creative economy, social and economic transformations" [47, p. 59]. From the perspective of digitisation and innovation for promoting cultural heritage, these challenges are meant to take the opportunities of digital transformation to the fullest, combining traditional with "cutting edge and digital technologies" and "innovative techniques", and capture technical, economic and social value. The cultural and creative industries are said to be a vital source for creative economy and innovation, which need to cross-link to other sectors in the economy [47, p. 59, 60].

Horizon Europe will be the main instrument to fund research and innovation actions and cooperation among key actors of digitisation and cultural heritage across Europe. On the one hand, it has a broad scope for shaping the research and innovation processes and framework conditions in support of relevant EU policy objectives. On the other hand, projects funded by Horizon Europe could feed into evidence-based policy making with regards to digitisation and cultural heritage. Horizon 2020 also plays this role for European research and innovation. Given the specific reference to cultural heritage under Cluster 2 of Pillar 2, the recent policy framework for a stronger system of innovation for cultural and creative sector, and the new momentum for enhanced digitisation given the crisis caused by COVID-19, Horizon Europe has significant scope for impact.

### 3.3 Discussion

Digitisation and cultural heritage are expected to gain weight on the European research and innovation policy space due to the COVID-19 crisis. The growth of advanced technologies and digitisation opens up new avenues for applying these technologies in the advanced use and reuse of cultural assets. Policy makers face a new challenge due to the COVID-19 pandemic. The first circle of response is about refocusing resources and actions to cope with the immediate challenges of the crisis. Longer-term policies will need to be calibrated due to the changes in social and economic context.

The European policy agenda in relation to cultural heritage refers to digitisation and favourable framework conditions to support creativity and innovation. Digital technologies are presented as enhancing access to and use of cultural assets, and thus as an important driver of culture-based innovations and the resulting social and economic benefits.

The most recent policy tools and initiatives discussed in this article call for synergy among policy actors and in legal and financial frameworks (Strategy 21, New Agenda for Culture); to capture the value of a shared culture in Europe (EYCH 2018); to enable a productive ecosystem for cultural heritage innovators and innovations (Work Plan for Culture 2019–2022); and to support innovations stemming from coupling cultural heritage with digital transformation to benefit the economy and society (Strategy 21, New Agenda for Culture, Work Plan for Culture, Recovery Plan, Horizon Europe).

The COVID-19 crisis showed the immediate need to act on the digitisation of cultural heritage within a supportive policy, legal and financial framework. The public consultation launched by the European Commission on opportunities offered by digital technologies for cultural heritage is intended to offer insights within this context.

The current policy landscape provides a favourable framework to support the digitisation of cultural heritage, harnessing its economic and social benefits to combat negative effects of the COVID-19 crisis. To achieve their desired objectives and to address the community needs raised in this article, the policies need to be implemented in practice. This requires two interwoven areas of intervention: EU funding programmes and bottom-up community initiatives. Horizon Europe plays a key role in implementing DCH policy in practice, given its significant reference to digitisation and cultural heritage and planned impact trajectory.

## 4    State of the Art and Analysis of Legal Frameworks

### 4.1    Theoretical Framework

At EU level, the recent Open Data Directive [49] and the Digital Single Market Directive [50] establish the substantive political and legal framework supporting the development and the growth of digital humanities and DCH research. In the forthcoming years, both directives can be expected to strongly influence Member States' policies and legislations related to open access and the sustainable digitisation and preservation of cultural heritage assets for future generations. For cultural heritage institutions, the directives create important opportunities to exploit digitised datasets for many different purposes in galleries, libraries, archives and museums, also referred as GALM domain.

Both directives are concerned with the economic impact of the use, reuse and exploitation of digital cultural resources to contribute to economic growth and job creation. In particular, both directives falls under the Digital Single Market Strategy recently replaced by the strategy "2030 Digital Compass: the European way for the Digital Decade" [51]. In this context, the European Commission is promoting a coherent approach at EU level to improve the framework conditions for digitisation and digital preservation of the European cultural heritage assets. As Recital 65 of the Open Data Directive states "one of the principal aims of the establishment of the internal market is the creation of conditions conducive to the development of Union-wide services" [54]. In this respect, it is important to mention the European Commission Recommendation 2011/711/EU on the digitisation and online accessibility of cultural material and digital preservation of 27 October 2011 [45]. The new Digital Cultural

Heritage and European Expert Group [52] will provide a forum for member states' bodies and the European Commission to cooperate on digitisation, online accessibility of cultural material and digital preservation.

In this section, we draw up an inventory of related legal issues, and analyse how each issue may positively or negatively affect DCH studies and research. Our aim is to identify and develop ways to address policy, legal and ethical issues in the DCH environment.

## 4.2 Methodology

At European Union level, the most relevant regulatory provisions are laid down by the two key directives which govern the digitisation of the cultural heritage resources. In terms of methodological premises, norms are scrutinised and explained based using legal informatics methodology [53–55]. Legal informatics is a discipline familiar with future scenario analysis and aimed at exploiting technology to the maximum extent possible, while minimising the legal, ethical, social and economic risks. The methodology is based upon a multidisciplinary, international and comparative approach. An ex-ante and proactive analysis and assessment of matters, whether they are legal, ethical, economic or technological, contribute to determining and preventing risks and barriers, and subsequently to exploiting opportunities. The legal informatics approach is grounded in philosophy of law (e.g. legal argumentation); it constitutes sceptical analysis of positive law and intensive hermeneutic interpretation of hard and soft law. In the last twenty years, legal informatics developed as discipline by embedding legal theory (e.g. the diachronic model of law), computer science paradigms (e.g. user experience and user interface design) and principles derived from philosophy of law. As a result, Legal informatics combines expertise in different disciplines – law, ethics, economics and technology.

In the Digital Cultural Heritage domain as Jon Bing wrote it is important to develop a project to make more Cultural Heritage content available in digital form and, "establish criteria and principles for computerisation, and coordinating this (project) on a national" and EU level [56]. According to Bing "this involves libraries, but also archives and museums – illustrating the converging force of information technology". Bing maintains that "this poses new issues on several fronts". Therefore; "a methodology is required to secure a representative picture at appropriate intervals. And the legal question related to copyright in the material acquired have to be met; though the legal basis for deposit is extend to digital material, this material also should be available for researchers and other relevant users". As a result, due to its multidisciplinary and interdisciplinarity approach, legal informatics methodology it is beneficial when applied to Digital Humanities domain as it contributes to provide a common holistic approach to the digital lifecycle of Cultural Heritage datasets.

Referring to research and innovation in Digital Cultural Heritage, legal informatics methodology should be used as complementary method for the implementation of the above mentioned Recommendation 2011/711/EU [57] in terms of providing the general framework for digitisation, online accessibility and digital preservation of cultural heritage resources. In this respect it is crucial to mention that the EU Commission has recently sets up a Centre for digital preservation of cultural heritage aiming to preserve and conserve European Cultural Heritage and has launched projects supporting digital innovation in schools [58].

### 4.3    The Open Data Directive and Digitisation of Cultural Heritage

The updated Open Data (OD) Directive, EU Directive 2019/1024 [49], lays down a set of specific rules and exceptions for the datasets collected, produced, reproduced, released and disseminated by cultural institutions. The normative in this context is the rules governing the digitisation of cultural heritage assets.

In the following, we explain the most relevant regulatory provisions laid down by the OD Directive at EU level: open access, exclusive arrangements, use of standard licences, protection of personal data, principle of charging for the reuse of documents, semantic web applications (see Sect. 4.3.1) and use of artificial intelligence (AI) technologies (see Sect. 4.3.2).

The OD Directive highlights the fundamental role of cultural heritage institutions. As stated in Recital 65, "libraries, including university libraries, museums and archives hold a significant amount of valuable public sector information resources, in particular since digitisation projects have multiplied the amount of digital public domain material" [49]. DCH collections and their related metadata have economic value according to Recital 65: they constitute "a potential base for digital content products and services and have a huge potential for innovative reuse in sectors such as learning and tourism".

**Open access** to information and the right to knowledge are fundamental rights according to the OD Directive. Currently, we can assume that the right of access to the information along with the principle of transparency constitute common legal bases in EU member states. Indeed, in all member states both principles have a constitutional basis and are embedded in the fundamental legal framework for the administrative action and policy.

Recital 5 of the OD Directive expressively states that "access to information is a fundamental right", linking it to Article 11 "Freedom of expression and information" of the Charter of Fundamental Rights of the European Union.

In addition, the right to knowledge is a is a basic principle of democracy that covers a wider area compared with the right to access and is expressed in Recital 43 of the OD Directive. The right to knowledge implies instruments to understand, use and reuse the data. Moreover, the quality and the truthfulness of the data should be guaranteed: to cite Recital 43, "that objective is applicable to institutions at every level, be it local, national or international".

In terms of research data, Article 10 of the OD Directive supports open access policies at local level: publicly funded research data should be made openly available "following the principle of open by default and compatible with the FAIR principles" [59]. Particular attention shall be considered in relation with "intellectual property rights, personal data protection and confidentiality, security and legitimate commercial interests".

**Standard licences** should be used. Article 8 and Recital 44 of the OD Directive clearly states the principle that "the reuse of documents shall not be subject to conditions" unless "justified on grounds of a public interest objective". Moreover, the conditions should be "objective, proportionate, non-discriminatory" and "not unnecessarily restrict possibilities for reuse and shall not be used to restrict competition".

As a consequence, as Recital 44 continues, when the reuse of documents is subject to conditions the use of standard licences is recommended "dealing with issues such as liability, the protection of personal data, the proper use of documents, guaranteeing non-alteration and the acknowledgement of source". The standard licence is defined in Article 2 point 5 of the OD Directive as "a set of predefined reuse conditions in a digital format, preferably compatible with standardised public licences available online".

At EU level the "European Commission's guidelines on recommended standard licences, datasets and charging for the reuse of documents" [60] remain the basic document regulating the use licences. In this respect we should also consider the European Commission "Decision of 22.2.2019 adopting Creative Commons as an open licence under the European Commission's reuse policy" [61]. According to Article 1 of this decision, the Commission has adopted Creative Commons Attribution 4.0 International Public License (CC-BY 4.0) as an open license for the Commission's reuse policy. In addition, Article 2 of the Decision asserts that, "without prejudice to the preceding article, raw data, metadata or other documents of comparable nature may alternatively be distributed under the provisions of the Creative Commons Universal Public Domain Dedication deed (CC0 1.0)".

As practical option for publishing both data and content, the Open Knowledge Foundation [62] recommends Creative Commons Licences CC0 1.0, CC-BY 4.0 and CC-BY-SA 4.0 as conformant with the principles set forth in the Open Definition [64]. Within this framework, we should mention Europeana [65] (Europe's digital library) as an example of an organisation that releases its metadata into the public domain using CC0.

**Exclusive arrangements** include exclusion of the digitisation of cultural resources. The general principle of the prohibition of granting exclusive rights for the reuse of public digital datasets, except for specific conditions, laid down in Article 12 of the OD Directive on "exclusive arrangements", does not apply to digitisation of cultural resources.

Recital 49 of the OD Directive acknowledges the importance of private partnerships to facilitate and accelerate the process of digitising cultural resources and therefore the need to grant a certain period of exclusivity that "might be necessary in order to give the private partner the possibility to recoup its investment". On the other hand, paragraph 3 of Article 12 introduces notwithstanding procedural safeguards to limit exclusive arrangements up to 10 years. Accordingly, if the period of exclusivity "exceeds 10 years, its duration shall be subject to review during the 11th year and, if applicable, every seven years thereafter". Moreover, the arrangements granting exclusive rights shall be transparent and made publicly available. Finally, the cultural institution "concerned shall be provided free of charge with a copy of the digitised cultural resources as part of those arrangement" and "that copy shall be available for reuse at the end of the period of exclusivity".

Aspects and issues related to the **protection of personal data** are to be accurately scrutinised when doing research in the DCH field. Regarding this matter the OD Directive clarifies that the reuse of datasets containing personal data shall be processed in full compliance with the General Data Protection Regulation (GDPR) [66], the

Directive on privacy and electronic communications [67] and any supplementing provisions of national law.

Accordingly, the OD Directive is grounded in the concept of anonymisation of data, as stated in Article 2 point 7. Notably, emphasising the risk of identification, Recital 16 asserts that "Member States are therefore encouraged to promote the creation of datasets based on the principle of 'open by design and by default', with regard to all documents falling within the scope of this Directive. Moreover, Member States shall prevent the risk of reidentification or deanonymisation ensuring 'the protection of personal data, including where information in an individual data set does not present a risk of identifying or singling out a natural person, but when that information is combined with other available information, it could entail such a risk'". Concerning anonymisation of datasets we shall recall Article 29 of Data Protection Working Party Opinion 05/2014 on Anonymisation Techniques [68], which "acknowledges the potential value of anonymisation in particular as a strategy to reap the benefits of 'open data' for individuals and society at large whilst mitigating the risks for the individuals concerned".

Article 6 of the OD Directive on "principles governing charging" advocates the general principle that the re-use of open data datasets shall be free of charge [69]. However, this principle is not mandatory. In fact, public sector bodies still allowed to charge the marginal costs incurred "for the reproduction, provision and dissemination of documents as well as for anonymisation of personal data and measures taken to protect commercially confidential information" (Article 6, paragraph 2 1). An exception is made for libraries, including university libraries, museums and archives to charge more than the marginal costs of dissemination for the reuse of their data (Article 6, paragraph 2, letter b). The fees charged "shall not exceed the cost of collection, production, reproduction, dissemination, data storage, preservation and rights clearance and, where applicable, the anonymisation of personal data and measures taken to protect commercially confidential information, together with a reasonable return on investment" (Article 6 paragraph 5). In the scope of the OD Directive, research outputs and datasets will have to be made available online and free of charge to end users, as is stated in Recital 27 and Article 6, paragraph, 6 letter b).

Besides the OD Directive, it is worth mentioning the Digital Governance Act [70], the latest European Commission proposal to regulate the digital space in Europe. Additional relevant aspects to consider can be found in the European Data Strategy Communication [71]. These two documents point out the value of data as economic assets. Moreover, the documents raise an interesting and new concept: "data sharing: means the provision by a data holder of data to a data user for the purpose of joint or individual use of the shared data, based on voluntary agreements, directly or through an intermediary" [71, Article 2]; that enlarges the future scenarios for G2B or B2G (government to business or vice versa) reusers of data. However, neither documents specifically refer to or dedicate space to cultural heritage (although they do refer e.g. to an Open Science Data Space).

Technological issues for open DCH datasets in the semantic web must also briefly be considered [72]. Technological methodologies that enable the opening, releasing and dissemination of reusable public DCH datasets and ensure their interoperability in the semantic web are needed.

### 4.3.1 European Data Strategy: Technological and Semantic Web Applications

As defined in the Open Data Handbook [73], "interoperability denotes the ability of diverse systems and organisations to work together (interoperate), to cooperate, to exchange information automatically, to interact seamlessly anywhere, anytime on the base of common rules". In the case of open data, interoperability is the ability to interoperate – or intermix – different datasets. «The core of a "commons" of data (or code) is that one piece of "open" material contained therein can be freely intermixed with other "open" material. This interoperability is key to realising the main practical benefits of "openness": the dramatically enhanced ability to combine different datasets together and thereby to develop more and better products and services. Providing a clear definition of openness ensures that when you get two open datasets from two different sources, you will be able to combine them together, and it ensures that we avoid our own 'tower of babel': lots of datasets but little or no ability to combine them together into the larger systems where the real value lies» [73].

Accordingly, Recital 34 of the OD Directive reads: «to facilitate reuse, public sector bodies should, where possible and appropriate, make documents, including those published on websites, available through an open and machine-readable format and together with their metadata, at the best level of precision and granularity, in a format that ensures interoperability». In Recital 16, the machine-readability recommendation is stressed jointly with the principles of "open data by design and open by default" to be applied to the creation of all the datasets falling within the scope of the OD Directive. This means designing information systems capable of automatically extracting datasets in open data format.

Article 2 of the OD Directive defines a format as machine-readable when the «file format structured so that software applications can easily identify, recognise and extract specific data, including individual statements of fact, and their internal structure». Additionally, Article 2 defines "open format" as a «file format that is platform-independent and made available to the public without any restriction that impedes the reuse of documents». Finally, in Article 2 «formal open standard means a standard which has been laid down in written form, detailing specifications for the requirements on how to ensure software interoperability» [63].

In the light of all these legal provisions, from a technical perspective, in the semantic web environment, there are four main principles to consider:

1. Open formats;
2. Metadata;
3. Ontologies;
4. Persistent Uniform Resource Identifiers (URIs).

Besides the legal definition, in computer science "open formats" also mean well documented, easily applicable, non-proprietary data representations, neutral with respect to the technology environment. Examples of open formats are: CSV, JSON, XML and RDF.

The dataset itself is not enough to ensure reusability: semantics also play a role. Two more elements are necessary: metadata and ontologies. Metadata corresponds to information on the dataset that is machine understandable in the semantic web platform

[74] and expressed according to standard vocabularies to facilitate searching and interoperability. Without metadata, the dataset is only a list of values without meaning and contextualisation. Without precise metadata, reuse can produce corrupted results and datasets are prone to the manipulation, mystification and misinterpretation. One of the most important methods for providing metadata is RDF, that permits making assertions on the main source using simple triple: subject (the entity being described), predicate (relationship) and object (a value or another entity associated within the relationship).

A paradigmatic example of ontology is DCAT [75] that "is an RDF vocabulary" developed by W3C "designed to facilitate interoperability between data catalogues published on the Web". Besides the datasets, sometimes it is fundamental to annotate also the schema, the vocabulary and taxonomies. ADMS [76] is a specific application of DCAT, used to describe semantic assets defined as highly reusable metadata (e.g. xml schemata, generic data models) and reference data (e.g. code lists, taxonomies, dictionaries, vocabularies) that are used to develop eGovernment systems. In this way, we can describe the dataset (e.g. with XML), the metadata of the dataset (e.g. with DCAT) and finally the vocabulary or schema for interpreting the dataset (e.g. with ADMS). A computational ontology is the abstract representation a specific domain using classes, attributes and relationships [77]. A computational ontology sets up a semantic model of a domain of the reality that, when shared inside a community, can create a common meaningful map of concepts. In addition, when using axioms, it is possible to create inferential rules about the objects connected to the classes of the ontology.

The possibility to have persistent, meaningful, semantic URIs for each different web resource is the main method to make RDF and ontology statements actually useful.

By managing these components it is possible to create an interoperable infrastructure that can be connected with the constellation of data in the semantic web, defined by Tim Berners-Lee as "a web of data that can be processed directly and indirectly by machines" [78]. "The Semantic Web is a Web of Data – of dates and titles and part numbers and chemical properties and any other data one might conceive of" [78]. The semantic web stack [79] (URI, XML, RDF, OWL, Logic, Proof, Trust) is meant to provide a complete environment where data can be referenced, modelled, enriched, inferenced and associated to their provenance.

The linked open data [80] methodology provides the best way to publish datasets and is particularly suitable for releasing DCH datasets.

Briefly, linked open data publication requires four rules:

1. To provide a persistent URI for each dataset;
2. The URI should be based on http;
3. Use RDF metadata connected to the dataset;
4. Reuse other ontologies when appropriate.

Linked open data is the accepted best practice worldwide for open data; however it is not easy to implement, so it is possible to apply this paradigm step by step following Tim Berners-Lee's five-star method [81]:

1. Provide the dataset on the web with an open license;

2. Provide the dataset in machine-readable open format;
3. The open format should be non-proprietary;
4. Link the data to RDF metadata;
5. Link the data to other data available in the linked open cloud.

All in all, we can surely assert that publishing datasets in the Cultural Heritage domain [82] adopting the principles of Linked Open Data, is an ethical imperative to support the full scholarly exploration and interconnection of the artefacts and assets of our heritage and is a key requirement for their sustainable preservation for our future generations.

### 4.3.2    AI-Related Technologies in the Cultural Heritage Sector

Finally, several points of the OD Directive emphasise the potential role of AI in the full economic exploitation of public open datasets. Recital 10 asserts that "the amount of data in the world, including public data, has increased exponentially and new types of data are being generated and collected" and that "there is a continuous evolution in technologies for analysis, exploitation and processing of data, such as machine learning, AI and the internet of things". These include "distributed ledger technologies", as added in Recital 13.

Another important reference to mention is the White Paper on AI proposed by the European Commission [83]. The White Paper defines AI as an "ecosystem that brings the benefits of the technology to the whole of European society and economy" [83 p. 2], for citizens in order to have better public services, for business in the tourism sector, and for public administration to reinforce the public interest, as in transport and education.

Recently the EU Commission has enacted a proposal for a Regulation laying down harmonised rules on artificial intelligence (Artificial Intelligence Act) [84].

Article 3 point 1, of the proposal states that "artificial intelligence system (AI system) means software that is developed with one or more of the techniques and approaches listed in Annex I and can, for a given set of human-defined objectives, generate outputs such as content, predictions, recommendations, or decisions influencing the environments they interact with". Annex I [84] clearly lists the following AI techniques and approaches: (a) Machine learning approaches, including supervised, unsupervised and reinforcement learning, using a wide variety of methods including deep learning; (b) Logic- and knowledge-based approaches, including knowledge representation, inductive (logic) programming, knowledge bases, inference and deductive engines, (symbolic) reasoning and expert systems; (c) Statistical approaches, Bayesian estimation, search and optimization methods. As it is pointed put in the Explanatory memorandum of the Proposal the promotion of AI-driven innovation is closely linked to the above-mentioned Data Governance Act, the Open Data Directive and other initiatives under the EU strategy for data, which will establish trusted mechanisms and services for the re-use, sharing and pooling of data that are essential for the development of data-driven AI models of high quality.

AI applications using open data datasets made available by Libraries, Archives, Museums, could significantly improve studies and research in the Digital Humanities domain. Cultural heritage institutions at large will benefit at different levels from using

AI-related technologies. Besides the digitisation of cultural heritage resources, AI leads the way to enhance the quality of datasets and their related metadata, to analyse and process an enormous amount of data and consequently, to preserve cultural heritage for the next generations.

However, AI applications give rise to numerous legal, ethical and technical issues that should be assessed according to the requirements set forth in the Ethics Guidelines for Trustworthy AI framed by the High-Level Expert Group on AI [85].

## 4.4   The Directive on Copyright and Related Rights in the Digital Single Market

EU Directive 2019/790 on the Digital Single Market (DSM) [50], hereinafter the DSM Directive, was designed to reform copyright laws that had become inadequate in an increasingly digital environment. This Directive is the first broad review of copyright in the European Union. It aims to harmonise copyright in the EU, and to update the copyright framework. As it is clarified in the Explanatory Memorandum of the Directive "the evolution of digital technologies has changed the way works and other protected subject matter are created, produced, distributed and exploited. New uses have emerged as well as new actors and new business models" [86, Article 2]. Recital 5 more specifically asserts that "in the field of research, innovation, education and preservation of cultural heritage" digital technologies permit new types of uses that are not clearly covered by the existing EU rules.

In the following paragraphs, we outline the most relevant provisions of the DSM Directive for cultural heritage institutions: text and data mining, preservation of copies, use of out-of-commerce works by cultural heritage institutions, collective licensing with an extended effect and works of visual art in the public domain.

### 4.4.1   Text and Data Mining

As defined in Article 2 paragraph 2 of the DSM Directive, text and data mining (TDM) "means any automated analytical technique aimed at analysing text and data in digital form in order to generate information which includes but is not limited to patterns, trends and correlations". A further definition is found on the website of the UK Intellectual Property Office: "text and data mining is the process of deriving information from machine-read material. It works by copying large quantities of material, extracting the data, and recombining it to identify patterns" [87].

It is therefore evident that the metadata provenance should be extended to TDM activity and this technical measure is an important complementary instrument for explaining the lifecycle of intellectual property rights and proving the origin of the data extracted from copyrighted collections. This is especially recommended when multiple resources are combined using TDM techniques.

According to Article 3 of the DSM Directive, member states should make an exception for "extractions and reproductions" of copyright protected works to which they have lawful access in order to allow "text and data mining activities" carried out by "research organisations and cultural heritage institutions". Under this exception "copies of works or other subject matter made in compliance with paragraph 1 shall be stored" by the cultural heritage institutions "with an appropriate level of security and may be retained for the purposes of scientific research, including for the verification of research results".

According to Article 4 of the DSM Directive "Member States shall provide for an exception or limitation" for anyone, individuals or cultural heritage institutions, for any purpose, to benefit from an exception to copyright for text and data mining of legally accessed works. However, in this case rightsholders will have the possibility to expressly reserve this right "in an appropriate manner, such as machine-readable means in the case of content made publicly available online". Finally, if the TDM is copyrighted itself the previous exceptions are limited by the existing InfoSoc Directive [88].

### 4.4.2 Preservation of Cultural Heritage: Exception for Preservation Copies

For a long time, the digital preservation of cultural heritage material has been a central policy of the EU. Now, the majority of member states report a variety and combinations of action plans, strategies and initiatives for the long-term preservation of digital material. Article 6 of the DSM Directive makes it mandatory that "Member States shall provide for an exception [...] the rights in order to allow cultural heritage institutions to make copies of any works or other subject matter that are permanently in their collections, in any format or medium, for purposes of preservation of such works or other subject matter and to the extent necessary for such preservation".

### 4.4.3 Use of Out-of-Commerce Works by Cultural Heritage Institutions

Articles 8–11 and the corresponding recitals 29–43 of the DSM Directive lay down the provisions aimed at authorising the cultural heritage institutions to make available out-of-commerce works in the institutions' permanent collections. Article 8 paragraph 5 defines that out-of-commerce works are "work or other subject matter [...] when it can be presumed in good faith that the whole work or other subject matter is not available to the public through customary channels of commerce, after a reasonable effort has been made to determine whether it is available to the public".

According to Recital 29 "works and other subject matter should be considered to be permanently in the collection of a cultural heritage institution when copies of such works or other subject matter are owned or permanently held by that institution, for example as a result of a transfer of ownership or a licence agreement, legal deposit obligations or permanent custody arrangements". As stated in Article 8 collective management organisation "may conclude a non-exclusive licence for non-commercial purposes with a cultural heritage institution for the reproduction, distribution, communication to the public or making available to the public of out-of-commerce works or other subject matter". Collective management organisation may conclude the agreement with the cultural heritage institution on condition that: "(a) the collective management organisation is, on the basis of its mandates, sufficiently representative of rightsholders in the relevant type of works or other subject matter and of the rights that are the subject of the licence; and (b) all rightsholders are guaranteed equal treatment in relation to the terms of the licence".

Therefore, Article 10 lays down "publicity measures" to ensure that in both cases rightsholders are able to prevent cultural heritage institutions from making their works available. Article 10 than states that the European Union Intellectual Property Office establishes and administers a "public single online portal where cultural heritage institutions and collective management organisations must publish information about the out-of-commerce works [...] six months before they make the works available online".

To prevent liability issues with rightsholders, Recital 42 and Article 11 of the DSM Directive specify a set of provisions to ensure that member states establish a "stakeholder dialogue". In this respect Article 11 specifies that "Member States shall consult rightsholders, collective management organisations and cultural heritage institutions in each sector before establishing specific requirements pursuant to Article 8(5)". Moreover, Article 11 continues that member states "shall encourage regular dialogue between representative users' and rightsholders' organisations, including collective management organisations, and any other relevant stakeholder organisations, on a sector-specific basis, to foster the relevance and usability of the licensing mechanisms set out in Article 8(1) and to ensure that the safeguards for rightsholders referred to in this Chapter are effective".

### 4.4.4 Collective Licensing with an Extended Effect

Article 12 of the DSM Directive contains provisions on collective licensing with extended effect that are quite similar to and inspired by the models of extended collective licensing (ECL). This is meant to ensure that member states implementing the DSM Directive in the domestic legislation, "may provide, as far as the use on their territory is concerned and subject to the safeguards provided for in this Article, that where a collective management organisation that is subject to the national rules implementing Directive 2014/26/EU [89], in accordance with its mandates from rightsholders, enters into a licensing agreement for the exploitation of works or other subject matter".

Member states shall provide safeguards that are set down in Article 12 paragraph 3 to ensure that the ECL mechanism "is only applied within well-defined areas of use, where obtaining authorisations from rightsholders on an individual basis is typically onerous and impractical to a degree that makes the required licensing transaction unlikely, due to the nature of the use or of the types of works or other subject matter concerned, and shall ensure that such licensing mechanism safeguards the legitimate interests of rightsholders".

### 4.4.5 Protection of Public Domain Works and Visual Art

According to Article 14 of the DSM Directive "when the term of protection of a work of visual art has expired, any material resulting from an act of reproduction of that work is not subject to copyright or related rights, unless the material resulting from that act of reproduction is original in the sense that it is the author's own intellectual creation".

Recital 53 of the Directive clearly explains the rationale of Article 14 in the field of visual art: "the expiry of the term of protection of a work entails the entry of that work into the public domain and the expiry of the rights that Union copyright law provides in relation to that work". In the visual arts, circulation of faithful reproductions of works in the public domain contributes to the access to and promotion of culture and cultural heritage. In a digital environment, the protection of such reproductions through copyright or related rights is inconsistent with the expiry of the copyright protection of works. In addition, differences between the national copyright laws governing the protection of such reproductions give rise to legal uncertainty and affect the cross-border dissemination of works of visual arts in the public domain. Certain reproductions of works of visual arts in the public domain should, therefore, not be protected by copyright or related rights" [50, Recital 53]. However, cultural heritage institutions remain free to sell reproductions, such as postcards, posters and books.

For the sake of completeness, we should point out that the DSM Directive has provided specific disciplines for "the protection of press publications concerning online uses" in Article 15 and on the "use of protected content by online content-sharing service providers" in Article 17. In these cases, care is needed to ensure that the safeguards for libraries in the Directive are present in national implementation.

Title II of the DSM Directive introduces "measures to adapt exceptions and limitations to the digital and cross-border environment" [50, Title II], also concerning cultural heritage.

## 4.5 Discussion

We can forecast that in the coming years the digital data policy and strategy of the EU member states will be strongly affected by transposition of the OD Directive and the DSM Directive, together with the upcoming Digital Governance Act. As a consequence, member states, both at central and local level, should adopt transparent, clear, coherent, applicable and effective legal provisions, in order to ensure the development of a robust and mature digital data market in the EU.

Accordingly, the European Commission should monitor progress, at member state level, in terms of digitisation, online access and digital preservation of DCH assets. The monitoring should focus on how member states transpose the two directives and implement the Recommendation on the digitisation and online accessibility of cultural material and digital preservation [90]. Both directives leave room to different degrees of transposition into the domestic legislative system of the member states. Notably, as to Recital 64 of the OD Directive "the Commission may assist the Member States in implementing this Directive in a consistent way by issuing and updating existing guidelines, particularly on recommended standard licences, datasets and charging for the reuse of documents, after consulting interested parties".

In this respect, several relevant issues related to supporting digital humanities and cultural heritage studies research must be pointed out.

The issue of licences is increasingly essential, since the Public Sector Information Directive 2013/37/EU [91] has been extended in scope "to libraries, including university libraries, museums and archives". Particularly, in the light of the Commission Decision adopting Creative Commons [92] as an open license to enable European Commission's reuse policy [cf. 93], it is fundamental to scrutinise the legal implications of transposing this measure within the EU legal framework. In this respect it is necessary to recall the critical issues related to the possibility that re-copyright of a dataset available in the public domain may deprive public sector bodies of an important asset. Thus, specific attention must be paid to governance of the use of the CC0 as a standard licence.

In terms of competition law, it is important to consider the implementation of the provisions on charging and exclusive arrangements to avoid market distortions at EU level. Implementation of ECL is territorial, so this can potentially distort market competition in the cultural heritage context. In this respect, member states' competition authorities will play an important monitoring role.

Considering the impact of the DSM Directive on the member states' legislations, Recital 5 states that "in the fields of research, innovation, education and preservation of cultural heritage, digital technologies permit new types of uses that are not clearly covered by the existing Union rules on exceptions and limitations". Moreover, according to Article 1, the "Directive lays down rules which aim to harmonise further Union law applicable to copyright and related rights in the framework of the internal market, considering, in particular, digital and cross-border uses of protected content. It also lays down rules on exceptions and limitations to copyright and related rights, on the facilitation of licences, as well as rules which aim to ensure a well-functioning marketplace for the exploitation of works and other subject matter".

In respect of AI, explicability is one of the key principles. The principle is introduced by the High-Level Expert Group on AI of the European Commission with the intention to reinforce its ethical instruments in the AI domain and to support transparency, accountability of the automatic decision system and auditability of the black box of algorithms. Explicability in this definition also applies to the lifecycle of DCH datasets: this should be traceable, transparent in the semantic and in the data model, and transparent in provenance and in modifications over time. This means explaining the method of anonymisation, the algorithm of aggregation, the model of classification of the datasets and the training set in cases of machine learning or deep learning.

In addition, the principle of knowability of the dataset used by the AI process is relevant, as it enables each data subject to act in accordance with Article 22 of the GDPR in the event that cultural data (e.g. museum visit data) are used against the individual (e.g. if all people attending a particular exhibition are classified according to the ideological opinions of the artist).

The White Paper on AI proposed by the European Commission [83] is an additional significant reference to mention. The White Paper defines AI as an "ecosystem that brings the benefits of the technology to the whole of European society and economy" [83 p. 2], for citizens to have better public services, for business in the tourism sector and for public administration to reinforce the public interest as transport and education. As a consequence, AI applications using open DCH datasets could significantly improve education, tourism and transportation – and thus quality of life.

Finally, cultural heritage institutions need to adopt a data ethics policy to ensure responsible and sustainable reuse of open datasets [94]. Implementing a data ethics policy constitutes a step forward besides the compliance with the legal framework on this issue, e.g. the GDPR. In this respect rules and technical mechanisms need to be defined to detect cognitive bias in the creation of the dataset in order to avoid discrimination, stereotyping, crystallisation, distortion of history, misrepresentation of reality and manipulation of the cultural identity of a country or a community. A data ethics policy is crucial to good practices around how data is collected, reused and shared. This is of particular relevance when data activities have the potential to impact on people and society, directly or indirectly. Specifically regarding AI-related applications it is essential to prevent cognitive bias in the creation of datasets.

## 5 Conclusions

Through recent policies and initiatives, the EU has sought to develop a holistic and complementary approach to create a strong system for cultural heritage-led innovations across Europe. At the EU level, legal initiatives and directives forms a supportive framework for digital humanities and digitisation of cultural heritage with the associated benefits of digitised assets. This setting could be said to be a conducive environment for European-scale services and intervention to facilitate community engagement in digitisation of cultural heritage.

A critical mass of policies and legal initiatives aim to support digitisation of cultural heritage and exploit its benefits. The EU has sought to create favourable and supportive structures and conditions for this in terms of access to finance, legal framework, enhanced skills, online accessibility, standardisation, citizen engagement and tailored policies. The COVID-19 crisis is expected to further enforce new business models and innovation support mechanisms to stimulate digital transformations and innovations. This context sets favourable framework conditions for capturing the value of digitisation and cultural heritage of Europe for innovation and creativity.

Horizon Europe, together with other Union Programmes, plays a critical role here as the funding it mobilises can be directed to develop and disseminate legal standards in relation to digitisation and access to data, copyright issues, access to finance and scaling up cultural heritage-led innovations for market uptake, strengthening the innovation ecosystem for the cultural and creative sectors.

This context can also be seen as an opportunity to fertilise research and innovation policies, legislative frameworks and funding structures to make a greater impact on innovation performance in Europe.

The analysis presented in this article is bounded within the contextual framework and based on a community use survey, but not on impact assessment of the policy and funding landscape. The policy and legal frameworks have not been evaluated at a sufficient scale to determine their role and influence on practice, such as funding. Future research would examine the effects of restructuring on research and innovation ecosystems and the community needs identified in the survey.

## References

1. Becher, T.: Academic disciplines. In: Becher, T. (ed.) Academic Tribes and Territories : Intellectual Enquiry and the Cultures of Disciplines, pp. 19–35. Open University Press, Milton Keynes (1989)
2. Krishnan, A.: What are academic disciplines. Some observations on the Disciplinarity vs. Interdisciplinarity debate. University of Southampton. National Centre for Research Methods, Southhampton (2009)

3. Knorr-Cetina, K.: Epistemic Cultures. How the Sciences make Knowledge. Harvard University Press, Cambridge (1999)
4. Knorr-Cetina, K., Reichmann, W.: Epistemic cultures. Int. Encyclopedia Soc. Behav. Sci. **7**, 873–880. Elsevier, Amsterdam (2015). https://doi.org/10.1016/b978-0-08-097086-8.10454-4
5. Digital Methods and Practices Observatory Working Group DARIAH-EU European Research Infrastructure Consortium: European survey on scholarly practices and digital needs in the arts and humanities (2016)
6. Albrecht, S.: Adoption of escience practices among scholars in the humanities and social sciences (Presentation). In: 2nd Network Conference des E-Science Forschungsnetzwerks Sachsen, 11th–13th June 2013, Dresden (2013)
7. Münster, S., Ioannides, M., Davies, R.: International stakeholder survey on demands in the field of digital cultural heritage (2017). https://doi.org/10.13140/RG.2.2.20179.07208
8. Fernie, K., et al.: 3D content in Europeana task force. The Hague (2020)
9. Weingart, S.: Submissions to DH2017. The Scottbot Irregular (2016)
10. Leydesdorff, L., Hammarfelt, B., Salah, A.: The structure of the arts & humanities citation index: a mapping on the basis of aggregated citations among 1,157 journals. J. Am. Soc. Inform. Sci. Technol. **62**(12), 2414–2426 (2011). https://doi.org/10.1002/asi.21636
11. Sprugnoli, R., Pardelli, G., Boschetti, F., Gratta, R.D.: Un' Analisi Multidimensionale della Ricerca Italiana nel Campo delle Digital Humanities e della Linguistica Computazionale Umanistica Digitale (2019). https://doi.org/10.6092/issn.2532-8816/8581
12. Münster, S.: Digital cultural heritage as scholarly field – topics, researchers and perspectives from a bibliometric point of view. J. Comput. Cult. Herit. **12**(3), 22–49 (2019)
13. Münster, S., Ioannides, M.: The scientific community of digital heritage in time and space. In: Guidi, G., Scopigno, R., Torres, J.C., Graf, H. (eds.) 2nd International Congress on Digital Heritage 2015. IEEE, Granada (2015). 978-1-5090-0048-7/15
14. Münster, S.: A survey on topics, researchers and cultures in the field of digital heritage. ISPRS Ann. Photogramm. Remote Sens. Spat. Inf. Sci. **IV-2/W2**, 157–162 (2017). https://doi.org/10.5194/isprs-annals-IV-2-W2-157-2017
15. Münster, S., Ioannides, M., Davies, R.: Internationale Umfrage zu Stakeholdern und Perspektiven im Bereich des digitalen Kulturerbes (2018)
16. Reja, U., Manfreda, K.L., Hlebec, V., Vehovar, V.: Open-ended vs. close-ended questions in web questionnaires. Dev. Appl. Stat. **19**, 159–177 (2003)
17. Mayring, P.: Qualitative content analysis [28 paragraphs]. Forum Qualitative Sozialforschung/Forum Qual. Soc. Res. **1**(2) (2000). Art. 20. http://nbnresolving.de/urn:nbn:de:0114-fqs0002204
18. Rigauts, T., Ioannides, M.: Web-based platforms and metadata for 3D cultural heritage models: a critical review. In: Proceedings of the 25th International Conference on Cultural Heritage and New Technologies (2020)
19. Zabeo, S., Pellizzon, D.: Cultural heritage in the frame of European funding programmes: challenges and opportunities. Sapere l'Europa, sapere d'Europa **4**, 69 (2017)
20. Petković, J.S.: European cultural policy: priorities and practices in the field of cultural heritage. FACTA Univ. Philos. Sociol. Psychol. Hist. **18**(03), 115–130 (2019)
21. Hristova, S.: The European model of cultural heritage policy. Zarządzanie w kulturze **18**(1), 1–16 (2017)
22. Sciacchitano, E.: The European year of cultural heritage 2018. A laboratory for heritage-based innovation. SCIRES-IT **9**(1) (2019)

23. Ross, S.: Progress from national initiatives towards European strategies for digitisation. In: Towards a Continuum of Digital Heritage: Strategies for a European Area of Digital Cultural Resources, European Conference, pp. 88–98, September 2004

24. Marinković, A., Mirić, A., Mirić, F.: European policy on digitisation of cultural heritage from 2005. onwards. Facta Univ. Ser.: Law Polit., 97–103 (2016)

25. Bachi, V., Fresa, A., Pierotti, C., Prandoni, C.: The digitization age: mass culture is quality culture. Challenges for cultural heritage and society. In: Ioannides, M., Magnenat-Thalmann, N., Fink, E., Žarnić, R., Yen, A.Y., Quak, E. (eds.) Digital Heritage. Progress in Cultural Heritage: Documentation, Preservation, and Protection. EuroMed 2014. LNCS, vol. 8740, pp. 786–801. Springer, Cham (2014). https://doi.org/10.1007/978-3-319-13695-0_81

26. Lykourentzou, I., Antoniou, A.: Digital innovation for cultural heritage: lessons from the European year of cultural heritage. SCIRES-IT-SCIentific RESearch Infor. Techno. 9(1), 91–98 (2019)

27. Filip, F.G., Ciurea, C., Dragomirescu, H., Ivan, I.: Cultural heritage and modern information and communication technologies. Technol. Econo. Dev. Econ. 21(3), 441–459 (2015)

28. Evens, T., Hauttekeete, L.: Challenges of digital preservation for cultural heritage institutions. J. Librariansh. Inf. Sci. 43(3), 157–165 (2011)

29. Tariffi, F., Morganti, B., Segbert, M.: Digital cultural heritage projects in Europe: an overview of TRIS and the take-up trial projects. Program (2004)

30. Commission of the European Communities (2005): Communication on i2010: Digital Libraries, Com (2005). 465 final

31. European Commission (2010): Communication on A Digital Agenda for Europe, Com (2010). 245 final

32. European Commission, Culture and Creativity Website, The European Year of Cultural Heritage (2018) section. https://ec.europa.eu/culture/cultural-heritage/eu-policy-for-cultural-heritage/european-year-of-cultural-heritage-2018

33. Council of Europe (2017): Recommendation of the Committee of Ministers to Member States on the European Cultural Heritage Strategy for the 21st century CM/Rec(2017)1

34. European Commission (2019): The European Framework for Action on Cultural Heritage, Comission Staff Working Document. https://doi.org/10.2766/949707. ISBN 978-92-76-03453-7

35. European Council (2019): A new strategic agenda for the EU, 2019–2024

36. Council of the European Union (2018): Council conclusions on the Work Plan for Culture 2019–2022, T/14984/2018/INIT, OJ C 460, pp. 12–25, 21 December 2018

37. European Commission (2017): Mapping of Cultural Heritage actions in European Union policies, programmes and activities

38. Romme, G., Meijer, A.: Applying design science in public policy and administration research. Policy Politics 48, 149–165 (2020). https://doi.org/10.1332/030557319X15613699981234

39. European Commission (2019): Report from The Commission to The European Parliament, The Council, The European Economic and Social Committee and The Committee of The Regions on the implementation, results and overall assessment of the European Year of Cultural Heritage 2018 COM (2019). 548 final

40. European Union, European Commission (2018) Fact Sheet: Building the legacy of the European Year of Cultural Heritage 2018: 10 European Initiatives – Overview • 4 Principles. https://europa.eu/cultural-heritage/sites/eych/files/overview-10-european-initiatives-factsheet_en_2.pdf

41. European Commission (2018): Communication from The Commission to The European Parliament, The European Council, The Council, The European Economic and Social Committee and The Committee of The Regions, A New European Agenda for Culture, Com (2018). 267 final

42. European Council (2017): European Council meeting (14 December 2017) – Conclusions on security and defence, social dimension, education and culture, climate change, Jerusalem, EUCO 19/1/17 REV 1, CO EUR 24 CONCL 7

43. European Commission (2020). Communication from the Commission to the European Parliament, the European Council, the Council, the European Economic and Social Committee and the Committee of the Regions. Europe's moment: Repair and prepare for the next generation, COM (2020). 456 final

44. European Commission (2020): Communication From The Commission to The European Parliament, The European Council, The Council, The European Economic and Social Committee and The Committee of The Regions, The EU budget powering the recovery plan for Europe, Com (2020). 442 final

45. European Commission (2011): Commission Recommendation of 27 October 2011 on the digitisation and online accessibility of cultural material and digital preservation, OJ L 283, pp. 39–45, 29 October 2011

46. European Commission, Webpage on Public Consultation, Digitisation and online access of cultural material and digital preservation (evaluation). https://ec.europa.eu/info/law/better-regulation/have-your-say/initiatives/11837-Evaluation-of-the-Recommendation-on-digitisation-and-online-accessibility-of-cultural-material-and-digital-preservation/public-consultation_en

47. European Commission (2019): Orientations towards the first Strategic Plan for Horizon Europe, Revised following the co-design process, Version of 31 October 2019. https://ec.europa.eu/info/sites/default/files/research_and_innovation/strategy_on_research_and_innovation/documents/ec_rtd_he-orientations-towards-strategic-plan_102019.pdf

48. European Commission, webpage, Strategic plan, what Horizon Europe's first strategic plan is, how it was developed, strategic planning and download the plan, The first Horizon Europe strategic plan (2021–2024). https://ec.europa.eu/info/research-and-innovation/funding/funding-opportunities/funding-programmes-and-open-calls/horizon-europe/strategic-plan_en

49. The European Parliament and The Council of the European Union (2019): Directive (EU) 2019/1024 of The European Parliament and of The Council of 20 June 2019 on open data and the re-use of public sector information (recast)

50. The European Parliament and The Council of the European Union (2019): Directive (EU) 2019/790 of The European Parliament and of The Council of 17 April 2019 on copyright and related rights in the Digital Single Market and amending Directives 96/9/EC and 2001/29/EC (Text with EEA relevance)

51. European Commission (2021): Communication from The Commission to The European Parliament, The Council, The European Economic and Social Committee and The Committee of the Regions 2030 Digital Compass: the European way for the Digital Decade, Com (2021). 118 final

52. European Commission (2021): Expert Group on Digital Cultural Heritage and Europeana (DCHE)

53. Leith P, Paliwala A.: Special issue on legal informatics. Eur. J. Law Technol. 1(1) (2010)

54. Biasotti, A., Francesconi, E., Palmirani, M., Sartor, G., Vitali, F.: Legal Informatics and Management of Legislative Documents (2008)

55. Saarenpää, A.: Does legal informatics have a method in the new network society? In: Society Trapped in the Network Does it have a Future? University of Lapland Printing Centre, Rovaniemi (2016)
56. Bing, J.: The Norwegian national library: poised on the threshold of the twenty-first century. Alexandria **17**, 123–131 (2005)
57. European Commission (2011): Recommendation on digitisation and online accessibility and digital preservation of cultural material (2011/711/EU)
58. European Commission (2021): Press Release "Commission sets up a Centre for digital preservation of cultural heritage and launches projects supporting digital innovation in schools", Last Update 8 March 2021, available at: Commission sets up a Centre for digital preservation of cultural heritage and launches projects supporting digital innovation in schools | Shaping Europe's digital future
59. Wilkinson, M.D., et al.: The FAIR Guiding Principles for scientific data management and stewardship. Sci. Data **3**(1), 1–9 (2016)
60. European Commission (2014): Commission Notice: 'Guidelines on recommended standard licences, datasets and charging for the re-use of documents'
61. European Commission (2019): Commission Decision of 22.2.2019 adopting Creative Commons as an open licence under the European Commission's reuse policy, C(2019) 1655 final
62. Open Knowledge Foundation website. https://okfn.org/
63. Casanovas, P., Palmirani, M., Peroni, S., Engers, T.V., Vitali, F.: Semantic web for the legal domain: the next step. Semant. Web **7**, 213–227 (2016)
64. Open Knowledge Foundation, Open definition. http://opendefinition.org/licenses/
65. Europeana Europeana Website. http://www.europeana.eu/portal/
66. The European Parliament and the Council of The European Union (2016): Regulation (EU) 2016/679 of The European Parliament and of The Council of 27 April 2016 on the protection of natural persons with regard to the processing of personal data and on the free movement of such data, and repealing Directive 95/46/EC (General Data Protection Regulation) (Text with EEA relevance)
67. The European Parliament and The Council of The European Union (2002): Directive 2002/58/EC of The European Parliament and of The Council of 12 July 2002 concerning the processing of personal data and the protection of privacy in the electronic communications sector (Directive on privacy and electronic communications)
68. Article 29 Data Protection Working Party (2014): Opinion 05/2014 on Anonymisation Techniques, 0829/14/EN WP216
69. European Data Portal (2020): The Economic Impact of Open Data Opportunities for value creation in Europe. https://data.europa.eu/en/highlights/the-economic-impact-of-open-data
70. European Commission (2020): Proposal for a Regulation OF The European Parliament and of The Council on European data governance (Data Governance Act), Com (2020) 767 final
71. European Commission (2020): Communication from The Commission to The European Parliament, The Council, The European Economic and Social Committee and The Committee of The Regions a European strategy for data, Com/2020/66 final
72. Palmirani, M., Girardi, D.: Open government data: legal, economical and semantic web aspects. In: Saarenpää, A., Sztobryn, K. (eds.) Lawyers in the Media Society. The Legal Challenges of the Media Society, pp. 187–205. University of Lapland, Rovaniemi (2016)
73. Open Data Handbook Webpage. http://opendatahandbook.org/
74. W3C (2001): Metadata and Resource Description. https://www.w3.org/Metadata/

75. W3C (2020): Data Catalog Vocabulary (DCAT) - Version 2 W3C Recommendation 04 February 2020. http://www.w3.org/TR/vocab-dcat/
76. W3C (2013): Asset Description Metadata Schema (ADMS) W3C Working Group Note 01 August 2013. http://www.w3.org/TR/vocab-adms/
77. Gruber, T.: Ontology. Encyclopedia Database Syst. 1, 1963–1965 (2009)
78. Berners-Lee, T., Hendler, J., Lassila, O.: The semantic web. J. Sci. Am. 284(5), 34–43 (2001)
79. Wikipedia Semantic Web Stack. https://en.wikipedia.org/wiki/Semantic_Web_Stack
80. W3C: Linked Data. https://www.w3.org/standards/semanticweb/data,https://www.w3.org/DesignIssues/LinkedData.html
81. Berners-Lee, T.: Linked Data (2009). https://www.w3.org/DesignIssues/LinkedData.html
82. Daquino, M., Mambelli, F., Peroni, S., Tomasi, F., Vitali, F.: Enhancing semantic expressivity in the cultural heritage domain: exposing the zeri photo archive as linked open data. J. Comput. Cult. Herit. (JOCCH) 10, 1–21 (2017)
83. European Commission (2020): White Paper on Artificial Intelligence - A European approach to excellence and trust, COM (2020) 65 final
84. The European Parlament and The Council of The European Union (2001): Laying Down Harmonised Rules on Artificial Intelligence (Artificial Intelligence Act) and Amending Certain Union Legislative Acts, Brussels
85. Independent High-Level Expert Groups on Artifical Intelligence Set Up By The European Commission (2019) Ethics Guidelines for Trustworthy AI. https://digital-strategy.ec.europa.eu/en/policies/expert-group-ai
86. European Commission (2016): Proposal for a Directive of the European Parliament and of the Council on copyright in the Digital Single Market (Text with EEA relevance), Com (2016) 593 final, 2016/0280 (COD)
87. GOV.UK Intellectual property, Copyright: detailed information. https://www.gov.uk/topic/intellectual-property/copyright
88. The European Parliemant and The Council of The European Union (2001): Directive 2001/29/EC of the European Parliament and of the Council of 22 May 2001 on the harmonisation of certain aspects of copyright and related rights in the information society, L 167/10
89. European Parliament and of the Council (2014): Directive on collective management of copyright and related rights and multi-territorial licensing of rights in musical works for online use in the internal market Text with EEA relevance (2014/26/EU)
90. European Commission (2019): The Report on Cultural Heritage: Digitisation, Online Accessibility and Digital Preservation
91. The European Parliament and The Council of The European Union (2013): Directive 2013/37/EU of the European Parliament and of the Council of 26 June 2013 amending Directive 2003/98/EC on the re-use of public sector information Text with EEA relevance, OJ L 175, 27 June 2013
92. Cerative Commons About CC Licenses. https://creativecommons.org/about/cclicenses/
93. Vollmer, T.: European Commission adopts CC BY and CC0 for sharing information. Creative Commons (2019). https://creativecommons.org/2019/04/02/european-commission-adopts-cc-by-and-cc0-for-sharing-information/
94. Granickas, K.: European Public Sector Information Platform Topic Report No. 2015/02, Ethical and Responsible Use of Open Government Data (2015)

95. European Commission, webpage, shaping Europe's digital future, consultation | Publication 22 June 2020, public consultation on opportunities offered by digital technologies for the culture heritage sector. https://digital-strategy.ec.europa.eu/en/consultations/public-consultation-opportunities-offered-digital-technologies-culture-heritage-sector

96. The Factual Summary Report on the open public consultation on digital for Cultural Heritage, Ref. Ares (2020) 6653094 - 12/11/2020. https://ec.europa.eu/info/law/better-regulation/have-your-say/initiatives/11837-Evaluation-of-the-Recommendation-on-digitisation-and-online-accessibility-of-cultural-material-and-digital-preservation/public-consultation_en

# Author Index

Apollonio, Fabrizio I.  3
Assendelft, Brenda  191

Bajena, Igor  25
Baptist, Vincent  191
Bruschke, Jonas  129

Dewitz, Leyla  46
Doreleijers, Kristel  191

Fallavollita, Federico  3
Filz, Nicole  46
Foschi, Riccardo  3

Giordano, Andrea  171
Girardi, Dino  237
Große, Peggy  25

Hammel, Katharina  46
Huffman, Kristin L.  171

Jara, Karolina  25

Karsten, Susanne  106
Khademi, Seyran  213
Kisjes, Ivan  191
Koszewski, Krzysztof  87
Kröber, Cindy  46
Kuroczyński, Piotr  25

Lazariv, Taras  106
Lehmann, Christoph  106

Mager, Tino  213
Maiwald, Ferdinand  106
Mol, Hans  191
Münster, Sander  106, 237

Niebling, Florian  129
Noordegraaf, Julia  191

Palmirani, Monica  237

Raat, Mark  191
Rasterhoff, Claartje  191

Schade, Cornelia  46
Siebes, Ronald  213
Suazo, Antonio  152

Ulutas Aydogan, Selda  237

van der Sijs, Nicoline  191
van Erp, Marieke  191
van Oort, Thunnis  191

Vermaut, Thomas  191
Vitali, Fabio  237
Vrielink, Charlotte  191

Wacker, Markus  129
Wnęk, Kinga  25

Zandhuis, Ivo  191
Zijdeman, Richard  191

Printed in the United States
by Baker & Taylor Publisher Services

Printed in the United States
by Baker & Taylor Publisher Services